Labour Rights in Crisis

Labour Rights in Crisis

Measuring the Achievement of Human Rights in the World of Work

W. R. Böhning

331.011
B67L

First published 2005 by
PALGRAVE MACMILLAN
Houndmills, Basingstoke, Hampshire RG21 6XS and
175 Fifth Avenue, New York, N. Y. 10010
Companies and representatives throughout the world

PALGRAVE MACMILLAN is the global academic imprint of the Palgrave Macmillan division of St. Martin's Press, LLC and of Palgrave Macmillan Ltd. Macmillan® is a registered trademark in the United States, United Kingdom and other countries. Palgrave is a registered trademark in the European Union and other countries.

ISBN-13: 978-1-4039-9075-4   hardback
ISBN-10: 1-4039-9075-1   hardback

This book is printed on paper suitable for recycling and made from fully managed and sustained forest sources.

A catalogue record for this book is available from the British Library.

Library of Congress Cataloging-in-Publication Data
Böhning, W. R.
    Labour rights in crisis : measuring the achievement of human rights in the world of work / W. R. Böhning.
        p. cm.
    Includes bibliographical references and index.
    ISBN 1-4039-9075-1
    1. Employee rights. 2. Human rights. 3. Labor laws and legislation, International. I. Title.

HD6971.8.B643 2005
331'.01'1–dc22   2005049811

10   9   8   7   6   5   4   3   2   1
14   13   12   11   10   09   08   07   06   05

Printed and bound in Great Britain by
Antony Rowe Ltd, Chippenham and Eastbourne

Contents

v

List of Boxes

List of Tables

List of Figures

List of Abbreviations

CEACR	ILO Committee of Experts on the Application of Conventions and Recommendations, also referred to for short as 'Committee of Experts'
CFA	ILO Committee on Freedom of Association
CIRI	Cingranelli and Richards Human Rights Dataset
Convention No. 29	International Labour Organization Forced Labour Convention, 1930, in force since 1932
Convention No. 87	International Labour Organization Freedom of Association and Protection of the Right to Organize Convention, 1948, in force since 1950
Convention No. 98	International Labour Organization Right to Organize and Collective Bargaining Convention, 1949, in force since 1951
Convention No. 100	International Labour Organization Equal Remuneration Convention, 1951, in force since 1953
Convention No. 105	International Labour Organization Abolition of Forced Labour Convention, 1957, in force since 1959
Convention No. 111	International Labour Organization Discrimination (Employment and Occupation) Convention, 1958, in force since 1960
Convention No. 138	International Labour Organization Minimum Age Convention, 1973, in force since 1976
Convention No. 182	International Labour Organization Abolition of the Worst Forms of Child Labour Convention, 1999, in force since 2000
CPI	Corruption Perceptions Index of Transparency International
CRG	Core Rights Gap
Declaration	International Labour Organization Declaration on Fundamental Principles and Rights at Work and its Follow-up, 1998
FDI	Foreign Direct Investment
ICCPR	United Nations International Covenant on Civil and Political Rights, 1966, in force since 1976

ICESCR	United Nations International Covenant on Economic, Social and Cultural Rights, 1966, in force since 1976
ICFTU	International Confederation of Free Trade Unions
ILO	International Labour Office (Secretariat of the International Labour Organization)
OECD	Organization for Economic Cooperation and Development
Organization	International Labour Organization
NGO	Non-Governmental Organization
UDHR	Universal Declaration of Human Rights
UNDP	United Nations Development Programme
UNESCO	United Nations Educational, Scientific and Cultural Organization

Preface

Why a book about measuring fundamental rights in the world or work? Because it is high time! Indicator development in the labour field has been the poor cousin of recent advances in other fields of human rights. Even the body in which I served the bulk of my professional life, the ILO, experiences great difficulties in spelling out the extent to which labour rights are realized in law and in practice. The short time-span since the recent consensus on what constitutes fundamental rights in the labour field is but a feeble explanation for the lack of indicator development because most of these rights date back to the beginning or middle of the 19th century. The complexity of measuring human rights is part of the reason why the literature is barren. However, difficulties must be tackled, and novel ideas should be put forward, which is the purpose of this book. Its underlying purpose was well captured by UNDP in the following words: 'Statistical indicators are a powerful tool in the struggle for human rights. They make it possible for people and organizations – from grass-roots activists and civil society to governments and the United Nations – to identify important actors and hold them accountable for their actions. That is why developing and using indicators for human rights has become a cutting-edge area of advocacy' (UNDP, 2000, p. 89).

While the new indicators, which I call the 'gap' system, are still at the infant and development stage, it is not too early to throw the bones of their structure to the academic and political communities interested in the subject. But it is too early to take all the empirical meat on their bones as ready for consumption, notably when countries are ranked. I expect the empirical results to be fully digestible when the time lags have worked themselves out of the system by the second half of the decade.

I should like to thank former ILO colleagues Zafar Shaheed and Peter Peek, who benignly looked upon my extra-curricular activities, and David Kucera, who extensively commented on my initial elaborations. Thanks are also due to Christiane Veltsos, who set up an Excel programme to handle the thousands of data in such a way that I could handle them as well, to Prof. Dieter Senghaas and Dr. Bernhard Zangl, both of the University of Bremen, and to an anonymous reader for helpful suggestions. All remaining errors and shortcomings are mine.

Roger Böhning

1
Basic Labour Rights are Human Rights

1.1 Introduction

After World War I, the League of Nations and the International Labour Organization set in motion a global codification process of human rights. It was given new urgency by the 'barbarous acts which have outraged the conscience of mankind' perpetrated by European and East Asian fascist regimes. The 1948 Universal Declaration of Human Rights (UDHR), from which these words are quoted, re-launched the codification that, 18 years later, gave rise to the International Covenant on Civil and Political Rights (ICCPR) and the International Covenant on Economic, Social and Cultural Rights (ICESCR). A number of Conventions and Declarations have since been elaborated on specific subjects under the auspices of the United Nations and some of its agencies, notably the International Labour Organization.

During the Cold War, national and international human rights bodies, activists and scholars, especially in developed countries, focused primarily on the assertion and development of civil and political rights. The labour field attracted comparatively little attention. The more recent political and academic concern with 'governance' has likewise not paid much attention to the world of work. Numerous analytical and empirical studies exist that dissect and measure notions such as democracy, development and corruption (see for example Landman and Häusermann, 2003). But the human rights of workers, which protect them as social and economic actors or as the subjects of employers' decisions or of governmental action or inaction, continue to lead the life of a wallflower – nice to know they are there, but of little interest to the uninitiated. The fact that the most fundamental of them are expressions of cherished civil and political rights is barely noticed.

The World Summit for Social Development held in Copenhagen in 1995 gave labour rights a political boost when Heads of State committed their countries to respecting a set of fundamental International Labour Organization Conventions.[1] Discussions had been underway for a while in the Secretariat, the ILO, to give certain values and rights more importance than others. In 1998 this resulted in the adoption by the Organization of the Declaration on Fundamental Principles and Rights at Work and its Follow-up, as well as in the designation of selected Conventions as 'fundamental'. Much of the Anglo-Saxon world refers to them as 'core labour standards', especially economists and politicians. Some legal cultures feel more at ease with words such as 'basic' rights. While linguists and specialists may consider 'fundamental' to be narrower and more specific in meaning than 'basic', and 'basic' to be more precise and broader than 'core', or *vice versa*, this book uses all three terms interchangeably.

What is characteristic of fundamental human rights in the labour field is that they are universal rights in the sense that they are applicable regardless of a country's level of economic, political or other development. Unlike the economic, social and cultural rights enunciated in the ICESCR, which can as a matter of law be achieved 'progressively' (article 2(1)), the fundamental principles and rights for which the International Labour Organization stands cannot be made subject to prior economic development. The principles apply in full here and today, the rights specified in international labour standards apply in full one year after ratification.

Most core labour standards that are held today to be of key importance date back to the early years of the codification process of human rights: the rights of workers to associate in the defence of their interests; freedom from slavery or forced labour; and everyone's right to equal opportunity and treatment. Children, by contrast, are newcomers to the world of international human rights. They owe their addition to both humanistic concerns and worries about physical, educational and economic development. The 1989 Convention on the Rights of the Child signalled this elevation to human rights status. The International Labour Organization, almost a generation earlier, had adopted an international standard designed 'to ensure the effective abolition of child labour and to raise progressively the minimum age for admission to employment or work to a level consistent with the fullest physical and mental development of young persons' (Convention No. 138, article 1). When in the 1990s newspapers and TV increasingly featured children who were trafficked into debt bondage

or made to work as prostitutes or perform hazardous industrial or
agricultural work, the Organization's members elaborated a further
standard that obliges ratifying countries to eliminate as a priority the
worst forms of child labour (Convention No. 182). 1998 marks the step
of elevating the abolition of child labour to a fundamental principle
and right in the International Labour Organization when it became
one of the four subject matters singled out by the Declaration on
Fundamental Principles and Rights at Work and its Follow-up. Convention No. 138 thus joined the ranks of core labour standards, and
Convention No. 182 became part of them when it entered into force in
2000.

By no means all the human rights enunciated in the UDHR and the
two 1966 Covenants that relate to the world of work enjoy high status
today. Some seem to enjoy little status in practice. For example, the
rights to social security (UDHR, articles 22 and 25, and ICESCR, article 9),
to work (UDHR, article 23, and ICESCR, article 6), to free choice of
employment and just conditions of work (ICESCR, article 7) had pre-
occupied the post-World War II generation. But their aura of important
human rights seems to have evaporated. Growth and investment are
terms heard more often in their context than the word right.

The discussions surrounding globalization in the 1990s led to a distinction between labour rights that are fundamental and others that
have lower status. The dice have been cast and are unlikely to be
juggled again for a while. Exactly which rights in the labour field are
fundamental human rights is indicated hereunder. Suffice it to use as
headings the terms of the Declaration and then list the titles or
selected provisions of key instruments of the League of Nations, the
UN and of the relevant core Conventions of the International Labour
Organization.[2]

1.2   Freedom of association[3]

It was the UDHR that boldly proclaimed that 'everyone has the right to
freedom of assembly and association', and 'everyone has the right to
form and to join trade unions for the protection of his interests' (articles 20(1) and 23(4), respectively). The two 1966 Covenants reiterated
these principles in slightly different and still gender-insensitive language. 'Everyone shall have the right to freedom of association with
others, including the right to form and join trade unions for the protection of his interests' (ICCPR, article 22 (1)). 'States Parties...under-
take to ensure: (a) The right of everyone to form trade unions and join

the trade union of his choice, subject only to the rules of the organization concerned, for the promotion and protection of his economic and social interests' (ICESCR, article 8 (1)).

The International Labour Organization's two core standards in this field are Convention Nos. 87 and 98.[4] The key provisions of Convention No. 87 lay down that 'workers and employers, without distinction whatsoever, shall have the right to establish and, subject only to the rules of the organization concerned, to join organizations of their own choosing without previous authorisation'. They specify that 'public authorities shall refrain from any interference which would restrict this right or impede the lawful exercise thereof' (articles 2 and 3(2), respectively). Convention No. 98 protects workers against, *inter alia*, 'acts calculated to (a) make the employment of a worker subject to the condition that he shall not join a union or shall relinquish trade union membership; (b) cause the dismissal...of a worker by reason of union membership' (article 1(2)).

1.3   Elimination of all forms of forced or compulsory labour[5]

The global human rights codification in this area began with the League of Nations Slavery Convention, 1926. Twenty-seven years later, the UN General Assembly amended this Convention by a Protocol. In 1956, it supplemented it by the Supplementary Convention on the Abolition of Slavery, the Slave Trade, and Institutions and Practices Similar to Slavery. The UDHR affirmed the basic principles summarily by stating: 'No one shall be held in slavery or servitude; slavery and the slave trade shall be prohibited in all their forms' (article 4). The ICCPR covered slavery and forced labour in one comprehensive article. 'No one shall be held in slavery; slavery and the slave trade in all their forms shall be prohibited'; and 'No one shall be required to perform forced or compulsory labour' (articles 8(1) and 8(3)(a), respectively).

The two core standards of the International Labour Organization in this area followed those of the League of Nations and United Nations with a short time lag and by focusing on work.[6] Convention No. 29 prohibits public and private employers from exacting any 'work or service...from any person under the menace of any penalty and for which the said person has not offered himself voluntarily' (article 2(1)). While there are certain exceptions to this principle, such as work imposed in cases of emergency, the notion of penalty is not limited to penal sanctions but extends to, for instance, withdrawal of traditional privileges, withholding of identity papers and the locking up of workers on private premises. Convention No. 105 lays down that workers cannot be compelled to work as a means of political coercion, labour discipline or racial, social, national or religious discrimination; as a method of mobilizing and using labour for purposes of economic development; and as a punishment for having participated in strikes.

1.4   Effective abolition of child labour[7]

While children were the first subject of protective labour legislation at the national level (see Engermann, 2003), 174 years elapsed before article 24(1) of the ICCPR recognized children as a possessor of human rights at the international level. A further 13 years later, in 1989, the wide-ranging Convention on the Rights of the Child was adopted by the United Nations. Article 32 contains its wording regarding child labour:

1. *States Parties recognize the right of the child to be protected from economic exploitation and from performing any work that is likely to be hazardous or to interfere with the child's education, or to be harmful to the child's health or physical, mental, spiritual, moral or social development.*
2. *States Parties shall take legislative, administrative, social and educational measures to ensure the implementation of the present article. To this end, and having regard to the relevant provision of other international instruments, States Parties shall in particular*
   (a) *provide for a minimum age or minimum ages for admission to employment;*
   (b) *provide for appropriate regulation of the hours and conditions of employment;*
   (c) *provide for appropriate penalties or other sanctions to ensure the effective enforcement of the present article.*

The International Labour Organization's core standards in this field are Convention Nos. 138 and 182.[8] The first of this pair of Conventions requires governments to set and enforce a minimum age or ages at which children can enter into different kinds of work. The general minimum age for admission to employment should not be less than 15 years, though developing countries may make certain exceptions to this rule, and a minimum age of 14 years may be applied where the economy and education system are insufficiently advanced. Household chores, work in family undertakings and work that is part of education are excluded from minimum age requirements. Convention No. 182 obliges ratifying countries to 'take immediate and effective measures to secure the prohibition and elimination of the worst forms of child labour as a matter of urgency' (article 1). Article 3 describes these 'worst forms' as:

(a) *all forms of slavery or practices similar to slavery, such as the sale and trafficking of children, debt bondage and serfdom and forced or compulsory labour, including forced or compulsory recruitment of children for use in armed conflict;*

(b) *the use, procuring or offering of a child for prostitution, for the production of pornography or for pornographic performances;*

(c) *the use, procuring or offering of a child for illicit activities, in particular for the production and trafficking of drugs as defined in the relevant international treaties;*

(d) *work which, by its nature or the circumstances in which it is carried out, is likely to harm the health, safety or morals of children.*

1.5   Elimination of discrimination in respect of employment and occupation[9]

UN instruments usually have a general non-discrimination clause among their initial provisions. Examples are UNDHR, article 2; ICCPR, articles 2(1) and 3; and ICESCR articles 2(2) and 3. They also contain specific equality provisions aimed at men and women or that extend to specific categories or which are open-ended in terms of the scope of their application. The UDHR lays down a long-cherished principle of the workers' movement: 'Everyone, without any discrimination, has the right to equal pay for equal work' (article 23(2)). The two Covenants are broader:

All persons are equal before the law and are entitled without any discrimination to the equal protection of the law. In this respect, the law shall prohibit any discrimination and guarantee to all persons equal and effective protection against discrimination on any ground such as race, colour, sex, language, religion, political or other opinion, national or social origin, property, birth or other status. (ICCPR, article 26); and

The States Parties to the present Covenant recognize the right of everyone to the enjoyment of just and favourable conditions of work which ensure, in particular:

> *(a) (i) Fair wages and equal remuneration for work of equal value without distinction of any kind, in particular women being guaranteed conditions of work not inferior to those enjoyed by men, with equal pay for equal work...*
>
> *(c) Equal opportunity for everyone to be promoted in his employment to an appropriate higher level, subject to no considerations other than those of seniority and competence* (ICESCR, article 7).

Two United Nations Conventions cover areas in which discrimination has existed since time immemorial: the International Convention on the Elimination of All Forms of Racial Discrimination, 1965, and the Convention on the Elimination of all Forms of Discrimination against Women, 1979.

The International Labour Organization's two core standards in this field are Convention Nos. 100 and 111.[10] The first of this pair of Conventions lays down that rates of remuneration are to be established without discrimination based on the sex of the worker. It requires that men and women obtain equal pay for work of equal value and not just for the same or similar work. The second, broader Convention outlaws all discrimination on seven grounds: 'race, colour, sex, religion, political opinion, national extraction, social origin' (Convention No. 111, article 1). It also encourages governments to add further grounds after consultation with employers' and workers' organizations, which means that countries can commit themselves internationally to, for instance, disability, age or HIV/AIDS as criteria for not permitting discrimination in the labour field.

It is worth insisting that the 1998 Declaration brought about a global consensus on the four fundamental freedoms in the world of work – freedom of association, freedom from forced labour, freedom from child labour and freedom from discrimination. These freedoms are not subject to Asian values, African traditions, OECD specifications, negotiations in the European Union or any region's or country's preferences.[11] They take as a minimum the general principles and rights enshrined in the Declaration and as a maximum the details specified in the aforementioned eight core Conventions. The UN's Global Compact launched in 1999 includes the Declaration's fundamental principles and rights at work. The Global Reporting Initiative includes them under human rights (although it is somewhat unspecific about non-discrimination, see GRI, 2002). Even the World Bank not only acknowledges that freedom of association is a human right that requires no further justification, but it also increasingly recognizes it as being economically beneficial to countries' development.[12]

1.6   Basic labour rights matter

Why in the contemporary world should one want to measure the achievement of these rights? Essentially, because their non-achievement cripples millions of lives[13] and many economies, too – and that is well worth documenting. Take the right to organize and bargain. Well-heeled 'western' neo-liberals decry unions as interfering in the workings of the market, and they hold up the ideal of atomized labour markets where individuals are traded like apples and oranges. In labour markets, ordinary workers do get gobbled up like apples and oranges. In single party/ single union regimes, they are herded like sheep to where they are told to go. Ordinary workers need independent organizations to protect themselves against the imbalances and injustices inherent in labour markets. Assured of having a real voice, trade unions are responsible and respected partners for both employers and governments; their loyalty to deals struck pays handsome productivity gains (Sengenberger, 2002). As Mark Malloch Brown, Administrator of UNDP, put it when introducing the Human Development Report of 2000 on human rights and development: 'Only when people feel they have a stake and a voice will they throw themselves wholeheartedly into development. Rights make human beings better economic actors' (UNDP, 2000, p. iii).[14]

Forced labour is morally reprehensible to all except those who perpetrate it and profit from it. Economically, it is actually inefficient. It can also be downright criminal in nature. The profits that landlords, recruiters, middlemen, traffickers and others make on the back of the poor are not legitimate by the mere fact of being profits. Traditional forms of bonding individuals or families for a season or for life have the effect of tying up capital sub-optimally and preventing both the workers and the capital from becoming more productive and gaining higher returns. Modern forms of trafficking boys and girls, adult men and women into brothels or sweatshops generally deprive the workers of protection in the event of accident or illness and the State of revenue. Failing to achieve the elimination of forced labour in all its forms means closing one's eye to work that is both immoral and uneconomic.

Across the globe, a quarter of a billion children labour in activities they should not be engaged in, about 180 million in what Convention No. 182 calls the worst forms of child labour (ILO, 2002b and 2002c). Unacceptable work stunts children's bodies, minds and mortgages their future, often leaving an indelible mark on their lives, sometimes even on the lives of their own children. While it is clear that poverty breeds child labour, it is equally clear that child labour perpetuates poverty. Until unacceptable work by children is effectively marginalized, development will suffer – the development of the children themselves and the development of their countries.

Most of today's workers encounter discrimination in access to work and while being employed – women, racial, ethnic, social or religious minorities, among others. Deeply seated traditions and status ascriptions have only recently come to be challenged. The horrors of fascism were sufficiently powerful to propel equality questions on the political agendas of some countries. South Africa's *apartheid* re-kindled the flames of moral outrage, as did the Khmer regime in Cambodia, Suharto's soldiers in Indonesia and Saddam Hussein's terror in Iraq. The economics of modern production processes call into question the written and unwritten rules of whom to employ and under what conditions. Cutting-edge enterprises need access to all available human resources, and they need to motivate and keep the workers they invest in. The threat of being branded a discriminator renders modern managers gender-friendly and open to the employment, training and promotion of groups formerly looked down upon. Where discrimination occurs, public opprobrium and economic losses may threaten.

The moral force of human rights and their economic utility combine to make the measurement of the achievement of basic labour rights a compelling – indeed an urgent – task.

1.7 Purposes of measuring human rights achievements

What purpose should the construction of human rights indicators have? The first and primary objective is to document empirically where countries stand today on scales measuring the realization of the four fundamental freedoms, and to monitor future progress in the achievement of rights. Aggregations of countries' scores to regions and the world at large enables one to perceive more generally whether this or that freedom is increasingly respected or encounters growing problems of giving it practical effect. This is not the same, however, as verifying theoretical constructs that seek to explain why countries are good or bad achievers, nor is it the same as analysing how effective international procedures are in ensuring compliance with core Conventions. The latter was attempted not long ago for a slightly different set of human rights Conventions of the International Labour Organization by Weisband, 2000.

The second purpose is advocacy – to stir the drum publicly about identified shortfalls. Naming and shaming can induce individual governments, employers' and workers' organizations or other non-State actors to change the *status quo*. A country can, of its own volition, set time-bound targets and adopt measures to achieve them progressively; and it can appeal to other countries or international organizations for assistance in moving forward.

Documentation and advocacy are the two aims underpinning this book, which will eschew complicated mathematical formulae so as to permit non-specialists to follow the logic and the actual results of the new indicator system.

2
Can the Achievement of Rights be Measured Quantitatively?

2.1 Credible outcome measurements are lacking

By which method is one to measure the achievement of basic rights in the world of work? Against which precise objective is one to place the measuring rod of indicators? Which kind of indicator should be used? Ideally, one should look for outcome indicators that reflect the reality of rights 'on the ground', that is, in the daily lives of individuals. Actual objectives to be assessed would include: do all workers in country X fully enjoy the freedom to organize and bargain? Is that country free from all forms of forced labour? Are its less-than-18-years-old employed or self-employed in activities that are harmful to health, safety or morals? Are certain groups discriminated when looking for work or when at work?

Straightforward questions – for which there are, to date, only unsatisfactory answers. Consider, to start with, freedom of association. The first on-the-ground indicator that comes to mind is union density. This is generally defined as the proportion of the (non-agricultural?) labour force or wage employees who are (currently? paid-up?) members of trade unions. For such an important phenomenon, union density is excruciatingly badly documented; and in one third or so of today's States it is not all documented (ILO, 2004b). What intrinsically invalidates this indicator as a measurement of freedom of association is the fact that there is no linear relationship between the extent of this freedom and the degree of union density because the latter is primarily a function of how countries' political regimes and traditions have evolved in the course of history and how their industrial relations systems are structured. For example, countries that were formerly part of the Soviet Union and some developing countries with single party

11

regimes have very high double-digit union density figures; by contrast, democratic countries such as France and Spain merely have single-digit union density figures.

Are there proxy indicators of freedom of association? It may be tempting to turn to the civil liberties and political rights indexes elaborated since 1972 by Freedom House, a US-based NGO, which include association and organizational rights. However, multiple weaknesses are associated with Freedom House's indexes. A panel of specialists from the same geo-political background uses different measuring rods for different countries but does not permit proper public scrutiny of their assessments. Objectivity and replicability are not ensured. Moreover, the actual freedom of association rights make up only 1/14 of the overall civil liberties index and cannot be extracted separately. This source is clearly unsuitable as a valid measure of achievements of basic labour rights.

The OECD elaborated a proxy by adopting a similar method, choosing a panel of evaluators from among its Secretariat staff who rated 79 countries and grouped them into four clusters (OECD, 1996). The OECD made clear, however, on which sources (including ILO sources) its judgements were based. Four years later the OECD published an update for 69 countries that rated observations made during 1989–99 by the ILO's Committee of Experts on the Application of Conventions and Recommendations (hereafter Committee of Experts or CEACR). The OECD Secretariat assigned a first score based on its appreciation of the type and degree of restriction of freedom of association rights commented upon by the Committee of Experts, followed by a second score based on the Secretariat's interpretation of the Committee of Expert's evaluation of the situation and required remedy (OECD, 2000, pp. 85–86). Combined scores vary from 0 ('full compliance') to 20 ('extreme non-compliance'). However, panel judgements by culturally homogeneous groups tend to be subjective, even where they give the appearance of sophistication. They are insufficiently objective and replicable to serve as a valid proxy for the measurement of freedom of association rights; and they cover less than the half of the world's States. The OECD did not actually dare to publish country-level data. While this book will construct two indicators that make use of the same Committee of Experts comments, I shall abstain from judging their contents and, instead, assign different weights to one form of comment as opposed to the other – as determined by the Committee of Experts itself – thereby safeguarding objectivity and inter-coder reliability (see Chapter 5).

When one searches for on-the-ground collective bargaining data, one is struck by the poverty of existing information and the difficulty of assigning outcome values to distinct but overlapping levels of collective bargaining. Collective bargaining can take place in individual enterprises, an industry or a region, the country as whole and, in a rudimentary form, even internationally in the sense that enterprises in several countries are involved simultaneously. Countries' mix of systems may change in the course of time. It is rather unclear what a certain degree of this or that form of coverage of collective bargaining actually represents in terms of the achievement of basic rights in the labour field.

Six sets of indicators purport to measure freedom of association and collective bargaining rights (Verité, 2004; CIRI, n.d.; Kucera, forthcoming; Cuyvers and van den Bulcke, forthcoming; Botero *et al.*, 2003) or could be taken as a proxy (ILO, 2004d). Since they will be tested later in the necessary detail (Chapter 8), suffice it to state here that none of them comes close to satisfying the requirements to which human rights indicators must submit. It must, unfortunately, be concluded that valid, replicable and objective country-level indicators measuring on-the-ground outcomes in the area of freedom of association and collective bargaining are at present not available.

As regards forced labourers, counting them in at least a quasi-scientific way is something that few (except Bales, 1999) have tried. The fact that some traditional forms of bonding which give rise to forced labour are outlawed in a number of countries and that trafficking is increasingly stamped as criminal has not enticed much academic interest nor has it entailed many solid assessments by NGOs. Interest was high in India for a while (see Mishra, 2001 and 2002). The forced-labour-outcomes of bonding, which follow time-honoured seasonal or other production patterns, could be documented with tailor-made surveys; and the ILO has now launched original research in a few countries. The forced-labour-outcomes of trafficking within and across countries are more difficult to capture and render scientifically defensible.

Proxy measurements of bonding have been put forward by reference to certain types of landholding in Pakistan (Ercelawn and Jauman, 2001). But the same kind of landholding can historically, socially and regionally produce quite different bonding outcomes (see follow-up research by Hussein *et al.*, 2004, and Arif, 2004). It is much too broad a measure. As regards within-country or across-border trafficking, proxy measurements would have to look into the underground economy, parcel out how much of it is due to trafficking and how much results

in forced labour, and then establish a more-or-less-invariable relationship between these variables, which is too far-fetched an idea to
warrant being pursued.

In the area of forced labour, too, outcome indicators do not exist at
present and are unlikely to be available on a regular basis in the fore-
seeable future.

The estimate of a quarter of a billion child labourers mentioned
earlier is extrapolated from a representative set of 29 national household surveys (see ILO, 2002b, 2002c and 2004c, figures relate to the
turn of the century). Most of these surveys were conducted by the ILO
and the World Bank. They may be repeated from time to time. A
number of countries include some young age groups in regular labour
force or establishment surveys, though these catch child labour in a
more limited way. Direct on-the-ground measurements are too spotty
to follow developments in a sufficient number of countries at short
intervals.

Several proxy indicators have been proposed for child labour.
Richard Anker has pointed to employed children who are not in school
and to children who are in wage employment or self-employment
(Anker *et al.*, 2003). Such data would approximate some but not all
forms of unacceptable work that is undertaken by children.
And they contain inherent flaws that render them unsuitable as on-
the-ground measures of various child labour phenomena: (a) non-
enrolment in schools or non-attendance may in developing countries
or transition economies be due to the lack of schools or the existence
of schools of such low quality that parents (or grandparents in the case
of the growing number of HIV/AIDS orphans) refrain from sending
their children there; (b) there are child labourers who combine work
and school (1 in 10 in a typical survey quoted in ILO, 2002c, table 14);
and (c) there may be others who are neither at work nor at school (1 in
7 in the same survey).

The OECD elaborated another proxy for child labour, applying the
methodology that it first developed for freedom of association.
Analysing the observations by the ILO's Committee of Experts on Convention No. 138 during 1992–2002 for 26 countries, its Secretariat
rated the type and restriction identified by the Committee of Experts as
well as the situation and requested remedy (OECD, 2003, pp. 118–120).
However, OECD staff is drawn from the same cultural background and
its interpretations are culture specific; they are not available on a
country-level basis; and they cannot serve as valid proxies to assess the
abolition of child labour on the ground.

In the area of non-discrimination, one would have to capture on-the-ground achievements with regard to three aspects: (i) equal pay for equal work or for work of equal value, (ii) equal access to employment in its manifold forms, and (iii) equal treatment once a worker is employed or self-employed. All of these aspects should be documented with respect to men and women, workers of different races, ethnic or social origin, religion and so on. Quite a tall order!

Pay differentials by sex can be inferred from average earnings of men and women in selected occupations or sectors of a fair number of countries. By contrast, pay differentials by racial, ethnic or other characteristics are almost entirely undocumented. In any case, averages are not really a valid measuring rod; the distribution of earnings would be; but distributional data are practically inexistent.

As regards equal access to work, discrimination is to some – but unknown – extent reflected in labour force participation rates and employment-to-population ratios. Although widely available by sex, these two indicators are influenced by so many factors other than equality measures that their value as proxies is, in fact, highly limited.[1] Some of these other factors – economic growth is an example – do not impact uniformly on the labour force participation rates of men compared with women. Labour force participation rates or employment-to-population ratios by racial, ethnic and other discrimination dimensions are unfortunately not available for most countries.[2] A group's share in non-agricultural wage employment could provide a more defensible proxy of the achievement of the basic right to equality in access to employment. Even though widely available on a gender basis, regular data of this kind for different races, ethnic, social, religious or other groups are lacking.

As regards the achievement of equality during employment, there are no time series that document differential conditions of work, training opportunities, promotion to higher-level jobs, termination of the employment relationship and so on. For women, discrimination could be said to be mirrored indirectly and rather approximately in their share among professional and technical workers.[3] However, this indicator reflects not only equality during employment but also equality in access to employment; it measures two aspects simultaneously that, though not unrelated, are distinct. Racial, ethnic or other characteristics, again, cannot be discerned in published statistics of professional and technical workers.

Two sets of indicators that assess the basic labour or economic rights of women (CIRI, n.d., and Cuyvers and van den Bulcke, forthcoming),

and UNDP's Gender-related Development Index or its Gender Empowerment Measure, may be viewed as proxies. When tested, however,
all of them turn out to be flawed in relation to the achievement of the
fundamental human right of non-discrimination in the labour field
(see Chapter 11.5). Thus, as for the other three freedoms, so for the
freedom from discrimination: on-the-ground indicators to measure
progress throughout the world are at present unavailable.

As regards indicators that cover all relevant core labour standards as
a whole, to the best of my knowledge only two sets full measurements
exist: Verité, 2004, and CIRI. n.d. Proxies of labour rights may be
assumed to exist in a truncated version in the form of ILO's Representation Security Index (ILO, 2004d), in the form of assessments of
political regimes (Freedom House, 1999, and Polity, n.d.) or in the
form of economic and development indicators (FDI, value added per
worker and Gini coefficients, UNDP's Human Development Index
(HDI) and ILO's Economic Security Index). But when all of them
are tested later in some detail (Chapter 7.5), it is clear that none comes
close to matching the validity, transparency, replicability, non-
truncation and, importantly, the objectivity of the new indicators
presented in the book, which have the added advantage that their data
are easy and cost-effective to collect.

2.2   Foundations of the new indicator system

This book puts forward a new system of indicators to credibly measure
real achievements with identical measuring rods each year for all countries at the same time. It is justified to speak of a system because all the
factors involved will be endogenous and inter-related. As it is intuitively easier to grasp, I turn things around to depict the extent of *non*-
achievement, which one could also refer to as *lack of* or *shortfall in* or
deficit of or in similar terms. I prefer the word *gap*, which is italicized
when it refers to the indicators constructed here.

The *gap* system is built on two dimensions. One is the enunciation of
rights in law, which I call *adherence*, italicized when used in the context
of this indicator system. The other concerns what actually happens on
the ground, which I call *implementation,* also italicized when used in
the new indicator system. In the field of human and labour rights it
rarely suffices to formulate a norm for it to become reality. Abolition of
the death penalty is an exception. None of the four freedoms this book
deals with comes about by mere legislative fiat.

The distinction between *adherence* and *implementation* enables one to
see at a glance which factor is responsible for the non-achievement of

rights: whether it is an *adherence gap*, an *implementing gap* or a combination of the two. Depending on the answer, quite different responses may be called for to close *gaps*. The indicators put forward here can then be used to monitor the results of remedial measures taken.

The first dimension measures the extent to which a country *adheres* to fundamental rights in the labour field. At the national level, this would put the spotlight on laws and other forms of legislation, at the international level on ratification and related reporting obligations. *Adherence* reflects political willingness or commitment, which may be full or partial. *Adherence gaps* indicate the extent of a country's unwillingness or lack of commitment.

Can the residents of an independent country enjoy fundamental human rights if they are not laid down in law? They cannot. Mere statements by political leaders are not enough. And, while small groups may manage during times of political transition to carve out for themselves small islands of rights (as certain unions did, for instance, at the end of Franco's regime in Spain and at the beginning of the 1980s in communist Poland), they are not secured by legislation and can be invaded at any time by the government without restraint (as the Jaruzelski government did in Poland). Freedoms need to be grounded in law, and their application has to be ensured in practice by public support and effective penalties in case of infringement, whether by private citizens or the police. Whatever might happen outside of the law, in contemporary States rights do not 'happen' – they are not gifts from heaven. The freedom to organize and bargain, the freedoms from forced labour, child labour and discrimination will remain unattainable until, as a result of a political process, each is firmly and correctly enshrined in law.

Economists nurture the hope that fundamental rights are byproducts of economic growth or development. But growth or development do not somehow cause or entail freedom of association. Workers' movements see to that or insightful governments enable it to happen. Nor does growth or development wipe out forced labour, though they may change some of its forms and sectoral distribution in the economy. Growth and development can actually entail new forms of forced labour, which happened for example in Brazil with charcoal burning for furnaces and car production, and the clearing of the Amazon forest for cattle ranching and meat exports. Likewise, growth or development do not abolish child labour, but they may change some of its forms or move children from, for instance, traditional carpet weaving to soccer-ball stitching or garment production for rich-countries' markets. Whether in Kolkata, Johannesburg, Naples or elsewhere, societies invariably have poor people with parents desperate enough to send their children out to work; and poor children themselves will look for work or fall prey to tempting offers. As regards discrimination, growth or development will not dissolve prejudices, for there is no factor inherent in either that would have such consequences. Historically, the boot has been on the other foot: Growth and development have in the past frequently proceeded on the basis of labour discrimination – for example, in South Africa during 100 years. Human rights pressure from the outside made the difference in that country. Such pressure has not been applied to many other parts of the world. The fact that a number of modern, notably multinational, enterprises nowadays seek to tap into all available human resources and adopt non-discriminatory policies should not blind one to the fact that this is quite exceptional, and costly. Not every small or medium-size enterprise, nor even all governments, can readily invest in equality measures.

At any rate, development is not a cure-all of basic rights in the labour field. Legislation is indispensable. The standard for national legislation is international human rights law.

The *gap* system's second dimension measures the extent to which countries give practical effect to basic freedoms. National legislation and international commitments will remain a dead letter unless appropriate follow-up steps are taken. Depending on the specific area of basic rights, these may comprise (i) compliance of national legislation with international standards, (ii) actual enforcement and (iii) institutional support mechanisms. *Implementation gaps* indicate the extent of non-compliance, of lack of enforcement and of deficits in institutional support.

The first of these aspects concerns the subordinate relationship of national legislation to internationally agreed minimum human rights standards. To enjoy freedom of association, for example, national law should not withhold from any category what international law accords to all workers, with the possible exception of the armed forces and the police (Convention No. 87, article 9). Agricultural workers, civil servants, migrant workers and workers in Export-Processing Zones should not be deprived nationally of fundamental rights that were enshrined internationally. In the area of forced labour, national laws would not comply with international standards if they did not ensure that landlords, recruiters, middlemen, traffickers and others give workers a reasonable chance to pay off their debts, to get their identity papers when they want them and to move around freely. In the area of child labour, national laws would be deficient if they did not spell out that children of certain ages should not be working in a number of activities. National laws would not afford equality of opportunity and treatment if their specifications did not properly cover remuneration, access to work and equality during employment in respect of race, colour, sex, religion, political opinion, national extraction and social origin. If national legislation were narrower in scope or more limited in content than the relevant international standard, an *implementation gap* would exist.

The second aspect of *implementation* involves the standard law enforcement function of States, which is exercised by way of administrative supervision and judicial challenge of violators, including private persons (see Box 2.1). International law almost always leaves the choice of means to national practices. Several core Conventions refer explicitly to monitoring the provisions that give effect to it (Convention No. 182, article 5), to labour inspectors (Convention No. 29, article 24) and to appropriate penalties such as the provision and application of penal sanctions (Convention No. 138, article 9, and Convention No. 182, article 7(1)). If such measures are absent in any of the four areas of freedoms, the Conventions are not fully *implemented* and *gaps* exist.

Box 2.1 Human rights commit governments to their application in the private sector

All fundamental rights in the labour field apply both to public employment or para-statal enterprises and to private enterprises of any size, cooperatives, self-employed, own-account workers, and so on. For example, governments should not tolerate private employers who unjustifiably punish trade unionists to keep workers' organizations out of enterprises or to minimize their influence. 'Facts imputable to individuals incur the responsibility of States because of their obligation to remain vigilant and take action to prevent violations of human rights' (ILO, 1996, p. 19). As regards forced labour, while decolonization and the demise of the communist system have much reduced the number of governments that knowingly engage in forced labour practices, today it is primarily private individuals who compel millions to work against their will, which governments must prevent. In the area of child labour, the private sector is almost exclusively responsible for the work of children that they should not carry out. As regards discrimination, most of it occurs outside government offices and workshops, although the public sector is not by any means beyond reproach in every country.

The third aspect concerns more far-reaching institutional measures. All four freedoms are positive rights in the sense that they require governments to establish systems for complaints about violation, adjudication and remedies or the setting up and staffing of special machinery or bodies to undertake promotional and monitoring activities. Where that is not the case or where the machinery or body in question does not actually contribute to realizing relevant freedoms, the *implementation* dimension of the new indicator system should record this as a problem in achieving the human right concerned.

A further aspect is conceptually relevant only to forced labour, child labour and discrimination. This comprises broad economic and social policies or programmes to combat these phenomena. For example, forced labourers who are freed may need to be provided with alternative opportunities to gain income and to receive training or education for themselves and their families. Child labourers and their families are likely to require educational support, poverty alleviation measures, and so on. Convention No. 182 mentions access to free basic education and vocational training (article 7(2)(c)) but also 'direct assistance for the removal of children from the worst forms of child labour and for their rehabilitation and social integration' (article 7(2)(b)).[4] In the area of non-discrimination, the State will certainly have to go beyond awareness raising and, among other things, plough human and financial resources into its educational and training systems to move lastingly towards more equality in the world or work. Convention No. 111, article 3(e), explicitly refers to vocational guidance, training and placement services. Any such measure entails public expenditure, probably sizeable expenditure, which explains why international human rights law tends to be silent on this subject. However, in the absence of specific international injunctions, the lack of specific policies or programmes will not enter the system as an *implementation* problem. The *gap* system measures the lack of achievement only in relation to specified obligations.

Once a country's *adherence* and *implementation gaps* have been estimated, they are summed to yield the *Core Rights Gap* (CRG). The CRG is a two-dimensional notion that is synthetic in nature and which, as such, cannot be measured in the real world. In this sense it is comparable to, for instance, UNDP's HDI that merges three distinct dimensions and to Wall Street's Dow Jones Index that sums the results of trading in important stocks. Neither of these two indexes is measurable directly.

If there is an *adherence* or *implementation gap*, it will show up in the system as a number larger than 0, and there will consequently be a

CRG. At 0 there is no *adherence gap*, no *implementation gap* and no CRG. Unlike the HDI and many other indicators, the lower the number that the *gap* system calculates, the better the country's performance. Ideally, a country should have no *adherence gap*, no *implementation gap* and, therefore, no CRG.

2.3   Human rights indicators must fulfil certain criteria

Indicators select the most representative or important aspects of the phenomenon studied. They suggest what is happening but do not necessarily reflect reality fully or exhaustively. Indicators suck up and simplify dispersed information that is complex in nature and which they display in an intuitively understandable form. At a glance, indicators help to gain a picture of where things stand and how they change over time.[5]

To be credible, indicators have to fulfil certain criteria. For example, they have to be valid, transparent, replicable and be applied potentially to all countries. Human rights indicators have to fulfil further criteria: they should not use biased sources or reflect the subjective views of a select few among the initiated or from the same cultural or political background. They must be objective and use identical measuring rods. They ought to be useful as well in the sense of providing timely information that is relatively easy and cost-effective to collect.

First and foremost, indicators have to be valid. Adcock and Collier (2001, p. 531) define a measurement as 'valid when the scores...derived from a given indicator...can meaningfully be interpreted in terms of the systematized concept...that the indicator seeks to operationalize'. The *gap* system fully satisfies this definition, as will be seen when its concept is set out in the next Chapter with the help of the logical structure developed by Adcock and Collier.

Second, indicators and their sources must be transparent. This means the internal structure of indicators and the relationships or weights among their constituent elements must be revealed. Readers must not be left in the dark as to what is involved – as is the case, for example, with the democracy index put out by Freedom House. I take great care to spell out each detail of the *gap* system, which draws its data solely from ILO sources that are in the public domain, in printed form or through the ILO's public website.

Third, inter-coder reliability must be ensured, that is researchers must be able not only to replicate the constructs of the *gap* system but also to reach the same results. This is easily ensured here by the use of binary indicators based on yes/no distinctions that record whether something happens or does not happen. Ratification is an example of a binary indicator: Either a country ratifies a Convention or it does not. A comment put out by the Committee of Experts is another example: Either the CEACR addresses a critical comment to a government or it does not. As binary indicators do not really give rise to interpretation questions or subjective judgements, other researchers should come to the same results. Inter-coder reliability of the *gap* system should, in principle, be 100 per cent.

Fourth, the basic data that serve to grade human rights achievements must not be truncated in the two-fold sense that (i) the data should not implicitly or explicitly select a few or a minority of countries but potentially bring all of them into the scoring range, and (ii) the actual results should not bunch countries at the top or bottom end of the scale or in the middle for that matter. The seven-point scale of Freedom House (1999) is an example of a heavily truncated scale. Indicators that quite indistinguishably select some countries as good performers and most others as poor performers do not measure the achievement of human rights across the board but draw political distinctions. My binary indicators cast some countries into one category and the others into another category, but they string them across the whole scale.

Fifth and importantly as far as human rights are concerned, the information on which the indicator system is based must be objective, and identical measuring rods must be applied to all countries at all times. This book eschews data put out by national governments, nongovernmental organizations, research institutes, and so on, for fear that biases may be associated with them. Information is drawn from a universal body, the ILO, where objectified data are available for indicator purposes, as will be detailed and tested later. Suffice it to say here that the actual data being fed into the new indicator system do not derive from subjective judgements or personal interpretations of staff members of the ILO – unlike the aforementioned OECD measurements of freedom of association or child labour and the Freedom House indexes. The objective facts captured by the *adherence* dimension are ratification and various forms of reporting on Conventions. The objective facts captured by the *implementation* dimension are problems identified by the Committee of Experts or the CFA, whereby the importance of the problems is weighted by these bodies themselves rather than by researchers.

Sixth, indicators should be useful, that is to say they should provide information at short intervals that is easy and cost-effective to collect.

This would not be the case for in-depth studies or detailed surveys. Although exceedingly helpful, they simply could not be repeated sufficiently often to permit the continuous tracing of developments in the human rights field that is called for. Even census intervals are too long. Annual data would be ideal. The *gap* system is fortunate to be fed with new data each year that cost practically nothing to collect. Software programmes that churn through the data can be elaborated without great difficulty and cheaply.[6]

Seventh, indicators ought to be relevant in the sense of linking data to policies. The *gap* system foresees exactly that. Its two constituent dimensions, *adherence* and *implementation*, are central to any human rights. One or the other or both variables may need to be operated upon to improve a country's situation.

Is it pertinent to distinguish among input, process and outcome indicators? That depends. Guy Standing and his group draws distinctions among input indicators such as laws and Conventions, process indicators such as the existence of labour inspectors and of labour-related boards, and outcome indicators such as the percentage of workers covered by collective agreements (Bonnet, Figueiredo and Standing, 2003, p. 216, and ILO, 2004d, p. 51). In my view, whether an indicator represents an input, process or outcome depends on the purpose of the investigation. For example, investment can be looked at as an input to an enterprise's future growth, as an output of a managerial process or as an outcome of economic conditions. By the same token, *adherence* could be viewed as a one-time input or as the outcome of a political process at a certain point of time. Likewise, the *gap* system's *implementation* dimension could be seen as an outcome of a never-ending political process, but it could equally be labeled an annual input to the realization of workers' rights.

Each of the indicators on which the *gap* system is based will be tested to see whether it fulfils the criteria postulated here. The applicability or limitations of ILO data will be examined at the same time.

3
The Architecture and Scope of the Gap System

3.1 Concepts and principles of measurement

Indicators compare an ideal world with the real world. In the field of fundamental labour rights, the ideal world is represented by freedom of association, freedom from forced labour, freedom from child labour and freedom from discrimination as enunciated by the International Labour Organization. The real world is represented by the extent of countries' *adherence* to these freedoms and the degree to which they *implement* them in practice. A *gap* is the distance between the ideal and the real world.

The freedoms are systematized as the prescriptions and proscriptions that are contained in the Organization's eight core Conventions and the related four principles and rights of the Declaration. Conventions become binding on countries when the competent legislative or executive authority ratifies them. The Declaration's principles and rights are binding by virtue of countries' membership of the Organization.

The *adherence* dimension starts with the all-important ratification indicator and comprises three others that scale obligations to report or to progress along the lines foreseen by the Declaration.

The *implementation* dimension comprises three indicators in relation to freedom of association but only two in relation to the freedoms from forced labour, child labour and discrimination. The *implementation* dimension thus has a wider scope as far as freedom of association is concerned. It would have been perfect had the other freedoms also been covered by three indicators. But the International Labour Organization has not established a complaints mechanism that is independent of ratification in respect of forced labour, child labour or discrimination. This makes the *gap* system's *implementation* dimension asymmetric, though tolerably so.

24

Inclusion of the CFA's complaints machinery bestows advantages. First, it potentially extends the assessment of *implementation* problems to countries that have not ratified either or both of the freedom of association Conventions, which matters because by the end of 2004 Convention No. 87 had not been ratified by a certain number of countries included in the *gap* system, 26. Second, it gives freedom of association greater importance than the other freedoms in the calculation of overall *gaps* when the data for all areas are combined. This is defensible because of the special importance attached to freedom of association and because it renders the *implementation* dimension more informative and complete. Freedom of association is a constitutional principle that every member State is supposed to respect by virtue of its entry into the Organization. That special importance warrants to be recognized by the indicator system.[1] Regrettably, it is the other three freedoms that are under-represented rather than freedom of association being over-represented, as it were.

The different levels of conceptualization and measurement are shown in Box 3.1, which owes its inspiration to Adcock and Collier (2001). The lightly shaded area identifies a proxy of measuring *implementation gaps* that will later be elaborated. The strongly shaded area draws attention to the fact that the CFA component concerns only freedom of association.

Several novel aspects in the development of human rights indicators characterize the system. The first is the fixed relationship between the ratification indicator of the *adherence* dimension and the other six indicators. Ratification of an international Convention scales all other indicators of the *gap* system in the sense that this decisive national act is accorded a certain value and the other indicators are expressed as a percentage of that value. The detailed reasons for this will become clear when each indicator is elaborated in detail. Suffice it to say here that any problem of reporting or *implementation* can call into question only a portion of the political commitment that is made when a country accepts a core Convention. If there were a small problem, only a small portion of the value of ratifying that Convention would be questionable. If there were broad violations of the letter and spirit of a ratified Convention, the act of ratifying it might be said to have lost much of its value.[2] The *implementation* dimension is thus inextricably linked to the *adherence* dimension – it depends on it.

If ratification of a core Convention is the lynchpin of the system, what value should it be accorded? One could choose any number between 0 and 1 or 0 and 100 or along another scale. The size of the

Box 3.1 Levels of conceptualization, measurement, disaggregation and reaggregation of gaps

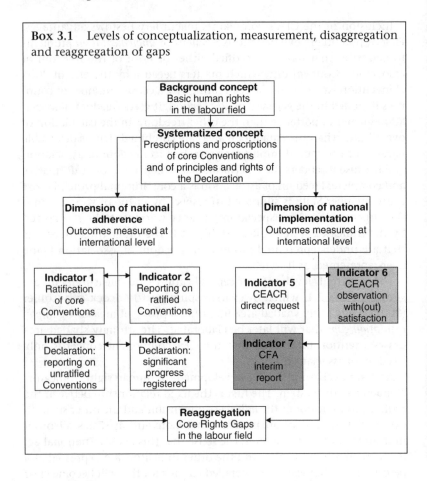

initial range is not important because all other indicators are a percentage of the standard value of ratifying a Convention – proportional relationships do not change with the size of the scale. I have chosen the range of 0 to100, which is an artificial but convenient scale that readers will find easy to follow when scoring is exemplified. Given the present high degree of ratifications of core Conventions, an *adherence gap* of 100 points could come about only if a new member State entered the Organization without ratifying a core Convention soon, which at the time of writing is the case for Timor Leste and Vanuatu, or if a current member State denounced all ratified core Conventions. Only one denunciation of a core Convention was registered during the review period: Malaysia denounced Convention No. 105 in 1990.

Furthermore, the absolute size becomes secondary when, at the end, all *gap* points are normalized, that is, compressed into a scale of 0 to 1 point. This range is frequently used when there is interest in comparing results of different indicators or for different countries.

Two values actually have to be fixed for ratification because seven core Conventions existed during the first 15 years covered by the *gap* system, 1985–99, and eight must be covered as from 2000 when Convention No. 182 came into force. The addition of a human rights standard during the period covered by an indicator system is not as extraordinary as it might appear at first sight and can be accommodated in various ways (see Box 3.2). The *gap* system opts for keeping the ratification scoring range of 0 to 100 unchanged and fitting into it seven Conventions up to 1999 and eight as from 2000. It follows that a single Convention's value comes to 14.3 points during 1985–99 and 12.5 points thereafter.

Box 3.2 Raising standards through the addition of Convention No. 182

The new indicator system has to allow for, and countries have to cope with, the raising of human rights ideals in the course of the 1985–2004 review period due to the adoption of Convention No. 182. One might argue that human rights standards should not change. However, the world would be poorer if they did not evolve and extended to more people or subject matters. Women, for example, were given the right to vote mostly long after men had enjoyed it, even in countries that considered themselves to be highly democratic. As regards the abolition of child labour, this subject has only very recently been accorded importance, joining the ranks of fundamental human rights in the labour field in the 1990s. Convention No. 182 itself was adopted as late as 1999. Countries are now called upon to live up to its requirements.

An indicator system can accommodate additional rights by having an open-ended additive scale where new data come on top of existing ones. This maximizes the effect of the internationally agreed raising of standards. Averaging would permit comparisons over time, though some loss of information is involved in calculating averages. Another approach would be to use a finite additive scale and to make the necessary adjustments within it. This reduces somewhat the effect of adding new standards, but it is more attuned to the 'new' Convention No. 182 because that standard was conceived as a specification of the 'old' Convention No. 138 of 1973 – the freedoms spelt out in the 'new' were at least implicit in the 'old' Convention. Keeping the same quantitative measure has the further advantage of allowing straightforward comparisons of how a country – or a region or the world at large – performs in the course of time. The second approach, therefore, is preferable for the *gap* system.

Box 3.2   Raising standards through the addition of Convention
No. 182 – *continued*

As regards the system's *adherence* dimension, two factors minimize unto-
ward effects on countries' scores of adding Convention No. 182: (i) the *gap*
system calculates five-year averages, with the year 2000 being a starting year;
and (ii) Convention No. 182 was blessed by the fastest rate of ratification of
any Convention of the International Labour Organization. By December
2004, 141 of the 159 countries covered by the system had ratified it. By comparison with the other fundamental labour Conventions, these are 16 more
ratifications than for the first child labour Convention of 1973, eight more
than for Convention No. 87, exactly as many as for Convention No. 98, four
less than for Convention No. 111, five less than for Convention No. 105,
seven less than for Convention No. 100 and eight less than for Convention
No. 29. A few years into its existence, therefore, Convention No. 182 was
ratified about as often as the other core Conventions, and countries' ratification records are, on average, not out of kilter. The impact of the ratification
indicator is negligible on overall CRGs that pull together all eight Conventions, though the scores of quite a number of countries will show a
'hump' for one, two or three years. Only countries not ratifying Convention
No. 182 will see their CRGs worsen significantly, which is due to the fact that
they failed to embrace the new prescriptions and proscriptions.

As regards the *implementation* dimension, it will be explained in Chapter 6.1
that scores under indicators 5 and 6 enter the *gap* system generally with a time
lag of between two and five years after ratification. Convention No. 182
will thus impact little on the overall 2000–04 *implementation gaps*; and their
contribution to CRGs will be very small indeed.

The second novelty is that the *adherence* dimension goes further than
measuring rights 'in principle' (to use the terminology of Todd
Landman, 2004). I have added not only an indicator that measures
whether or not countries report on ratified Conventions (indicator 2)
but also elaborated a component that brings into the picture the
International Labour Organization's Declaration on Fundamental
Principles and Rights at Work and its Follow-up, which obliges
member States that have not ratified particular core Conventions to
report on how they respect, promote and realize the principles and
rights that underpin those Conventions. If a country fulfils these
reporting obligations under the Declaration (indicator 3), and if it
significantly respects, promotes and realizes the relevant principles and
rights (indicator 4), the *gap* system accords it bonus points. Bonus
points reduce a portion of the country's *adherence gap*.

The third novelty in indicator development is that the *implementation* dimension objectively measures rights not at the national level but

at the international level. The *gap* system can take this approach because the national implementation of ratified Conventions is supervised internationally by an independent ILO body, the Committee of Experts, and because complaints alleging lack of respect of freedom of association are examined by another ILO body, the CFA. In essence, the *gap* system measures the frequency and degree of non-fulfilment of labour rights by weighting the form – not the contents – of selected pronouncements by the Committee of Experts (indicators 5 and 6) and CFA (indicator 7).

If the supervisory and complaints procedures operated by these bodies do not reveal any problems, there is no *implementation gap*. But if there are such problems, the *implementation* dimension can accumulate up to a maximum of 75 points. The maximum *implementation gap* is a function of the weights given to the Committee of Experts component, up to 60 points, and of the CFA component in the case of freedom of association, which has an upper limit of 15 points, just above the value of a Convention. More details will be given later.

Due to the interaction of the indicators and the weights chosen, *Core Rights Gaps* can reach a maximum of 115 points at the first stage of the system's elaboration. The maximum would be reached if no core Convention was ratified (entailing an *adherence gap* of 100 points), if no bonus points were earned under the Declaration and if the CFA component added as many as 15 points to the *implementation* dimension, which it can do even if no Convention is ratified.

Ratification of a single Convention would prevent the maximum CRG of 115 points being reached even where the Committee of Experts component and the CFA component gave rise to their respective maxima. This is due to the fact that the pronouncements of these two bodies can call into question no more than a – relatively small – portion of the value of a Convention, as will be explained in Chapter 5.

Box 3.3 summarizes how qualitative information is turned into numbers. Again, the lightly shaded area identifies where a shortcut to *implementation gaps* will later be situated, and the strongly shaded area draws attention to the fact that the CFA component applies only to freedom of association. The second stage of the construction of the new indicator system need not be explained right now and is left to Chapter 6.2.

An *adherence gap* can be either smaller or bigger than an *implementation gap*, the opposite holds true as well, and both can also have the same size. A country that has ratified all of the International Labour Organization's fundamental Conventions (and which reports dutifully

Box 3.3 Logical structure and method of calculating countries' gaps (rounded figures)

Dimension	Adherence to fundamental labour rights				Implementing basic labour rights in law and practice		
Measurement	International expression of national adherence				International verification of effect given nationally		
Component	Core Conventions (Nos. 29, 87, 98, 100, 105, 111, 138, 182)		Declaration: reporting and progressing on unratified Conventions		CEACR direct requests and/or observations and/or satisfaction on ratified Conventions		CFA interim reports
Indicator	1 = Annual (a) Ratification of seven or eight Conventions or (b) lack of ratification	2 = Biannual (a) Reporting on each ratified Convention or (b) failing to report	3 = Annual (a) Reporting on up to four principles and rights since 1999 or (b) failing to report	4 = Annual (a) Progressing on up to four principles and rights since 2004 or (b) not progressing	5 = Biannual (a) Direct request to government or (b) no direct request	6 = Biannual (a) Negative observation with or without positive satisfaction or (b) no such observation or only satisfaction	7 = *Ad hoc* (a) Interim report or (b) no such report
Mode of calculating gaps under each indicator	(a) No gap (b) Gap = points per unratified Convention	(a) No gap (b) Gap = 25% of Convention points	(a) 12.5% *bonus points per principle/right* (b) No bonus points	(a) 37.5 % *bonus points per principle/right* (b) No bonus points	(a) Gap = each direct request equal to 20% of Convention points (b) No gap	(a) Gap = each observation equal to 40% of Convention points. Satisfaction halves gap (b) No gap	(a) Gap = each such report is equal to 20% of Convention points (b) No gap

1st stage

Box 3.3 Logical structure and method of calculating countries' gaps (rounded figures) – *continued*

Dimension	Adherence to fundamental labour rights	Implementing basic labour rights in law and practice
1985–99 since 2000	0 14.3 0 3.6 *1.8* 0 – – 0 12.5 0 3.1 *1.6* 0 4.7 0	2.9 0 5.7 or 2.9 0 2.9 0 2.5 0 5.0 or 2.5 0 2.5 0
Maximum gap of component	100 points each year 25 points in 2 years or 12.5 annually *Can reduce ratification gaps by up to 50% each year*	20 + 40 = 60 points every two years or 10 + 20 = 30 on an annual basis Cap of 15 points in any year
Maximum gap of dimension	Adherence gap = interaction among indicators 1 to 4 = 100 points	Maximum implementation gap if all Conventions are ratified = interaction between indicator 1 and indicators 5 to 8 = 75 points. Maximum implementation gap if no Convention is ratified = 15 points
CRG	\multicolumn{2}{c}{CRG = adherence gap + implementation gap = scores range from 0 to 115 points}	

2nd stage	Reweighting Normalization	CRG = (adherence gap)/4 + implementation gap = scores range from 0 to 81.25 points CRG = Actual first stage gap/maximum gap = scores range from 0 to 1

on their application) has no *adherence gap*, but it may well have an *implementation gap* in respect of one, several or all of the ratified Conventions. Or it may have a large *adherence gap* and a small *implementation gap*. The interrelationships between the two scores will be exemplified several times throughout the book.

The method of calculating *implementation gaps* developed here for fundamental rights in the labour field lends itself to application to any human rights or other rights that are the object of supervisory procedures. Empirically speaking, near-universal levels of ratification yield the best results because, according to the system's logic, only ratification can reveal *implementation* problems – international supervisory bodies other than the CFA cannot look into *implementation* problems until a country has ratified or acceded to a human rights instrument. The fact that the ILO's Committee of Experts was the first important international supervisory body and has served as model for those that followed it at global and regional levels should encourage researchers to apply the logic and methodology of the *gap* system to other international instruments.

It is important to realize that the application of *gap* concepts and measurements has to take account of the duration of reporting cycles. The ILO today operates, in principle, a two-year reporting cycle for ratified core Conventions, though in practice countries that perform worst may have to report every year (Chapter 5.3.4 contains details about the reporting system). For indicators 2, 5 and 6 this means that data can be expected to be entered only every other year. While Declaration data (indicators 3 and 4) are generated every year and CFA data (indicator 7) accrue *ad hoc* year after year, it would be non-sensible to analyse and compare labour rights *gaps* during any single year. Tracing countries' – or regions' or global – achievements requires the comparison of two two-year averages as a minimum. But, instead of presenting many columns of two-year periods, the outputs of the new indicator system are shown here in the more compact form of five-year averages. Future editions of the book, depending on publication of the source material, may present new data limited to two- or three-year averages.

3.2 Unit of analysis – countries and years

The country-year format is used to determine scores. Every country is assigned values each year on all seven or eight indicators.

Calculation of *Core Rights Gaps* starts in 1985. By the mid-1980s contemporary globalization had influenced most countries' policy-making and had made itself felt in product and labour markets as well as relative to labour institutions (Ghose, 2003). Since then, most countries' workers have been faced with strong calls for more 'flexibility'. At around that time, authoritarian regimes gave way to democracies in a number of developing countries. Paradoxically, there was both a more enabling environment for values such as those upheld by the International Labour Organization and more pressure exerted on workers in general and on unions in particular to respect the 'laws of the market'. With the break-up of the Soviet Union and the old Yugoslavia at the beginning of the 1990s, contemporary globalization extended its reach and perfected its modes of operation; China's opening towards market forces and FDI came on top. Choosing 1985 as the starting date has the added advantages that the *implementation* data which will be fed into the new indicator system will be practically untainted by the politics surrounding the demise of colonialism and Cold War struggles.

As there is a time lag between the year to which some of the data relate and the year in which they are published, the last year for which a complete set of data can be fed into the *gap* system at the time of writing is 2004.

Indicators have to cover all countries with the same measuring rod, which makes me exclude non-metropolitan territories. If one were to include non-metropolitan territories, one would potentially score some countries twice or more often for the same basic fact, perhaps 'yes' in one territory but 'no' in another territory, which would give rise to attribution problems. Alternatively, one could set up a special sub-system for non-metropolitan territories, which I have found unappealing.

Also not covered are sub-units within existing States, namely China's special administrative regions, Hong Kong and Macau; Malaysia's three constituent regions, Peninsular Malaysia, Sabah and Sarawak (only Malaysia itself included); and Tanzania's two entities, that is, Tanganyika and Zanzibar (only Tanzania is included).

States that have ceased to exist are excluded from the system because, for advocacy and technical cooperation purposes, it would be pointless to analyse whether their *adherence* and *implementation gaps* are growing or declining. Cases in point are the Czech and Slovak Republic (which split in 1993 when each became a member of the International Labour Organization), the German Democratic Republic (which joined the Federal Republic of Germany in 1990), the Yemen Arab Republic and the People's Democratic Republic of Yemen (which united and joined the International Labour Organization as the Republic of Yemen in 1990) and the USSR (which dissolved in 1991, its successor States joined the International Labour Organization in 1992 and 1993).

New member States of the International Labour Organization ought to be exempted from *gap* assessments for a short while. The system accords them a grace period of a minimum of a year so as not to penalize them upon entry with high non-*adherence* scores. States that rejoined the Organization are also scored as from a year later. Box 3.4 contains relevant details.

Should indicators try to take into account a country's capacity to give effect to core Conventions such as the extent to which a

---

Box 3.4   Changes in membership of the International Labour Organization since 1985

Year	Country	Explanation and scoring
1985	All member States except	(153 member States).
	– Vietnam	Not scored. Membership terminated (but see under 1992).
	– Czech and Slovak Republic	Not scored. Czech and Slovak Republic split in 1993.
	– USSR	Not scored. Dissolved in 1991.
	– Yugoslavia	Not scored. Broke up early 1990s (see also under 2001).
	– German Democratic Republic	Not scored. German Democratic Republic joined the Federal Republic of Germany in 1990. Scored first with values of the Federal Republic and then with Germany's.
	– Yemen Arab Republic	Not scored.
	– People's Democratic Republic of Yemen	Not scored.
1986–89	No change –	
1990	Republic of Yemen	Yemen Arab Republic and People's Democratic Republic of Yemen united under new name of Republic of Yemen. Scored from 1992.
1991	Albania	Readmitted. Non-functioning State 1997–2000. Scored from 2002.
	Korea, Republic of	New member. Scored from 1992.
	Latvia	Rejoined. Scored from 1992.
	Lithuania	Rejoined. Scored from 1992.

Box 3.4   Changes in membership of the International Labour
Organization since 1985 – *continued*

Year	Country	Explanation and scoring
1992	Vietnam	Readmitted. Scored from 1993.
	Armenia	New member. Non-functioning State. Not scored.
	Azerbaijan	New member. Scored from 1993.
	Croatia	New member. Scored from 1993.
	Estonia	New member. Scored from 1993.
	Kyrgyzstan	New member. Scored from 1993.
	Moldova	New member. Non-functioning State. Not scored.
	Russian Federation	New member. Scored from 1993.
	Slovenia	New member. Scored from 1993.
	Uzbekistan	New member. Scored from 1993.
1993	Bosnia and Herzegovina	New member. Non-functioning till 1995. Scored from 1997.
	Czech Republic	New member. Scored from 1994.
	Eritrea	New member. Scored from 1994.
	Georgia	New member. Non-functioning State. Not scored.
	Kazakhstan	New member. Scored from 1994.
	Macedonia, Former Yugoslav Republic of	New member. Scored from 1994.
	Slovak Republic	New member. Scored from 1994.
	Tajikistan	New member. Non-functioning State. Not scored.
	Turkmenistan	New member. Scored from 1994.
1994	Oman	New member. Scored from 1995.
	South Africa	Resumed membership. Scored from 1995.
1996	St. Kitts and Nevis	New member. Scored from 1997.
1997–99	No change	–
2000	Kiribati	New member. Scored from 2001.
2001	Yugoslavia (renamed Serbia and Montenegro in February 2003)	New member. Non-functioning State. Not scored.
2002	No change	(175 member States)
2003	Timor-Leste	New member. Scored from 2004 but not yet presented.
	Vanuatu	New member. Scored from 2004 but not yet presented.

government can train labour inspectors to ensure their effective respect in enterprises or on plantations? The degree to which it can administer or enforce labour law? The extent to which it can mobilize the financial and human resources needed to staff equality-promotion bodies? I believe that they should. A country's capacity is bound to reflect, at least in part, its general level of development and its associated financial and human capabilities. A developing country such as Bolivia or a transition economy such as Tanzania will be challenged to a much larger extent than an advanced industrial country such as Canada when it has to cope with ratification, reporting and implementation questions.

My earlier attempt to take government's capacity into account with the help of ILO data did not come up to expectation (Böhning, 2003a).[3] This does not mean that countries' capacity plays no role. Of course, it does. But it will have to be measured differently. UNDP's HDI is probably the best available indicator of governments' capability to give effect to human rights.

As my ambition is to feed only ILO data into the *gap* system, I shall not pursue the capacity question in detail. However, the system deals with it broadly by not scoring what are often called failed States. I call them non-functioning or non-independent countries, which are defined by three criteria: (i) their governments lack the authority to administer their territories because deep-seated civil wars rage in large parts of the territory or are in the hands of secessionists or foreign powers,[4] (ii) they depend on foreign governments, or (iii) they are for other reasons incapable of implementing international commitments. A single criterion suffices to select a country as 'non-functioning or non-independent'. These States will be scored only if and when governments have managed to establish normal, continuing autonomous control, more precisely, two years after they may be considered to have reverted to the status of a normal State.[5] For example, if a country is held to be non-functioning or non-independent in the middle of the review period (say, during 1992–98), it will not be scored during the preceding years (1985–91) because it would not be informative to produce averages or trends based on end-points without data in the middle. Starting two years after its calamitous state has ended, the country would be scored from 2000 onward.

Sixteen countries are non-functioning or non-independent States throughout the review period. Five are from Africa (Angola, the Democratic Republic of Congo, Liberia, Somalia and Sudan), six from Asia (Afghanistan, Armenia, Iraq,[6] Nepal, Solomon Islands and Tajikistan), two from the Americas (Colombia and Haiti) and three from Europe (Georgia, Moldova, and Serbia and Montenegro, that is, the Former Republic of Yugoslavia that broke up in the early 1990s and changed its name to Serbia and Montenegro in February 2003). These 16 countries are excluded at present, nearly one in ten of all member States of the International Labour Organization, including some that are reputed to have the worst human rights record in recent decades.

Bosnia-Herzegovina, Congo, Cyprus, Pakistan (Tribal Areas) and Sri Lanka may be viewed as borderline cases, the Ivory Coast also since late 2002. Bosnia-Herzegovina has an international protection force (as opposed to an occupation force) on its soil. Congo went through a debilitating civil war but seems to have gained at least a semblance of stability. Cyprus, which has just joined the European Union, is assumed by the international community to be temporarily prevented from administering its Turkey-occupied part. Current indicator systems usually include all these countries, and so does the *gap* system.

Six non-functioning or non-independent States are included after expiration of the two-year grace period: Albania (scored as from 2002), Bosnia-Herzegovina (scored as from 1997), Cambodia (scored as from 1995), Lebanon (scored as from 1994), Mozambique (scored as from 1995) and Sierra-Leone (scored as from 2003).

As regards regional borders, those of Asia-Pacific and Europe differ from ILO groupings (including in my earlier working papers, see Böhning, 2003a and 2003b). In the ILO, Azerbaijan, Georgia (a non-functioning State), Israel, Kazakhstan, Kyrgyzstan, Tajikistan (a non-functioning and non-independent State), Turkey, Turkmenistan and Uzbekistan are part of the European region. In this book, only Turkey, which straddles geographic regions but has repeatedly expressed its wish to join the European Union, forms part of Europe. Azerbaijan, Israel, Kazakhstan, Kyrgyzstan, Turkmenistan and Uzbekistan are allocated to the Asian-Pacific region. As of 2004, the four major regions comprise 48 countries in Africa, 39 in the Asian-Pacific region, 33 in the whole of the Americas and 39 in Europe. Where the presentation allows it, the Americas are split into two subregions: 12 countries of the Caribbean plus Canada and the US are distinguished from 19 Latin American countries. The Asian-Pacific region is from time to time split into nine countries designated for want of a better term as 'favourably inclined' towards the values of the International Labour Organization (Australia, Bangladesh, India, Israel, Japan, New Zealand, Pakistan, Philippines and Sri Lanka) and the 'other' 30 countries of the major region.

In toto, the new indicator system covers 159 countries. When long-term trendlines are considered, which must cover a period of at least 10 years, five countries are left out: Albania, Bosnia-Herzegovina, Kiribati, St. Kitts and Nevis, and Sierra Leone. Data concerning the Organization's two newest members, Timor Leste and Vanuatu, are not presented in this book because they relate to a single year, 2004.

4
Measuring Adherence

4.1 Core Conventions component

The *adherence* dimension measures the extent to which countries commit themselves to the four freedoms in the world of work and report thereon. To do this credibly, its methodology must fulfil the demanding criteria for indicators in the human rights field postulated earlier (Chapter 2.3), notably validity, transparency, reliability and objectivity.

The *adherence* dimension first constructs a core Conventions component and then grafts onto it a Declaration component. The core Conventions component records whether countries ratify Conventions and fulfil the constitutional obligation to report to the ILO on how they apply these Conventions in law and in practice. As ratification and reporting are additive parts of the core Conventions component, the total core Conventions *gap* is the sum of the ratification *gap* and of the reporting *gap*. Zero points would be obtained where a State had ratified all fundamental Conventions and fulfilled its reporting obligations on them fully. In that case there would be no *adherence gap*. Non-ratification gives rise to a *gap*, maximally 100 points per year where no core Convention has been ratified. Not reporting when required to do so likewise gives rise to a *gap*, with a theoretical maximum of 25 points per year.

The two indicators of this component have to be calibrated on seven Conventions before the year 2000 and on eight thereafter because only seven core Conventions existed until Convention No. 182 entered into force in the year 2000 (see also Box 3.2 above).

4.1.1 Ratification indicator

The voluntary ratification of a core Convention is the most decisive initial step a country can take.[1] As almost everything else depends on it, nationally and internationally, it becomes the lynchpin of the *gap* system. The quantitative importance of (non-)ratification is fixed in abstract, as mentioned earlier, because it is not decisive in itself.[2] What matters is the proportional relationship of the other indicators to the value of ratification.

Do countries know that they should ratify Conventions? They certainly do. After the adoption of a new Convention, they are required by the constitution of the International Labour Organization to submit the question of ratification to the competent legislative or executive authority. In the case of fundamental Conventions, hardly a resolution by the Organization fails to ask non-ratifiers to consider ratification (and ratifiers to apply Conventions). Furthermore, since 1995 the Director-General of the ILO has sent a letter each year to the governments of countries that have not ratified all core Conventions, urging them to consider ratification.

Ratification is a credit to the country and reduces its *adherence gap* by a certain number of points, starting with the year in which the ratification was registered. As the Convention enters into force for the country one year after registration, one could choose that year to credit the country with ratification points. However, this might lend itself to confusion in different contexts, and I prefer the solution that favours countries' willingness to *adhere* to core Conventions. *Gap* reductions due to ratification stay on the indicator year after year. They would disappear only if a denunciation of the ratification were to occur, in which case the points would turn into an equivalent ratification *gap* as from the calendar year following the denunciation.[3]

Two values are fixed for a single ratification, 14.3 and 12.5 points, which sum to 100 when multiplied by seven or eight, respectively. To illustrate, a non-ratifier that decided in 1999 to ratify four of the seven fundamental Conventions would reduce its ratification *gap* from 100 to 3×14.3 or 42.9 points. One year later, due to the addition of Convention No. 182 and if no further Convention was ratified, the *gap* would amount to 4×12.5 or 50 points.

4.1.2 Reporting indicator

The core Conventions component's second indicator captures whether or not governments report on ratified Conventions. These reports, on which national workers' and employers' organizations have a right to comment, are scrutinized by the Committee of Experts with a view to determining whether countries' legal and factual situations correspond to the terms of the ratified Conventions. More will be explained in the next Chapter about these functions of the Committee of Experts.

Article 22 of the International Labour Organization's constitution obliges each member State to submit reports on the measures it has taken to give effect to the provisions of Conventions to which it is a party. In principle, governments are requested to report every other year on each core Convention.[4] They are asked to report more frequently if they have not done so when previously required or if the Committee of Experts has reason to ask for a report because it perceives serious discrepancies between the stipulations of a Convention and actual laws or practices (see also Chapter 5.3.4). Do governments know that they should report on ratified Conventions? Of course, they do. Countries receive a questionnaire from the ILO, with a dateline of when to report; and national and international organizations of workers and employers are informed which country is to report on which Conventions. The Committee of Experts regularly records whether reports that were due have been received on time (ILO CEACR, Appendix I).

Reporting is not unimportant because it forces governments to consider where they stand in relation to the prescriptions and proscriptions of Conventions. But it is much less important than the act of ratification itself. Therefore, the actual weight attached to reporting is set at 25 per cent of the value of a core Convention. The weight chosen reflects the biannual reporting rhythm and a desire to accord a similar importance to the two reporting procedures that form part of the *gap* system, that is, reporting on ratified Conventions and reporting on unratified Conventions under the Declaration component (see Chapter 4.2.2). The latter should not be more important than reporting on ratified Conventions. Failing to report when required to do so in relation to a ratified Convention becomes a *gap* of 3.6 points during 1985–99 and of 3.1 points as from the year 2000. Failing to report on all core Convention simultaneously sums to a maximum *gap* of 25 points.

To which year should the source's reporting data be attributed? Until March 1995 the Committee of Experts drafted its appraisals under cover pages that referred to the June session of the International Labour Conference in the same year; thereafter it drafted them in December under cover pages that refer to the Conference of the following year. In both cases the reporting data relate principally to the year preceding that of the Conference. Thus, if the report of the Committee of Experts is addressed to the Conference in year X, the data for the Convention reporting indicator concern year X–1.

4.1.3 Testing indicators 1 and 2

The binary ratification indicator is self-evidently valid, transparent, reliable, objective, and it is publicly and easily available. A country either ratifies or it does not. If ratification is in conformity with certain formal or substantive requirements (such as the specification of the general minimum age in the case of Convention No. 138), it is registered publicly.[5] The new indicator system does not even have to set up a complicated accounting mechanism for reservations. Reservations are not allowed in respect of the International Labour Organization's Conventions because representative organizations of workers and employers are associated as equal partners with governments in the elaboration and adoption of these instruments. Thus, the act of ratification cannot be limited by interpretations as to what the government alone intended to accept and what it intended to disregard.

As regards reporting on ratified Conventions, this binary indicator is likewise self-evidently valid, transparent, reliable, objective, publicly and easily available. A country either sends a report that is requested and the report arrives on time, or it does not. Assessments of the comprehensiveness and quality of a report would be subjective in nature and, therefore, cannot be entertained by the *gap* system.

4.2 Declaration component

The 1998 Declaration was politically aimed at countries that have not ratified the Organization's core Conventions. The text of the Declaration goes as far as stating in article 2 that member States, 'even if they have not ratified the Conventions in question, have an obligation, arising from the very fact of membership in the Organization, to respect, to promote and to realize...the principles concerning the fundamental rights which are the subject of those Conventions', namely freedom of association and the effective recognition of the right to collective bargaining, the elimination of all forms of forced or compulsory labour, the effective abolition of child labour and the elimination of discrimination in respect of employment and occupation (see also Box 4.1). Fulfilment of the Declaration is a step towards ratification. The new indicator system can operationalize this notion by according countries bonus points in certain circumstances.

Box 4.1 What does it mean 'to respect, to promote and to realize' the Declaration?

Respect, promotion and realization are three steps on a ladder or notions that are strung along a continuum which starts with 'respect' and ends with 'realization'. I would see the obligation 'to respect' as an obligation of conduct of a negative kind that requires governments to abstain from contravening fundamental principles or hindering the enjoyment of rights, and this with respect to both acts carried out in their name and acts carried out by private citizens. For example, the obligation 'to respect' is not fulfilled where governments deny civil liberties, or where they interfere in the establishment or running of worker's or employers' organizations, or where they engage in – or permit private employers to engage in – acts of anti-union discrimination. As regards the second step on the ladder, that is, the obligation 'to promote', this is an obligation of conduct of a positive kind that requires States to go further than 'to respect' by committing political, administrative and financial resources to enable the fundamental principles and rights to be attained. For example, a government cannot be said to promote the elimination of forced labour or the abolition of child labour where the country's basic legislation does not outlaw forced labour or child labour and where judges do not apply the law, or where governments do not from time to time survey different forms, sizes and characteristics of forced or child labour populations, or where they do not engage in awareness-raising activities or international cooperation. As regards the third step on the ladder, that is, the obligation 'to realize', this is an obligation of result that requires States to take specific legislative, administrative, budgetary, judicial and other measures towards the full achievement of fundamental principles and rights. For example, a government does not qualify as eliminating discrimination where it fails to take steps beyond proclaiming a general equality-promoting policy. To qualify, it would have to adopt specific labour market policies, set up equality-support bodies, and so on.

These distinctions have certain similarities with but also differ slightly from the *Maastricht guidelines on violations of economic, social and cultural rights* of 1996, which were published in, for instance, *Human Rights Quarterly*, 1998, and A. Chapman and S. Russell, 2002.

4.2.1 The Declaration's relationship to Conventions

While the Declaration component logically relates to core Conventions and the *gaps* that non-ratification entails, when a country observes the Declaration by reporting on how it respects, promotes and realizes the relevant principles and rights, this is not equivalent internationally to ratifying a binding Convention. It follows that proper observance of the Declaration can make good merely a portion of an existing ratification *gap*, not all of it. How much of a ratification *gap* can the Declaration component make good? Some observers might put the

Declaration's weight high, others low. I suggest that the whole of the Declaration component can make good maximally 50 per cent of such a *gap*, a proportion that one should consider to be an average for all countries during any year the Declaration indicators were active.

Given that the Declaration's four principles and rights each relate to a pair of core Conventions, one may wonder whether potential bonus points apply to a single or both Conventions. The answer is simple. It depends on how many of the relevant Conventions have not been ratified under the relevant principles and rights. If it is one, the ratification *gap* amounts to 14.3 in 1999 and 12.5 points thereafter, and the *gaps* would be reduced maximally by 7.1 and 6.3 points, respectively (differences due to rounding). If neither of the two Conventions has been ratified, the *gaps* come to 28.6 or 25 points, and in that case full observance of the Declaration would maximally make good 14.3 or 12.5 points, depending on the year.

The word 'maximally' is important because bonus points presuppose that a country performs perfectly under the Declaration component itself. Two performance indicators are involved: (i) reporting (indicator 3), and (ii) progressing in terms of the respect, promotion and realization of the relevant principles and rights (indicator 4). If a country did not perform as it should under either of the Declaration indicators, it could not be credited with any bonus points, and its non-ratification *gap* would stay unchanged. If it fulfilled its reporting obligations correctly but its legal and factual *status quo* remained unchanged, its bonus could maximally be 12.5 per cent of the existing *gap*. If it performed well under one set of principles and rights but not under another, one of its ratification *gaps* would benefit but not the other.

When a country has ratified all core Conventions it is no longer required to report under the Declaration. It then becomes subject to the reporting that is measured under the core Convention component (Chapter 4.1.2).

4.2.2   Declaration reporting

Reporting under the Declaration is not unimportant because it makes countries consider where they stand in relation to unratified Conventions. Correct reporting is credited with a bonus of 12.5 per cent of a ratification *gap* because the weights chosen for the system's two reporting indicators should be appropriately similar. Biannual reporting on ratified Conventions is worth 3.6 points prior to 1999 and 3.1 points afterwards; annual reporting on unratified Conventions under Declaration auspices is worth 1.8 points in 1999 and 1.6 points thereafter, equivalent to 3.6 and 3.2 points over a period of two years. To illustrate, the value of a single Convention is 14.3 points in 1999, and the mere fact of reporting under the Declaration would reduce a ratification *gap* that is due to a single Convention (14.3–1.8) to 12.5 points. From 2000 onward, when the value of a Convention is 12.5 points, it would reduce the *gap* (12.5–1.6) to 10.9 points. The difference between the full *adherence gap* and what is made good by observing correctly the reporting requirement under the Declaration remains a *gap* and would require progress to be recorded under the other Declaration indicator in order to diminish further, or ratification in order to disappear completely.

Do governments know that they should report under the follow-up of the Declaration? They assuredly do. Each year they receive a questionnaire from the ILO with specification of a dateline; and national and international organizations of workers and employers are informed which country is to report on which of the four principles and rights.

To which year should Declaration-reporting data be attributed? The source is the so-called Review of Annual Reports drafted in January each year by seven independent Declaration Expert-Advisers, a document that is submitted to the March session of the ILO Governing Body (ILO, 2000a, 2001a, 2002a, 2003a, 2004a and 2005). The Declaration Expert-Advisers, who are drawn from different regions of the world, examine information that was provided during the preceding year. It follows that – similar to the Committee of Experts reporting data – the Declaration-reporting data should be attributed to the year preceding the ILO source document. For example, the report published in the year 2000 supplies the data for the 1999 indicator.[6]

4.2.3 Declaration progress indicator

Starting in the middle of the decade, the Declaration's reporting procedure should lead to the identification of countries that make significant efforts to respect, promote and realize those of the Declaration's principles and rights that underpin Conventions they have not ratified. When countries in their annual reports inform the ILO of legislative changes, policies or other measures that significantly change the *status quo* along the lines foreseen by the Declaration, the countries warrant to be recognized for their efforts. The size of their ratification *gaps* should be reduced proportionately.

There should be no argument with the assumption that voluntarily taking steps to achieve the Declaration's objectives is several times more important than merely reporting on it to the ILO. The *gap* system, therefore, accords progress under the Declaration three times the weight, 37.5 per cent, of reporting under the Declaration.

If 37.5 per cent of the *gap* due to a single non-ratification could be made good by significantly changing the *status quo*, that *gap* would decrease from 12.5 to 7.8 points (in effect, it would be lowered by a further 1.6 points to 6.3 points – half the *adherence gap* – because reporting would have taken place, otherwise no assessment of progress could have been made). If progress were recognized under several fundamental principles and rights simultaneously, the country would be accorded bonus points under each of them.

Do countries know that they should progress along the lines foreseen by the Declaration? They are painfully aware that they should do so. The questionnaire they receive each year is a reminder, as are the discussions on the Declaration during the sessions of the ILO Governing Body and the International Labour Conference.

How is one to determine whether progress has occurred? A two-stage assessment process ought to take place (Böhning, 2003a), which is summarized in the ILO Programme and Budget for 2004–05 as follows:

> *...Reports under the Declaration follow-up will identify significant and definite steps being taken to observe fundamental principles and rights. They will include the following, undertaken during a pre-defined 12-month period: new or actual policies; practical measures such as programmes for spreading information on recent policy changes or training to implement policies; legislative changes and/or judicial decisions bringing member States closer to realizing the principles and rights; and new expressions of willingness to enter into a dialogue with the ILO on these issues* (ILO, 2003f, para. 143).

How many policies or measures a country adopts in a year and which form they take is not at issue. What matters is whether at least one such policy or measure passes the significance tests. The *gap* system should not subjectively determine how important one policy is compared with another measure, nor should it evaluate how important one country's policy is compared with another country's measure. It can only acknowledge objectively that significant progress has occurred. Mention of the country in the ILO Governing Body document containing information on the implementation of the Programme and Budget suffices to accord 4.7 bonus points under this indicator in respect of the relevant category of fundamental principles and rights.

Progress points count only once in the *gap* system, that is, they are not retained on the indicator year after year. Still, a country may well take further steps in subsequent years under the same category or under another category of principles and rights. If these new steps pass the test, the country would again make good a portion of its ratification *gap*.[7]

To which year should Declaration-progress data be attributed? The assessment tests that were at the outset foreseen to be the responsibility of the seven Declaration Expert-Advisers[8] but which will in future be undertaken by ILO staff, have to be based on responses to questionnaires that describe events in year X. The assessment itself will be prepared in year X+1 and published in March of year X+2 in the ILO Governing Body document on the implementation of the Programme and Budget. The first set of data that can be fed into the system, foreseen in March 2006, should be credited to countries in 2004.

4.2.4   Testing indicators 3 and 4

The binary Declaration reporting indicator is self-evidently valid, transparent, reliable, objective, and is publicly and easily available. A country either sends a report that is requested and the report arrives on time or it does not. Appraisals of the comprehensiveness and quality of a report would be subjective in nature, which the *gap* system seeks to avoid.

As regards progress concerning the respect, promotion and realization of relevant Declaration principles and rights, this is a valid binary indicator that is publicly and easily available. It is reliable to the extent that governments report on positive developments, which they are keen on doing. Unlike all other *gap* indicators, however, the Declaration progress indicator will obtain its data in the future on the basis of judgements made by ILO staff members. Still, the fact that some countries will be listed in a public ILO document and others not is a test on the veracity of the judgements made by the staff because the listing can be challenged – not only by governments but also by independent organizations of workers and employers.

5
Measuring Implementation

5.1 Starting points

The *implementation* dimension measures the degree to which countries give legal and practical effect to the commitments they make in international law by virtue of joining the International Labour Organization and by ratifying its core Conventions. The measurement method evaluates at the international level what happens at the national level. Given that this dimension is calibrated on ratifications in the sense that *implementation* problems are calculated as a fixed proportion of the value of a Convention, the detection of lack of *implementation* presupposes ratification except in respect of the principles and rights of freedom of association where the CFA's procedures enable international verification to take place even in countries that have not ratified the relevant Conventions (Nos. 87 and 98).

The CFA component apart, ratification is a prerequisite for the measurement of *implementation gaps*. Fortunately, the new indicator system is blessed by near-universal ratification of the International Labour Organization's core Conventions. At the end of 2004, of the 159 countries covered at present, 148 had ratified one or both of the non-discrimination Conventions (93 per cent), 146 one or both of the forced labour Conventions (92 per cent), 143 one or both of the freedom of association Conventions (90 per cent) and 134 one or both of the child labour Conventions (84 per cent).

International verification of national realities is accomplished through several supervisory and complaints procedures operated under the auspices of the Organization or its executive organ, the Governing Body, with the assistance of the ILO Secretariat.[1] Some of these procedures lend themselves to the elaboration of credible indicators; others do not satisfy the demanding criteria for indicator development in the human rights field that were stipulated earlier, notably objectivity and non-truncation. It is heuristically useful to start this Chapter by weeding out unsuitable procedures before introducing those in some detail that are retained for the purpose of supplying the *gap* system with data.

Procedures that are unsuitable, though they may be elaborate in conception and potentially far-reaching in impact, include the kind of finger-pointing engaged in by the Committee on the Application of Standards of the International Labour Conference, Representations lodged by employers' or workers' organizations, Direct Contact missions by the ILO Secretariat, General Surveys prepared by the Committee of Experts, Commissions of Inquiry, and the Fact Finding and Conciliation Commission on Freedom of Association that in over 50 years of history has dealt with only three member States of the Organization (Chile, Greece and Japan). It is today practically defunct, its fact-finding functions having been taken over for all practical purposes by the CFA.

All of these procedures lack objectivity in that they are politically inspired at the input and/or output stage. Most identify extreme cases and none satisfies the non-truncation criterion – measuring the achievement of human rights across the board and without bunching countries somewhere along the scale. For example, in more than 80 years of ILO history, Commissions of Inquiry have so far been concerned with only 11 countries.[2]

Representations are a form of complaint that employers' or workers' organization can submit to the ILO Governing Body to determine whether a country that has ratified a Convention effectively observes its provisions. However, two problems render Representations unsuitable for the *gap* system. One is that, empirically speaking, this procedure tends to be used mostly by trade unions from advanced industrial countries. The other is the relative small number of Representations. Since 1985, only nine Representations have been aimed at Convention No. 29, eight at Convention No. 87, seven at Convention No. 98, four at Convention No. 100, six at Convention No. 105, 19 at Convention No. 111, two at Convention No. 138 and none at Convention No. 182. Representations thus fail the test of wide applicability across the whole of membership of the Organization. From time to time, when representations raise legislative questions, the Committee of Experts may subsequently be asked to deal with them; and when they concern freedom of association, they are usually transmitted to the CFA. In both cases they indirectly enter the *gap* system.

Direct Contact missions are occasionally suggested by the Committee of Experts or the CFA as a way of solving legislative or other questions with the assistance of ILO staff. Formally, they presuppose that a willing government requests such a mission to take place. Incorporation in the *gap* system could theoretically be imagined on the lines of the bonus points method developed earlier for the Declaration component. But Direct Contact missions are rare events that do not apply to countries on a sufficiently widespread basis to be included in the system.

Questionnaire-based General Surveys by the Committee of Experts are drafted at irregular and long intervals. They are closer to occasional in-depth studies than to indicator material that can be mined on a continuous basis.

As regards the Committee on the Application of Standards of the International Labour Conference, this body performs functions in conjunction with the Committee of Experts and relies for its pronouncements largely on the findings contained in the CEACR's annual report. However, while the CEACR is entirely independent of the Committee on the Application of Standards and could exist without the latter, the reverse does not hold. Most of all, the Committee on the Application of Standards is a political body composed of delegates to the International Labour Conference who select from among the hundreds of comments made each year by the Committee of Experts a relatively small number – those they consider to be furthest removed from the norms – to discuss them in public, requesting concerned government representatives to be present.[3] Although core Conventions have been the object of most of its attention, its pronouncements must be excluded from the *gap* system because they are the result of political processes and fail the non-truncation criterion.[4]

5.2   Relevant supervisory and complaints procedures

Box 5.1 typifies the institutional features of the Committee on the Application of Standards and compares them with those of the supervisory and complaints procedures that are selected as sources of data to measure the achievement of *implementation*.

Box 5.1   Distinctions among the three principal supervisory and complaints bodies

	Application Committee	CEACR	CFA
Function	Putting pressure on governments held to be least compliant, to make the necessary changes	Biannual or more frequent examination of legislation and practice in light of ratified Conventions' provisions	Examination of merits of allegations filed *ad hoc* by workers' and employers' organizations
Appointment mode	Government, worker and employer delegates to the annual International Labour Conference	By the Director-General of the ILO, to ensure independence, impartiality and relevant qualifications	Three representatives each of governments, workers and employers of Governing Body, to act in personal capacity, plus an independent outsider as chairperson
Information basis	Mainly CEACR's appraisals of situation plus information supplied by governments or Conference delegates	Wide-ranging reports by governments, employers or workers plus information at disposal of ILO Secretariat	Basically written information contained in allegations and subsequent submissions by the parties to a case
Characterization	Politico-diplomatic process	Technical appraisal	Quasi-judicial assessment
Indicator suitability	Not on its own	High	Medium

5.2.1   Committee of Experts component

The Committee of Experts on the Application of Conventions and Recommendations was established in 1926 to examine whether the governments of countries that had ratified Conventions actually applied them in law and in practice. Committee members are selected, not on the basis of a list proposed by interested governments (as is usually the case in, for example, the UN system), but by the Director-General of the ILO whose senior colleagues in the relevant department first collect CVs and sometimes interview people to ensure that they have the requisite command of working languages and some international experience. The Director-General submits their résumés *pro forma* to the ILO Governing Body. In this way, Committee members are appointed in their individual capacity as impartial experts of technical competence and independent standing. Its contingent of 20 experts is drawn from all parts of the world so that the Committee may enjoy first-hand experience of different legal, economic and social systems. In the early 1960s, Haas (1964, p. 255) characterized its members as an 'uninstructed collegial group of specialists'. Representatives of democracies and legal systems stressing individual rights were heavily over-represented at that time. The CEACR eventually included two law professors from socialist States; the *sharia* legal system also became represented. At the start/end of the of the *gap* system's review period, the following number of experts hailed from the major regions distinguished in this book: Africa 2/3, Americas 5/4, Asia and the Pacific 5/5, and Europe 8/7.[5]

As regards its working methods, the Committee assigns to each of its members the 'initial responsibility for a group of Conventions or for a given subject' (ILO, 1995, p. 150). Experts from all major regions have been in charge of core Conventions. While 'the final wording of the drafts to be submitted to the Committee remains the sole responsibility of the expert entrusted with the examination... all draft findings are considered and approved by the Committee in plenary sittings' (*ibid.*, p. 151). To prevent pressure being exerted on individuals in respect of their decisions, the Committee of Experts' deliberations remain strictly confidential. It appears that no majority decisions ever had to be taken. Experts do not hesitate to consult colleagues from countries whose situations they examine, but they would look askance at attempts to spare their governments from justified criticism. Experts from socialist States have on several occasions dissented, according to Landy (1966, p. 31) 'not from the observations on ratified Conventions as a whole but from those regarding "the application of the freedom of association Conventions in the socialist countries".' The dissent has always been recorded in the Committee's published report (for the *gap* review period, see the CEACR reports concerning 1985–89).

The Committee's fundamental working principles call for impartiality and objectivity in pointing out the extent to which the legal and factual positions in a State having ratified a particular Convention are in conformity with the terms of that Convention and the obligations which that State has undertaken by virtue of the Organization's constitution. On the occasion of the 60th anniversary of its establishment, the Committee of Experts restated its fundamental principles, mandate and method of work: 'Subject only to any derogations which are expressly permitted by the Convention itself, these requirements (of a given Convention) remain constant and uniform for all countries. In carrying out its work, the Committee is guided by the standards laid down in the Convention alone, mindful, however, of the fact that the modes of their implementation may be different in different States' (CEACR, 1987, p. 12). Gravel and Charbonneau-Jobin recently confirmed that the Committee of Experts 'continues to examine the application of Conventions...in a uniform manner for all States. The rights and obligations under the instruments adopted by the International Labour Conference are the same for all, and should be applied in a uniform way in all member States' (Gravel and Charbonneau-Jobin, 2003, p. 14).

It may nevertheless be pertinent to draw a distinction between measuring rods, on the one hand, and focus or scope, on the other. The focus of the Committee of Experts may leave the narrow starting grid of applying certain Conventions when consciousness changes in the world at large. For example, women or gender questions have invariably been high on the list of the Experts in the case of Convention No. 111, and the global concern with apartheid has upheld issues of race or colour, too. But the other four grounds of impermissible discrimination under that Convention – religion, political opinion, national extraction and social origin – have apparently not been looked at with the same intensity, regularity or global sweep since that Convention entered into force. Some countries may not actually have different religions or significant groups of identifiable national extraction or social origin on their soil, which may spare them from getting into trouble with the Committee of Experts on those counts – unless their legislation draws illegitimate distinctions. In the case of the forced labour Conventions, children who are forced to work, and trafficking that results in forced labour, are either a relatively new phenomenon or have entered the Experts' frame of considerations only after they burst on the international scene – after today's globalization took hold and media reported on them.

Where the Committee of Experts detects something questionable, it comments publicly in two forms: through *direct requests* or *observations*. Both terms are italicized here when they refer to their function in the *gap* system. *Direct requests* and *observations* date back to the origin of the Committee. *Observations* were initially dubbed 'criticism', but this was not a very diplomatic term and it did not survive.

The Committee of Experts chooses the form of *direct requests* when it raises an issue of a technical nature or when it has doubts but is not sure about a particular question and wishes to obtain clarification before expressing an opinion (ILO, 1995, pp. 152–153, and Gravel and Charbonneau-Jobin, 2003, p. 13). It is a low-level form of suggesting to a government that *implementation* may not be what it should be. In the late 1950s the ILO decided not to publish any longer the text of *direct requests* in the increasingly bulky CEACR report but merely to record the fact that they were sent to governments.

Observations are the Committee of Experts' 'most important comments' (ILO, 1995 p. 163). The CEACR's report comprises both general observations and individual observations. The former are mainly concerned with broad questions of reporting on ratified Conventions, which the *adherence* dimension captures at the level of each country through indicator 2. General observations can therefore be disregarded. Where the Committee of Experts perceives significant non-compliance with ratified Conventions, it puts forward critical comments in the form of negative individual *observations* under the heading of the Convention in question. They are 'generally used in more serious or long-standing cases of failure to fulfil obligations' (ILO, n.d., paragraph 54, note 8). In its latest report the Committee of Experts itself formulated the distinction between *direct requests* and *observations* in a note to readers: 'The observations contain comments on fundamental questions raised by the application of a particular Convention... The direct requests usually relate to more technical questions or questions of lesser importance' (CEACR, 2004, p. 2).

Where a government responds to the criticism of the Committee of Experts, the Committee examines the measures taken to determine whether they constitute significant progress. If that is the case, it generally expresses its *satisfaction* in an individual comment when it deals with the Convention itself and, since 1964, has listed the country in a distinct section at the beginning of its report under 'Cases of progress'. *Satisfaction*, italicized when referred to in the context of the *gap* system, is the opposite of the criticism aired through *observations* and must therefore be taken into account, which the *gap* system does on the lines of bonus points.[6] Since *satisfaction* is expressed only in relation to preceding 'negative' *observations* (not in relation to *direct requests*), the *gap* system can combine the two comments in a single scale. Technically, this gives rise to *observations* corrected for *satisfaction* or *observations-cum-satisfaction*. Both terminologies being quite a mouthful, reference will be made merely to *observations* unless the clarity of the presentation requires otherwise.[7]

It is worth making clear that the new indicator system measures the formal existence of *satisfaction*, not the importance one might attribute to the actual words chosen. Gravel and Charbonneau-Jobin state: 'Even though the Committee endeavours to enumerate cases of progress, in so doing it does not establish a hierarchy between them. A case of progress is listed as such almost irrespective of the circumstances in which measures are taken by the government' (2003, p. 25).

The Committee of Experts clearly operates an ordinal scale of both criticism and approval. On the critical side, the Experts' ordinal scale consists of (i) making no comment, (ii) putting forward a direct request, (iii) addressing an observation to the government or combining (ii) and (iii). The words chosen to express a *direct request* or an *observation* are secondary to the classification of its comments. On the side of approval, the Experts' ordinal scale consists of finding (i) nothing to be *satisfied* about, (ii) everything having been dealt with *satisfactorily* and being (iii) *satisfied* with elements of what the government has done but not with everything.

5.2.2 CFA component

The Committee on Freedom of Association was established during the early years of the Cold War and has functioned in its present form since 1953. From them on, even if a country had not ratified the relevant Convention, the prior consent of the government was not required for a case to be looked at and pronounced upon by the CFA. Nor did national procedures have to be exhausted before a complaint could be examined. By contrast, the CFA cannot start the procedure of its own volition. It springs into action when complaints are submitted to it and determined to be receivable. National as well as international organizations of workers and employers have the right to lodge complaints. Workers' organizations account for the vast majority of complaints, including organizations that are not officially recognized by the government of the country concerned or which have been dissolved.[8] In terms of its composition, the CFA is a Committee of the executive organ of the ILO, the Governing Body, and meets during its three sessions in March, June and November of each year. Its nine regular members represent in equal proportion the governmental, worker and employer groups of the Governing Body. No special qualifications are required, but members should enjoy general confidence and impartiality – they should act in their personal capacity as the hallowed formula goes. In 1978 an independent Chairperson was added, somebody of the qualification and calibre of CEACR experts. A good 40 years ago, Haas (1964, p. 384) noted a preponderance of Europeans among CFA members. In the meantime, the Committee has become more representative. For example, Burundi, El Salvador and Pakistan filled the governmental slots in the most recent years.

The CFA's function is 'not to formulate general conclusions concerning the trade union situation...on the basis of vague general statements' (ILO, 1995, Committee's rules of procedure, Annex I, pp. 210–211) but to focus on the issues of fact raised by a particular allegation with the help of the specific documentary evidence that the ILO Secretariat obtains on its behalf from the complainant and the government, giving the latter ample opportunity to reply to the complaint as well as to the views of the CFA.[9] Even though governments sometimes delay their responses, almost all find it preferable to cooperate with the Committee because they are thus able to defend themselves against what they may consider to be unfounded accusations or to explain why they have adopted the measures objected to (Von Potobsky, 1998, p. 212). Where a government stoically refuses to reply, increasingly urgent and public admonitions or contacts are pursued; if all else fails, the CFA proceeds to examine the case by default. The Committee deliberates in private and confidentially. No CFA member from a country against which a complaint has been made is allowed to be present or even to see the documentation. If a worker or employer representative has been involved in launching the complaint through an international organization, that person may not participate in the deliberations. Even Governing Body members who do not sit on the CFA cannot be present. These and other safeguards are designed to uphold the integrity of the Committee, which to this day – often after long and intense discussions – has reached its decisions unanimously. The Governing Body has never called into question its Committee's judgement. The CFA's examinations, conclusions and recommendations are published, first of all in the form of a Governing Body paper and, several months later, in the ILO's *Official Bulletin* (ILO, various).

The CFA's institutional features make it perhaps not an ideal choice, like the Committee of Experts, for the potential extraction of data to feed the *gap* system (see Box 5.1). But, unlike the Committee on the Application of Standards of the International Labour Conference, they make it a defensible choice – subject to a satisfactory test of the credibility of the actual data that will be undertaken later.

Which of the CFA's input or output factors could yield suitable source material for a distinct set of indicators? It is useful to start again by weeding out unsuitable data. For example, researchers may be tempted to instrumentalize complaints by attributing numerical values to the mere fact that an allegation against a particular government has been made – at the input stage of the procedure. However, it would be difficult to determine objectively what weight to attach to this fact. Does the mere submission of a complaint call into question 0, 5, 25 or 50 per cent of the value of a core Convention? Nothing is certain at this stage. While some complaints raise broad and far-reaching policy issues, others involve an individual enterprise or person. It would be quite subjective to attach different weights to them at the moment of submission to the CFA. Another problem is that complaints may not fulfil receivability criteria or their initiators may withdraw them. Information on whether a complaint is receivable and on whether it has been withdrawn is not always clearly discernible in the published CFA's reports, which would incur scoring problems.

One might also be tempted to put numbers on the fact that the CFA uses the initial paragraphs of the Introduction of its report to identify serious and/or urgent cases which the Committee draws to the attention of the Governing Body, which generally involve matters of human life, liberty or new or changing conditions in a particular country that affect the freedom of action of a trade union movement as a whole. However, since this practice by the CFA is relatively new – it took that step for the first time in 1995 – and because it would fail the non-truncation test, it has to be left out of the *gap* system.[10] The so-called urgent appeals by the CFA can also not be instrumentalized. One reason is that they are of a purely procedural nature designed to induce governments not to delay their responses endlessly,[11] another that one should not clutter an indicator with minor items of little weight.

When the CFA receives information from a government, mostly as the result of a request that it be kept informed, or from the complainant submitting further evidence, it may not issue a full report but may note its views or reactions in a section of its report headed 'Effect given to the Recommendations of the Committee and the Governing Body'. It may express regret or satisfaction, hope or interest, simply take note or use a similar formula of this kind; or it may consider that a case does not call for further examination; or it may once again ask for information. The many variations of the words used mirror the nuances that lawyers or politicians excel in and the diplomatic language of international organizations with their implied assumed meanings. This section of the CFA's reports cannot be instrumentalized for indicator purposes because one would have to make a judgement as to what exactly the CFA had in mind.

One could perhaps think of instrumentalizing the several categories of complaints that are handled by the CFA as identified by the headings used in CFA reports, which ILO publications have recently referred to (ILO, 2000c, p. 26, and 2004b, p. 27) and which this book will later pick up for different purposes (see Table 8.3). For instance, general denial of the right to organize could be judged to be more important than refusal to recognize unions in a specific enterprise, which in turn could be judged to be more important than the dismissal of a single trade unionist following strike action. A scale could be established and different points could be accorded. But since the CFA itself does not provide an objective categorization of the relative importance of one kind of case relative to another – it merely lists the category into which a case falls – any such scale would be subjective.

To find data suitable for indicators, one's eyes must be turned to the output stage of the CFA's procedures. Its outputs are reports on individual cases that contain conclusions and recommendations and which appear under different headings. The *gap* system instrumentalizes the distinctions among them by converting one form of reports – the kind that identifies the most serious failures to realize freedom of association – into a binary indicator.

Since 1969, the CFA has issued its findings on cases under four (later three) headings in a document referred to as the Introduction to its report (ILO, various), namely:

- Reports on cases that do not call for further examination. This happens when the Committee 'finds, for example, that the alleged facts, if proved, would not constitute an infringement of the exercise of trade union rights, or that the allegations made are so purely political in character that it is undesirable to pursue the matter further, or that the allegations made are too vague to permit consideration of the case on its merit' (ILO, 1995, Committee's rules of procedure, Annex I, pp. 209);

- Reports containing definitive conclusions and recommendations. Such reports are issued 'where the government has been asked to take action and has reported back to the CFA on the measures taken. The case can be brought to its final conclusion in the eyes of the Committee' (Tajgman and Curtis, 2000, p. 66);
- Reports in which it requests to be kept informed of developments. Where the CFA categorizes its reports under this heading, the Committee considers that it has had sufficient information to adopt its conclusions and recommendations but prefers to follow the manner in which the government gives effect to its recommendations in order to encourage their full implementation before closing the case;
- Reports that contain interim conclusions and recommendations. Where the CFA issues an interim report it does so either because it needs further information in order to come to an assessment in knowledge of all the facts or when the problems raised, because of their seriousness, should continue to be subject to an in-depth examination by the Committee. The need to obtain further information is usually a reflection of the gravity of the case.

It would not make sense to set up a distinct set of indicators on cases that do not call for further examination because they normally concern unjustified allegations of infringement of freedom of association rights. Since 1996, the reports that were previously issued under this heading are put forward under the heading of definitive reports with conclusions and recommendations which clearly spell out that particular allegations do not call for further examination. When the CFA issues definitive reports on matters other than those that do not call for further examination, it has found violations of freedom of association rights. Still, this kind of output report officially closes the case. The temptation to determine whether definitive reports, which cover quite heterogeneous situations, characterize what governments did or did not do as somewhat or much or whatever in contravention of their obligations would require interpretation of the CFA's conclusions, which would involve subjective judgements that are incompatible with indicator systems in the field of human rights – one's political culture and geo-political preferences would fail the test of objectivity. The same holds true when the CFA issues reports in which it requests the government to be kept informed of developments. The only kind of report that can feed indicators with objective data is an *interim* report. Italicized in the context of the *gap* system, *interim* reports have sufficiently relevant and clear definitional boundaries to constitute suitable indicator material.

The CFA, like the Committee of Experts, operates an ordinal scale of criticism. The CFA's scale consists of (i) issuing an *interim report* or (ii) issuing no such report or another form of report. Here, too, the words chosen to express its findings are secondary to the decision to issue an *interim report*.

In summary, then, the Committee of Experts' *direct requests*, *observations* and *satisfaction* plus the CFA's *interim* reports are retained to measure countries' achievement of how they *implement* the policies, measures and sanctions they committed themselves to. While the Committee of Experts and the CFA interact, they function each in their own right and for their own specific purposes. Fundamental Conventions or the principles and rights of the Declaration take up much of the CEACR's and all of the CFA's time. The CFA regularly brings to the attention of the Committee of Experts cases of ratified Conventions where the CFA procedures have ended but where in the CFA's opinion the Committee of Experts ought to examine the legislative aspects involved and to watch whether the government concerned takes the measures appropriate to give effect to the recommendations of the CFA. This does not give rise to double counting in the *gap* system because the two Committees will not examine the same question at the same time.

5.3   Scoring

The first principle to be applied in scoring *implementation* problems is not to treat countries unfairly. The attribution of human rights *gaps* must proceed with prudence and err on the side of the government under scrutiny rather than on the side of 'mining the data' until they yield something quantifiable. We will shortly see what this means in practice.

5.3.1   Committee of Experts component

The *implementation* problems revealed by the Committee of Experts can validly be said to call into question a certain proportion of the policies that governments pursue when they ratify a Convention. What should the proportion be? It is clear from the preceding discussion that *observations* and expressions of *satisfaction* are more important than *direct requests*, and that *interim* reports are comparable in importance to negative *observations*. But it is not clear how much more important *observations* and *satisfaction* or *interim* reports are than *direct requests*, nor is it clear what weight the CEACR component should have relative to the

CFA component. Decisions will have to be taken to fix each indicator at a size that is reasonable in itself and comparable with the size of the others.

Direct requests are important in their own right but not overwhelmingly so. It is suggested that each time the Committee of Experts puts forward a *direct request* the *implementation gap* is equivalent to 20 per cent of the value of the relevant Convention. Twenty per cent should be seen as an average that applies to all countries alike, without distinction and exception, throughout the period 1985–2004. Due to the two-year reporting-cum-CEACR cycles, indicator 5 generates biannual data for almost all countries. During in-between years, a *direct request* would not be formulated and a *direct request gap* could not arise because of the fundamental scoring principle that, if there is no negative comment, there should be no *gap*. On an annual basis, given the country-year format chosen for the *gap* system, the effective weight of *direct requests* is thus half, 10 per cent, which is a level that would appear to be reasonable in relation to the political commitment made by governments when they ratify a Convention.

Observations represent a rather stronger form of questioning a country's legal or factual situation than *direct requests*, which means that the weight associated with *observations* must be significantly higher. It seems reasonable to fix the size of an *observation gap* at twice the size of the stipulated weight of *direct requests*, 40 per cent of a Convention's value. In the context of normal two-year reporting-cum-CEACR cycles, indicator 6 provides data every other year and its effective weight drops to 20 per cent on an annual basis.

When the Committee of Experts faces a particularly non-compliant or recalcitrant government, it requests a report straight away without waiting until it is normally due two years later; and in that case it is likely to address *observation* after *observation* to the country's government. In this way, the new indicator system captures the most serious *implementation* problems without having to look for separate sources of data. An example is Myanmar and Convention No. 87 on freedom of association, which the government has been asked to report on every year since 1994. During these 11 years Myanmar incurred *observations* that gave rise to *implementation gaps* of 40 per cent each. Its situation with regard to Convention No. 29 is very similar. Another example is Pakistan and Convention No. 87, which the government has been asked to report on every year between 1986 and 1992, then at two-yearly intervals, and again without interruption since 2000. *Observations* weighing 40 per cent each were formulated by the Committee of Experts during 17 of the 20 years; and in respect of a further year, 2000, the CEACR both expressed *satisfaction* and found that much remained to be done, which was confirmed by the *observations* put forward ever since.

If the Committee of Experts were to address simultaneously a *direct request* and an *observation* on the same Convention to a government, which happens not infrequently, the *implementation gap* would amount to 60 per cent of the Convention's value during the year in question. On an annual basis, a *direct request* plus an *observation* would come to 30 per cent.

Expressions of *satisfaction* have the same stipulated weight as *observations*, 40 per cent, but the opposite effect – they wipe them out. They, too, are a biannual indicator. On an annual basis, the effective weight of expressions of *satisfaction* is reduced to 20 per cent.

It is crucial to understand that the formal nature of the outputs of the supervisory machinery is instrumentalized for indicator purposes, not the contents of comments. To go deeper into each *direct request*, each *observation* or each *satisfaction* in order to determine which *direct request* is 'more important' than another or which *observation* incriminates a country 'more deeply' than another or which *satisfaction* deals with a 'more crucial' matter than another would inevitably become an arbitrary exercise, subjective personal preferences would creep in and superhuman efforts would be required to maintain identical measures for all countries at all times. The new indicator system objectifies the measurement of the achievement of human rights by relying on the formal distinctions of the comments put forward by the independent and impartial Committee of Experts. Objectivity requires that one does not interpret the contents or importance of a comment (see also Box 5.2). What matters is whether or not the Committee's review of a country's legal and factual situation leads it to formulate a comment on a pre-determined ordinal scale.

Box 5.2   Yes/No distinctions vs. further grading of the severity of implementation problems

Is it appropriate and sufficient to apply binary indicators to the various forms of Committee of Experts' comments or should one examine the contents of, for example, *observations* to further grade countries' achievement of fundamental human rights in terms of the proportion of their people or the percentage of territory involved or some such criterion? For example, should one relate Committee of Experts' *observations* in the area of freedom of association that concern a single category such as teachers to the whole of the

---

Box 5.2   Yes/No distinctions vs. further grading of the severity of implementation problems – *continued*

economically active population or *observations* that find infringements only in Export-Processing Zones to the violations-free remainder of the territory? Should degrees of severity be calculated when Committee of Experts' *observations* in the area of forced labour are limited to the sex sector or migrant workers or the poorest regions? Should proportions be established when the Committee of Experts' *observations* identify child labour only in the brick-making industry or private households or on plantations or in the informal as opposed to the formal economy? Should one relate Committee of Experts' *observations* in the area of non-discrimination to all working women or to men and women when the latter receive equal pay for work of equal value in the public but not in the private sector or when racially distinguished groups are discriminated in access to employment? Should one weight the fact that women are but one of seven groups – and race another – when the other six – or five or whatever – are not found to be discriminated against?

To pose such questions is to give the answer: One should not! An analogy with 'traditional' human rights demonstrates the superiority of the binary approach and the absurdity of opening the floodgates to subjective reference points. Can, for example, the number of death penalties carried out or the number of political opponents tortured or the number of arbitrary arrests of ethnic minorities members be weighted in terms of countries' population? Of course not! If executions, torture or arbitrary arrests are practiced, countries should find themselves on one side of the fence rather than straddling it. They are not struggling to achieve human rights, they are violating them – 'a little', 'much', 'to a great extent' or whatever is not the question. A violation is a violation and is sufficient to be scored as such and for as long as it is practiced or tolerated.

Given that the Committee of Experts determines in the most objective way possible whether something is questionable and determines how important the issue is, it is unnecessary to grade further the contents of its *direct requests*, *observations* or expressions of *satisfaction*, which would open the floodgates to conscious or unconscious political or personal preferences.

An analogy with GNP and unemployment data may be helpful here. Statisticians do not draw distinctions of 'importance', 'impact' or whatever when they add up goods and services produced. Statisticians count US Dollars for GNP purposes irrespective of whether they are earned by a lathe-machine operator, a prostitute or a banker laundering receipts of illegal drug trading. Likewise, statisticians count as one case each the desperately poor 20 years old bricklayer and the 60 years old high-level staff member of a large enterprise with a fat bank account who register as unemployed. The headcount does not evaluate any differential impact the loss of a job may have on peoples' lives. Like statisticians that count US Dollars or the number of unemployed, the *gap* system assesses *implementation* problems under the Committee of Experts component with measuring rods that apply to all countries in the same way.

The relative sizes of each binary indicator give rise to a sufficient number of combinations to assess the extent to which countries *implement* human rights in law and in practice with a degree of precision. The following six combinations are possible for any single Convention: (i) if there is no negative comment, there is no *gap*. The same holds true if a previous *observation* induces a government to resolve a problem to the CEACR's entire *satisfaction* and no other negative comment is issued at the same time; (ii) if there is a small problem, it is identified through a lightly weighted *direct request*. If such a *direct request* is issued and, at the same time, the resolution of a big problem is acknowledged by the CEACR through an expression of *satisfaction* without a further negative *observation*, only the *direct request* is keyed into the system. The *direct request* does not call into question the progress achieved that relates to a previous negative *observation*; (iii) if a big problem is perceived but no other comment made, an *observation* weighs in heavily and fully; (iv) if the *implementation* problems are such that the CEACR issues simultaneously an *observation* and a *direct request*, the two get added together; (v) if a big problem gets resolved *satisfactorily* in part or if a big problem gets resolved *satisfactorily* in its entirety but a new or different big problem is found at the same time, the size of the *gap* recorded by the system is half the size of an *observation*; (vi) if the CEACR issues simultaneously a *direct request*, a negative *observation* and a positive expression of *satisfaction*, the three comments are added together (see Table 5.1).

Taking into account the fact that combinations 5 and 6 yield the same scores as combinations 2 and 3, there can be seven distinct *implementation* scores per pair of Conventions that lay down the principles and rights in a particular area of freedom, 21 different *implementation* scores under the seven Conventions that existed up to 1999 and 24 different scores under the eight Conventions in force since 2000.

One could make these grades even more variable by choosing odd numbers. But not only are the selected weights easier to follow as they stand; what counts is that they are both defensible in themselves and when one compares the various indicators' weights across the system. They should be seen as averages that apply to all countries across all

Table 5.1 CEACR component: Six grades yielding four distinct implementation scores per Convention

Combinations of CEACR comments	Size of implementation gap measured as % of value of single Convention	
	Weight during normal two-year reporting cycle	Effective annual weight for 'normal' countries
No negative comment or only positive satisfaction expressed	0%	0%
Direct request or direct request plus positive satisfaction	20%	10%
Negative observation	40%	20%
Negative observation plus direct request	60%	30%
Positive satisfaction plus negative observation	20%	10%
Direct request and negative observation plus positive satisfaction	40%	20%

core Conventions at any point of time. They are the identical measuring rods that human rights assessment systems must use if they are to be credible.

As regards the actual size of *implementation gaps* at the first stage of the system's construction, from 1985 to 1999 a single *direct request* entails an *implementation gap* of 2.9 points, corresponding to 20 per cent of the value of one of the seven core Conventions during that period. As from 2000, when eight Conventions have to be taken into account, a single *direct request* entails a *gap* of 2.5 points. The maximum load that seven or eight *direct requests* can put on the *implementation* dimension during the respective periods is 20 points.

When the substance of a *direct request* changes in the light of new information that has come to the Committee of Experts' attention, the charge on the *implementation* dimension will nevertheless stay the same. It is the formal fact of making a *direct request*, not its contents, which matters.

When the government is the object of a single *observation*, 5.7 points will be charged to the *implementation* dimension during 1985–99 and 5 points in subsequent years. The maximum *implementation* load in any year that could derive from *observations* is 40 points.

If the content of an *observation* changes in the light of new information that has come to the Committee of Experts' attention, the charge on the indicator will stay the same. The CEACR can revert to an *implementation* problem as often as it receives new information or as a result of itself having asked for a further report, or as result of the normal core Convention reporting cycle of two years. Where a country has been the object of *observations* for many years, this evidently reflects a very unsatisfactory situation. The country will be scored as long as the Committee of Experts makes *observations* without being *satisfied*. The Committee does not stop asking for change until it has occurred.

If a country is listed under 'Cases of progress' in Part I of the Committee of Experts' report without a negative *observation* being made at the same time, no CEACR *gap* will be attributed to the Convention concerned. The Committee of Experts, under that Convention in Part II of its report, invariably explains what it is *satisfied* with. The distinction between positive *satisfaction* and negative *observation* is sufficiently clear in theory and practice that there should be no ambiguity when scoring.[12] If for one reason or another the *observation* does not contain the word *satisfaction*, the explicit listing under 'Cases of progress' should be taken as sufficient evidence that the Committee of Experts has, indeed, been *satisfied*.[13]

However, the Committee of Experts may not be entirely *satisfied* with the measures taken by the government. While it lists the country and Convention in Part I under cases of progress, it may well find that there are unresolved issues or that new questions have been raised by new measures or new information received – for example, through comments submitted by workers' organizations. The Committee will not hesitate to express its view that not everything is *satisfactory* in Part II of its report and will proceed to formulating an individual *observation* with distinctly positive and distinctly negative connotations, making it very clear that, while steps have been taken by the government to close the *gap* between the real world and the ideal world, there is not enough progress for the Committee of Experts to consider the question closed. In the event of a mixed comment of this kind, the system will halve the charge of a single *observation* on the *implementation* indicator to 2.9 or 2.5 points, depending on the year concerned.

If an *observation* on one core Convention contains a cross-reference to another core Convention, the *gap* system has to count them as two distinct *observations*. For example, the Committee of Experts may make a detailed *observation* on Convention No. 87 but under Convention No. 98 merely add a cross-reference: 'See under Convention No. 87'.

The four pairs of core standards consist each of two Conventions that are interlinked and which build on one another. When matters are questionable under one of them, they are sometimes also questionable under the other paired Convention. Where the Committee of Experts refers to both, it is entirely appropriate to score both.

To which year should the Committee of Experts' data be attributed? *Direct requests* and *observations* relate mostly to the situation during the year preceding the Conference referred to on the cover pages of its report. It follows that the data in the Committee of Experts' report to the International Labour Conference in year X have to be entered under year X – 1.[14]

The same rule applies to cases of progress. *Satisfaction* is expressed by the Committee of Experts when the government has correctly dealt with an *observation*. In the course of a normal reporting cycle this may be several years after the critical comment was made; in the course of heavily criticized countries' annual reporting requirements the change – if there is any – may be notified to the CEACR within a year. For simplicity's sake, the *gap* system assumes that expressions of *satisfaction* are time-lagged by the duration of a normal reporting cycle, that is, two years. Therefore, the first *satisfaction* data to be keyed into in the system relate to countries' 1987 situations and must be taken from the Committee of Experts' report addressed to the 1988 Conference. While there are 20 years of *observations* in the system, only 18 years of cases of progress have so far been keyed into it.

5.3.2 Committee on Freedom of Association component

The *implementation* problems examined by the CFA can validly be considered to call into question a proportion of the value of ratifying Convention No. 87 and/or Convention No. 98. Where neither of these Conventions has been ratified, CFA *interim* reports call into question a proportion of the International Labour Organization's constitutional principles and rights of freedom of association; and in that context the question is: to which quantitative reference value should one relate the weight of an *interim* report? One might be tempted by the fact that the constitutional principles and rights inspire two core Conventions, in which case the reference values would come to 28.6 until 1999 and 25 points thereafter. But this would be twice the value of any CFA case because one single case covering the two Conventions is not reported upon separately for Convention No. 87 and for Convention No. 98. A complaint is one event irrespective of coverage. The opposite option of putting the quantitative reference value at, say, half the level of a

Convention would incur the reverse inequity because a 'constitutional' case could effectively cover the same ground as a Convention case – or of two Conventions for that matter – but should not have a lower reference value. Logically, the most pertinent reference value in cases involving the constitutional principles and rights of freedom of association is the value of one Convention. Equally logically, the same reference values are applied to all eventualities that may arise under a CFA complaint – one or two ratified Conventions or none – 14.3 points up to 1999 and 12.5 points as from 2000.

Implementation problems brought to light by an *interim* report are given a weight of 20 per cent. This puts them at the same level of importance as CEACR *observations* on an annualized basis.[15] Identical annual weights are justified by the comparable degree of criticism implied – on average for all countries during all years covered – by CFA *interim* reports and CEACR *observations* concerning freedom of association.

In terms of absolute size, each *interim* report entails an *implementation gap* of 2.9 points up to 1999, thereafter of 2.5 points.

The logic of equalizing the annual weight of an *observation* by the Committee of Experts with the weight of an *interim* report makes me cap at 15 points the CFA component at the first stage of the system's construction. Why should no more than 15 points be charged to a country during any year under the CFA component? Because a *gap* of that size is equal to the Committee of Experts' maximum charge on the *implementation* dimension were it to issue simultaneously two *direct requests* and two *observations* on both freedom of association Conventions in the period starting with the year 2000. (The slightly higher maximum up to 1999 is disregarded and a uniform ceiling is fixed from 1985 onward, which has the effect of generating an identical maximum CRG throughout the review period – see Box 3.3.)

The ceiling of 15 points is reached when six *interim* reports are issued during a year on six different cases. If during any single year the CFA were to put out two or three *interim* reports on the same case, only one would be counted by the system as an *implementation gap*. This scoring decision is determined by the country-year format of measuring the achievement of human rights.

The CFA weights, too, should be seen as identical measuring rods and averages that apply to any country at any point of time irrespective of whether Convention No. 87 and/or Convention No. 98 or the constitutional principles and rights of freedom of association are involved. They reflect the time-honoured distinctions that the CFA makes as a collective body. To want to go deeper into each case would inevitably introduce subjective elements that an indicator system of human rights must avoid.

If in the course of a session the CFA issued reports under one heading covering several distinct cases, each case would be taken into account on its own. The CFA has an understandable habit of considering two, three or more country cases together. Where they are listed side-by-side under one heading, disentangling is necessary because the CFA sometimes concludes that there is no need for further examination of one or several of the cases, while it continues to examine one or several cases on which it has formulated *interim* conclusions. Each case must be scored separately according to the form of report adopted by the CFA.[16]

The notions of progress and satisfaction, which are also evoked in CFA pronouncements and reports, cannot be instrumentalized under this component of the *gap* system because they are not graded by the CFA itself with the same visibility and clarity as by the Committee of Experts.[17] Follow-up may be pursued by the CFA in the form of a dialogue with the government, which may well continue for years but without giving rise to further *interim* reports. The binary approach to scoring is simple: No such report, no *gap*.

To which year should the CFA data be attributed? Allegations that are filed in year X may sometimes not give rise to an *interim* report until a year or two later, especially where the CFA has to request further information from the complainant or the government in the course of its examination of the case. Highly complex or serious cases may take years to sort out, and more than one *interim* report may be issued on it. To be fair to countries, *implementation* problems should be attributed only to the year in which an *interim* report is issued.[18]

The CFA component starts in 1985 but disregards all cases pre-dating this year. Only new cases are taken into account. The first to enter the *gap* system is case 1326 concerning Bangladesh.

5.3.3 Combining the two components

According to the logic of the indicator system, *implementation gaps* start at 0. Zero points mean that no problems were identified by the Committee of Experts or the CFA during the year in question. If there were problems, the *implementation* dimension would get loaded with points according to the weight of the comment or report that revealed them.

Indicators 5, 6 and 7 each pick up *implementation* problems in their own right. They are therefore additive and points must be summed to estimate the total size of a country's *implementation gap*.

Given the proportional relationships involved, *implementation* has an upper limit of 75 points. This maximum would be reached (a) if in any single year a country incurred a full range of comments by the Committee of Experts on all core Conventions, which would sum to 60 points, and (b) if it was simultaneously the object of six *interim* reports, adding a further 15 points. Inspection of the database is reassuring in the sense that the Committee of Experts component does not generate scores of 60 *implementation* points. No country gets everything wrong once it has *adhered* to all fundamental human rights in the labour field. However, two countries reached the ceiling of the CFA component: Peru in 1993 and Guatemala in 1995–97.

5.3.4 Testing indicators 5 and 6

The Committee of Experts' task is to verify whether countries' legal or factual situations differ from the prescriptions and proscriptions of ratified Conventions. If it finds significant deviations, it grades them in terms of importance by addressing a *direct request* or an *observation* to the government. The Committee of Experts also assesses governments' responses and expresses *satisfaction* if problems are resolved. In principle, indicators 5 and 6 measure countries' *implementation* achievements validly.

Objectivity of measurement is ensured by the fact that the indicators are fed with data that reflect the judgements of high-calibre experts from all parts of the world who are appointed in their individual capacity rather than as representatives of governments or non-governmental organizations. They operate the verification process in the most independent and impartial way imaginable. The Committee of Experts' reasoning is published in full.

Do the Committee of Experts' sources mirror national realities reliably? This question can be elucidated by a brief explanation of the reporting system concerning ratified Conventions. Governments cannot simply send a bland or whitewash report but have to respond to a detailed questionnaire that reflects key provisions of the Convention and relevant information needs. Although ILO reporting intervals changed over the years, all core Conventions had to be reported upon every two years during the *gap* system's review period, except Convention No. 138 where regular reports were due every five years before 2001.[19] Even when a government's report is not normally due during in-between years, the Committee of Experts can – and often does – request a report when it believes it is faced with a particularly serious case of non-compliance or recalcitrant government (see the examples of Myanmar and Pakistan in Chapter 5.3.1). Of course, a government can chose not to send a report – in which case the Committee of Experts tends to remind it of this fact by way of an *observation* or by repeating its previous *observation*, both of which get scored by the *gap* system. Governments' response rates have been fairly high. They averaged well above 80 per cent for all Conventions in the 1950s (Landy, 1966, p. 26). The figures came down a little over the years. Towards the end of the 1990s, the indicator on ratified Conventions (indicator 2) puts the governmental reporting rate of the countries in the *gap* system at about two thirds for the then existing seven Conventions. Since the beginning of the 21st century, the rate has climbed back to around 75 per cent for the eight core Conventions as a whole.

The fact that a government fails to report is not, however, the end of it. National and international organizations of workers and employers not only have the right to comment on government reports but to send, at any time, views and information to the government or to the ILO directly. If sent directly to the ILO, the views or information are communicated by the Secretariat to the government to enable it to comment upon them, which is sometimes a more effective means of getting the government to explain what the situation is in the country than the receipt of an ILO questionnaire. Critical comments by employers' and workers' organizations tend to entail an *observation* by the Committee of Experts. Even in the absence of reports by governments and comments by workers' or employers' organizations, the Committee of Experts usually has some relevant information at its disposal through the services of the Secretariat, which performs something more than a clerical function in this context. ILO specialists may have texts of national legislation, collective agreements or court decisions relevant to the implementation of standards, information on the results of inspections, reports on ILO technical cooperation activities, published or unpublished research papers and material from other supervisory bodies such as those of the UN, which are made available to the Committee of Experts for potential use in appraising countries' situations (for a list of official and unofficial sources used with respect to the two non-discrimination Conventions, see Thomas, 2003). Landy's judgement of nearly 40 years ago still holds true today: 'Generally speaking supervision has never been impeded by any failure on the part of ratifying countries to send in their reports' (Landy, 1966, p. 151).

Could it be argued that the realities in this or that country are, in general, very much in line with the Conventions of the International

Labour Organization even though the country has failed to ratify them? One could make such an assertion. But it is unverifiable. The indicator system measures national political will through the *adherence* dimension; and political will to *adhere* internationally to the Organization's prescriptions and proscriptions is obviously absent where a country does not ratify Conventions that it claims to apply – largely or entirely – on its territory (see also Box 5.3). Without ratification, one cannot trace that country's realities relative to global ideals. Outside the system, subjective judgements hold sway.

Box 5.3 Commitment without ratification? The US and freedom of association

The US is frequently referred to as a country that embraces certain values without proceeding to ratification. Successive governments have been hostile to, for instance, ratification of the two Conventions on freedom of association. Although the country's main trade union, the AFL-CIO, is powerful internationally, in the US the principles and rights of freedom of association are highly contested by many employers; and this group is powerful enough domestically to forestall ratification of Convention Nos. 87 and 98. Compa recalled that farm workers, household domestic workers and low-level supervisors are legally barred from the right to organize and that 'in twenty-seven U.S. states, collective bargaining by public employees is prohibited' (Compa, 2002, p. 13). In another article he concluded that 'many workers who try to form trade unions are spied on, harassed, pressured, threatened, suspended, fired, deported, or otherwise victimized in reprisal for their exercise of the right to freedom of association. A culture of near-impunity has taken shape in much of U.S. labor law and practice' (Compa, 2003, pp. 32–33). A recent exercise in indicator construction stated that 'the US is generally considered by scholars to have fairly low levels of collective bargaining protection for workers, accompanied by a strong anti-union movement among employers' (Block, Berg and Roberts, 2003, p. 458). Even an official report by the government under the Declaration in 2000 coyly acknowledged that 'there are aspects of this system (in the US) that fail to fully protect the rights to organize and bargain collectively of all employees in all circumstances' (ILO, 2000b, p. 153). The ICFTU's comment on this report briefly summaries existing legal pitfalls and practical obstacles (*ibid.*, pp. 160–163).

Indicators 5 and 6 fully respect the non-truncation criterion. Thousands of *direct requests* and *observations* were made by the Committee of Experts during the review period. Only two of the 159 countries covered have not been the object of critical comments during the 20 years, Kiribati and Turkmenistan, which are recent member States and recent ratifiers who have so far benefited from the time lags associated with recent ratifications that will be explained in the next Chapter.

Finally, it is worth noting that indicators 5 and 6 are useful in the sense of providing timely information that is easy and cheap to collect.

5.3.5 Testing indicator 7

The test of the CFA indicator's validity has to verify whether the definitional selectivity of *interim* reports is borne out in practice. Are these reports addressed to countries with the worst freedom of association *implementation* problems or are they issued at random? Such a test can sensibly be carried out at the regional level because the regional distribution of *interim* reports should fit a certain pattern, which is set out in the first column of Table 5.2. As two of the four major regions normally distinguished in this book, the Americas and the Asian-Pacific region, are too heterogeneous as far as freedom of association questions are concerned, they will be split into subregions. In the Americas, I split off the Latin American countries from the rest, that is, the Caribbean countries, Canada and the US. In Latin America, several decades ago successive military regimes either subdued democratic workers' organizations or forced them into a corporatist structure, of which there are still many traces. Today, in the region with the most unequal income distribution in the world, many governments and employers remain hostile to independent trade unions whose battle cry is equality and solidarity. One must expect, therefore, strong tensions to erupt from time to time between the powers-that-be and countries' trade unions. The Caribbean-Canadian-US group, on the other hand, would be expected to be closer to Europe than to any other region as regards its laws and practices in the area of freedom of association. In the Asian-Pacific region, I separate out Australia, Israel, New Zealand, Japan, the Philippines, as well as four South Asian countries (Bangladesh, India, Pakistan and Sri Lanka) where unions in the private sector flourished until recently under an import-substitution policy. One could call this group 'favourably inclined' towards freedom of association in historical terms and by comparison with the 'other' Asian-Pacific countries. The latter include China and other communist countries where the party imposed and continues to enforce a single union system; the several Gulf countries where unions were anathema, at least until recently; formerly communist countries such as Azerbaijan and Kazakhstan whose leaders have scarcely loosened the reigns; and formerly military or authoritarian regimes such as the Republic of Korea, Indonesia and Thailand where various degrees of control and repression prevailed for a long time under export-oriented development strategies but where democratic changes started to take hold in recent years. As a whole, the 'other' Asian-Pacific subregion must be assumed to be the worst achiever of the principles and rights of freedom of association during the *gap* system's 20-year review period.

The regional ranking pattern is postulated in the first column of Table 5.2. It puts European countries as a whole closest to the require-

Table 5.2   CFA data ranking regions from hypothesized best to worst achiever of freedom of association

Assumed ranking of regions	Complaints registered			Interim reports 1985–2004			Actual ranking of regions
	1951–2000: 2,112 for all former and current member States	1985–2004: 993 for all 159 gap countries	1985–2004: average number of complaints per country in region	Cumulative number	Distribution	Average number of reports per country in region	Interim reports as % of complaints
1	2	3	4	5	6	7	8
Europe	31%	19.4%	4.9	25	6.5%	0.6	13.0%
Caribbean, Canada, US	–	9.3%	6.6	17	4.4%	1.2	18.5%
Asia-Pacific 'favourable'	–	8.6%	9.4	34	8.8%	3.8	40.0%
Africa	13%	13.2%	2.7	58	15.1%	1.2	44.3%
Latin America	44%	45.0%	23.5	218	56.6%	11.5	48.8%
Asia-Pacific 'other'	12%	4.5%	1.5	33	8.6%	1.1	73.3%
Total or average	100%	100.0%	6.2	385	100.0%	2.4	38.8%

N.B. For definitions of regions and subregions, see Chapter 3.2. In column 2, the Latin America figure includes the 14 countries of the Caribbean, Canada and the US as well as the 19 Latin American countries; and the Asian-Pacific figure includes the nine countries of the 'favourable' Asian-Pacific group as well as the 30 countries of the 'other' Asian-Pacific group.

ments of legal and practical respect for freedom of association and the 'other' Asian-Pacific group at the other end of the scale. The Latin American subregion is hypothesized to be the second worst achiever. Africa is situated closer to the worst achievers than to Europe or the Caribbean-Canadian-US group or even the 'favourably inclined' Asian-Pacific countries. Not long after independence, most African governments co-opted earlier freedom fighters or imposed single union systems and suppressed independent voices. The winds of democratization that blew across the continent in the late 1980s and early 1990s should have breathed new air into the once cherished freedom of workers to defend their interests. But in some countries old habits die hard.

Bearing in mind that all data in Table 5.2 are averages of sorts that lock countries into a ranked group even though there are significant differences within regions, what do they indicate? Columns 2 and 3 set the scene with reference figures, which show that Latin America has consistently been the object of almost half of all complaints. Europe's 1985–2004 share dropped by 12 per cent compared with the 50-year period that covers the Cold War and its immediate aftermath. In column 4, the incidence of complaints is divided by the number of countries in each region, which averages the number of complaints filed per country. The contrast between Latin America and the 'other' Asian-Pacific subregion is enormous. In Latin America governments were the object of a complaint about 16 times as often as in the 'other' Asian-Pacific subregion. The huge number of Latin American complaints reflects not only the fact that unions had no other recourse during the period when the military was in power but also their long-standing familiarity with the CFA machinery and the continuing utility of the system for them. The low number for 'other' Asian-Pacific countries reflects the tight political control exercised over trade unions by most governments. Africa's figure tells a similar story.

The actual *interim* report data are presented in columns 5–7 in different forms. The huge proportion of reports addressed to Latin American countries dominates the picture. But columns 5–7 do not measure sufficiently precisely where the problems revealed by CFA reports are gravest. Column 8 does this by relating the number of *interim* reports (output) to the number of complaints (input); and this column confirms the hypothesized ranking of the first column. Workers' organizations from the 'other' Asian-Pacific subregion have used the ILO's complaints procedures on freedom of association much less often than their Latin American counterparts, but when they did so nearly three quarters of the cases gave rise to *interim* reports, that is, they involved serious violations of freedom of association. Latin America's incidence of seriousness in column 8 is significantly lower than that of the 'other' Asian-Pacific subregion, and Africa's is a little lower still. All three regions are above the average figure, even the 'favourably inclined' Asian-Pacific subregion is. By contrast, the proportion of the Caribbean, Canada and US group is much lower, about half the figure of their southern neighbours; and it is lowest in Europe. This test confirms empirically that *interim* reports constitute a germane selection which picks up the gravest *implementation* problems.

Can complaints data be scored reliably? Scoring should pose no problem whatsoever because the categorization of reports is almost always visible in the heading of each case and spelt out in the CFA's conclusions or recommendations.

Do the CFA data measure freedom of association problems objectively? They certainly do. The CFA quasi-judicially verifies whether allegations are true and dismisses them if they are not. When the numerically equal representatives of governments, workers and employers who fill the benches of the CFA have reason to believe that violations have occurred, the accused governments are given ample opportunity to refute allegations. When these violations are particularly serious, this is almost invariably brought out into the open through an *interim* report. Governments could seek to overturn the CFA's findings when the report is presented in the ILO Governing Body. They could also appeal the findings to the International Court of Justice in The Hague, which none has done.

In testing indicator 7 for truncation it is worth recalling that *interim* reports measure *implementation* problems at the output rather than the input stage of the complaints procedure. However, there may not be any inputs – allegations of infringement – to start with, in which case there could not be any outputs either. One possibility is that, when no allegations are raised, freedom of association is actually complied with. The other possibility is that the lack of allegations is a reflection of a very understandable peculiarity affecting the ILO's complaints machinery, which is that allegations of infringements of freedom of association are mainly submitted by national organizations of workers and by their international confederations, notably the ICFTU, that have reason to believe the ILO offers them a better chance of righting wrongs than domestic dispute settlement procedures do. Where national trade unions are controlled by governments or fearful of them, they are highly unlikely to submit a complaint to any international body (see African and 'other' Asian-Pacific countries in Table 5.2, column 4). In some instances, notably in respect of 'big' countries such as China, the ICFTU occasionally complains to the ILO. All told, 69 of the *gap* system's 159 countries have been objects of complaints that have given rise to *interim* reports.[20] Given such differential propensities to complain, the test suggests that the non-truncation criterion is extensively but not entirely respected by indicator 7.

Finally, complaints procedures yield useful data in the sense that they are easy to collect without incurring particular costs.

In toto, it can be concluded that the incidence and size of *gaps* revealed by indicator 7 are determined by data that are valid but a little truncated. While not perfect, they are sufficiently satisfactory to press them into use.[21] The CFA component, which has the advantage of covering non-ratifiers, supplements the new system's measurement of *implementation gaps*. Neither overall data nor even the area of freedom of association depend on it for the measurement of *implementation gaps*. The CFA component's impact on the *implementation* dimension is limited in the sense that the *gap* which may derive from it is capped at 15 points – no more than roughly the value of an unratified core Convention. Researchers may disagree with the actual weights assigned to an *interim* report, 20 per cent of the value of a Convention, which they can change in the light of their own perception. Researchers may also not want to limit the overall importance of the CFA component to 15 points, which they can vary or dispense with altogether.

5.4   Shortcut to implementation gaps

The Committee of Experts' comments apply to the core Conventions without restrictions. They constitute, quantitatively speaking, the largest portion of all *implementation* points. Two of these comments – *observations* and expressions of *satisfaction* (the lightly shaded area in Boxes 3.1 and 3.2) – are selected to construct a shortcut or annual proxy variable that provides insights into *implementation* problems without having to work through all the details and variations of this dimension.

The *implementation* shortcut is a simplified version of indicator 6 that gives each 'negative' *observation* a value of 1, each expression of *satisfaction* a value of 0, and 'mixed' *observations* that contain both negative remarks and 'positive' *satisfaction* a value of 0.5. It disregards all *direct requests* (indicator 5), the different loads of *observations* and *satisfaction* during the *gap* system's two sub-periods, as well as all points generated by the CFA component (indicator 7). As for the full implementation variable so for the proxy: combinations of *observations* and *satisfaction* could be referred to as *observations* corrected for *satisfaction* or *observation-cum-satisfaction*, but the term *observation* will be used in the interest of intelligibility unless clarity demands otherwise.

The proxy also measures *satisfaction* separately according to the full or half values that obtain each year. This adds a distinct variable to the *gap* system.

Adding up each year's *observations*, deducting *satisfaction* and halving values when there are 'mixed' *observations* facilitates a presentation that will be resorted to several times in later Chapters when aggregate scores are strung along a time path to see how their path changes during the 20 years for which data have been entered into the *gap* system – whether regions' or global *implementation* problems are decreasing or increasing.

6
Time Lags and Finalization of the System's Features

6.1   Time-lag effects and extensive recent ratifiers

The new system's *implementation* and CRG scores are afflicted by time lags from the mid-1990s until the present time that are inherent in the reporting cycle on the application of ratified Conventions and certain working habits of the Committee of Experts. This gives rise to some temporarily odd scores until the time lags have worked their way out of the system. When the next round of five-year averages will be estimated in 2005–09, the effects should for all practical purposes have disappeared and the *gap* system should have reached its stage of maturity that fully and correctly measures the achievement of human rights in the labour field for all countries.

The origin of the time lags lies in the fact that a new ratification in year X lowers the *adherence gap* strongly, immediately and forever, reducing CRGs commensurately, while governmental reporting and the Committee of Experts' assessment of laws and practices do not follow suit as quickly as they do when reporting-cum-supervision has set into a pattern several years after ratification. Whereas the weights of *direct requests* and *observations* were fixed at a level to reflect the degree to which they might call into question the application of Conventions during a normal biannual reporting period, they may be hollowed out somewhat by governmental delays in reporting or by nonreporting as well as by the particular caution and diplomacy exercised by the CEACR when it examines a government's first report on a new ratification.

To illustrate, when a Convention is *adhered* to (say, in March of year X), the ratification enters into force for the country concerned one year later (March X+1), and the first governmental report on its application is due a year later. If the report arrives on time and the Committee of Experts in December X+2 has doubts about the country's legislative or factual situation in respect of the Convention's prescriptions and proscriptions, or if the government indicates that a process is underway of bringing laws and practices into line with the Convention, the CEACR will usually ask merely for additional information through a *direct request* and will diplomatically give the government more time to put its house in order. Thus, while ratification (indicator 1) strongly lowers the *adherence gap* from year X onward and the CRG registers a full reduction of 12.5 points in both X and X+1 because there can be no *implementation gap* during those years (disregarding CFA *interim* reports), a small *implementation gap* of 2.5 points feeding through to the country's CRG usually appears at the earliest in year X+2 under indicator 5 of the Convention concerned. This assumes that the government fulfils its reporting obligation, which is not always the case, and that the CEACR has the time to examine the occasionally voluminous first report, which is sometimes impossible.[1] When there are delays in reporting or when the government does not report at all or when many ratifications occur at the same time, the CEACR may get to grips with the realities of a country's situation only a year later, in X+3.

Should the Committee of Experts in year X+2 find stark discrepancies between the Convention's provisions and the country's situation without as much as a hint that the government intends to do anything about it, the CEACR might comment immediately by way of an *observation* (indicator 6), which would charge the *implementation* dimension and CRG immediately with 5 points. But the CEACR is not in the habit of formulating an *observation* until the second government report is due a further two years later. If in X+4 the government reported on time, and an *observation* was then formulated, it would increase the relevant CRG by 5 points. (In X+3, when a report is not due, the CEACR would not formulate a *direct request* or an *observation*, and neither the *implementation* dimension nor the CRG would be charged with points.) If the government did not report on time in X+4, the CEACR's report could not contain an *observation* until X+5.

The impact of time lags can most easily be demonstrated by choosing a pair of Conventions, such as Gambia's ratification of Convention Nos. 87 and 98 in 2000. The first report on the application of the Conventions were due in 2002 but not received. They were received in time for the Committee of Experts' session of 2003, and the CEACR promptly addressed two *direct requests* to the government on each Convention that charged the *implementation* dimension and the country's CRG with a total of 5 points. As far as the two freedom of association

Conventions are concerned, Gambia has a CRG of 0 points in 2000–01, 5 points in 2002 and will again have a CRG of 0 points in 2003–04 because the next reports on the two Conventions are not due until 2005. The average for the five year period would thus be 1 point. Comparing the pre-ratification average of 1995–99 (14.3 points) with the average of 2000–04, Gambia's CRG dropped by 13.3 points on account of two ratifications. This effect would be multiplied by four if the country ratified all core Conventions in one fell swoop. In Gambia's case, seven Conventions were ratified in 2000, the eight in 2001 and, as Table 1 of the Rights Gaps Indicators shows, time-lag effects catapulted it from CRG rank 126 in 1995–99 to rank one in 2000–04 – probably not the rank it really deserves and probably not the one it will occupy in years ahead.[2]

The normal workings of the new indicator system were blown out of proportion by the ratification campaign launched by the ILO's Director-General in 1995 and the adoption of the Declaration in 1998 that not only entailed a large jump in ratifications of core Conventions between the mid-1990s and the beginning of the 21st century[3] but also had the effect of bunching many ratifications in a very short time span. Fifty-one countries covered by the *gap* system (32 per cent) ratified three or more Conventions between January 1996 and December 2004, a group I call 'extensive recent ratifiers' in relation to the whole set of Conventions. They are identified in the Tables by capital letters. Only ten countries did not ratify any of the eight core Conventions between January 1996 and December 2004.[4] It is, therefore, inevitable that the new indicator system currently contains a large number of *implementation* scores and CRGs that favour recent ratifiers – at least temporarily, until the CEACR catches up with their realities.

Theoretically, if all countries ratified Conventions at about the same time, they would all be subject to similar time lags, enjoy large simultaneous drops in CRGs and their positions relative to each other would not be jumbled greatly. Reality is quite different. Compare Gambia with, for example, the Netherlands. Gambia's wholesale ratification occasioned a drop in its *adherence gap* of 87.5 points in 2000 and of another 12.5 points in 2001, moving it from near the back of the CRG ranking to up front. The Netherlands, on the other hand, had ratified seven core Conventions by 1993 and adhered to the eight, Convention No. 182, in 2002. The Netherlands benefited from a reduction in its CRG of 12.5 points in 2002, everything else being equal. As Table 1 of the Rights Gap Indicators shows, this had practically no effect on its

CRG rank (33 in 1995–99 and 32 in 2000–04) because many extensive recent ratifiers rushed past it – benefiting as they did from the cumulative time-lag effects associated with the recent ratification of many Conventions.

Time lags impact on a sliding scale according to the extent of preceding ratifications and the spacing of new ratifications. Where a country had previously *adhered* to three, four or five core Conventions, time-lag effects are less pronounced than where a country had ratified none or one or two. Similarly, where a country spaces its new ratification over several years, the time lags of the first and the next ratification begin to wane as the others take effect.

Sliding-scale impacts on *implementation* scores can be exemplified by reference to El Salvador. The country, having ratified Convention 105 in 1958, *adhered* to Convention Nos. 29 and 111 in 1995, No. 138 in 1996 and Nos. 100 and 182 in 2000. El Salvador's *implementation* scores (excluding a 2003 *interim* report) averaged 5.7 points during 1995–99 largely on account of Convention No. 105 since the new ratifications did not entail *implementation gaps* for two or three years, and when *implementation* was charged with points, this happened initially at the low level of *direct requests*. In 2000–01, *implementation* scores were not affected by the further ratifications and increased only marginally; but thereafter they jumped to 17.5 points in 2002–03 and to 15 points in 2004 when *observations* started to appear in 2002 on Convention Nos. 100, 138 and 182, in 2003 on Convention Nos. 29 and 111, and in 2004 again on Convention Nos. 138 and 182. The *implementation* average of 2000–04 was 13 points, 7.3 points higher than the average of 1995–99.

Ratification is the lynchpin of the *gap* system and, through the *adherence* dimension, is the biggest single determinant of the size of CRGs at the first stage of its construction. Over time, CRGs emancipate themselves from *adherence* and are influenced progressively by *implementation* problems. The new indicator system thus mirrors the shift from the importance of espousing a policy, which is the decisive first step, to giving it practical effect in all respects over an indefinite period of time.

The time lags will work themselves out of the new indicator system in the coming years. Even though universal ratification of the International Labour Organization's core Conventions is far from having been realized (see Table 6.1), by the time the next five-year averages of 2005–09 can be calculated few countries will have proceeded to new ratifications and few cumulative ratifications on the part of a single country will impact significantly on its *implementation gaps* and CRGs.

Table 6.1 Conventions not ratified by countries in the gap system as of January 2005[1]

Freedom of association		Forced labour		Child labour		Discrimination	
C. No. 87	C. No. 98	C. No. 29	C. No. 105	C. No. 138	C. No. 182	C. No. 100	C. No. 111
BAHRAIN	BAHRAIN			Australia	Australia	BAHRAIN	
		Bolivia		BAHRAIN			
Brazil				Bangladesh			
	Canada	Canada			CAMBODIA		
				Canada			
				Cape Verde			
China	China	China	China	Chad			China
				Czech Republic	Cuba		
				Djibouti	Djibouti		Djibouti
EL SALVADOR	EL SALVADOR			ESTONIA	ERITREA		ESTONIA
				Gabon			
				Ghana			
Guinea-Bissau				Guinea-Bissau	Guinea-Bissau		
India	India			India	India		
Iran	Iran			Iran			
					Israel		
Jordan			Japan				Japan
KENYA							

Table 6.1 Conventions not ratified by countries in the gap system as of January 2005[1] – continued

Freedom of association		Forced labour		Child labour		Discrimination	
C. No. 87	C. No. 98	C. No. 29	C. No. 105	C. No. 138	C. No. 182	C. No. 100	C. No. 111
KOREA, REP.	KOREA, REP.	KOREA, REP.	KOREA, REP.	KIRIBATI	KIRIBATI	KIRIBATI	KIRIBATI
	Kuwait					Kuwait	
Laos	Laos	Latvia	Laos	Laos	Laos	Laos	Laos
				Latvia	Latvia		
Lebanon			MADAGASCAR				MALAYSIA
MALAYSIA			MALAYSIA				
MAURITIUS	Mexico	Mongolia	Mongolia	Mexico			
Morocco	Myanmar		Myanmar	Myanmar	Myanmar	Myanmar NAMIBIA	Myanmar
New Zealand				New Zealand			
Oman	Oman	Philippines	Oman	Oman		Oman	Oman
				Pakistan			
Qatar	Qatar		Qatar	Qatar		Qatar	
				ST. KITTS & NEVIS			
				St. Lucia			
				ST. VINCENT & GRENADINES			

Table 6.1 Conventions not ratified by countries in the gap system as of January 2005[1] – continued

Freedom of association		Forced labour		Child labour		Discrimination	
C. No. 87	C. No. 98	C. No. 29	C. No. 105	C. No. 138	C. No. 182	C. No. 100	C. No. 111
		Sao Tome & P.	Sao Tome & P.	Sao Tome & P.	Sao Tome & P.		
Saudi Arabia	Saudi Arabia			Saudi Arabia			
				Sierra Leone	Sierra Leone		
Singapore			Singapore	Singapore			Singapore
				Surinam	Surinam	Surinam	Surinam
Thailand	Thailand						Thailand
				TURKMENISTAN	TURK-MENISTAN		
Uganda						Uganda	Uganda
U. ARAB EMIRATES	U. ARAB EMIRATES						
United States	United States	United States		United States		United States	United States
Uzbekistan				Uzbekistan	Uzbekistan		
					Venezuela		
VIETNAM	VIETNAM	VIETNAM	VIETNAM				
26	18	10	13	34	18	11	14

[1] New member States Timor Leste and Vanuatu are not taken into account; neither country had ratified any core Convention by the end of 2004. Countries shaded under Convention Nos. 87 and 98 have been object of CFA *interim* reports. Capitalized countries are extensive recent ratifiers, that is, countries which ratified three or more Conventions between the beginning of 1996 and the end of 2004.

What grounds are there for assuming that ratifications have ebbed off given that 60 countries are listed in Table 6.1 as having not yet *adhered* to one or several of the standards that specify the fundamental human rights in the labour field?[5] First of all, 17 countries are capitalized, that is, they are extensive recent ratifiers. Their governments have presumably studied seriously the question whether to ratify the outstanding Conventions – and decided against it. Of course, countries may change their minds or their governments.

Second, quite a number of the non-ratifiers have historically been – to put it diplomatically – reluctant to ratify international labour Conventions, notably Asian and Gulf countries. They are over-represented in Table 6.1 and unlikely to turn into enthusiastic ratifiers any time soon.

Third, it is unrealistic to expect a great many more *adherents* of one of the standards that has been lagging in ratification tables, Convention No. 87. Countries such as China, India, Saudi Arabia and the US are politically strongly opposed to ratification, in India's case on the ground that it would give its privileged civil servants yet more power than they already wield. The ratification prospects of the companion Convention, No. 98, are similarly bleak. Shading in Table 6.1 indicates that 14 of the 30 non-ratifiers of the two freedom of association Conventions have actually been at the receiving end of CFA *interim* reports (although some of the reports fall into the early years of the *gap* system), which will scarcely have endeared them to embracing fully any unratified freedom of association Convention.

Fourth, as regards the least ratified standard of all core Conventions, No. 138, insightful policies, a determination to put primary education high on the domestic agenda or fears of foreign boycotts of goods produced by children may induce some developing countries or transition economies to *adhere* to this Convention. Its companion, Convention No. 182, is also likely to be ratified by some of the 15 developing countries or transition economies that have not yet taken that step. But universal ratification is not on the horizon of either Convention.

Fifth, the forced labour and non-discrimination Conventions are already pretty close to universal *adherence*, which implies that one should not expect much ratification in the future. In the case of Convention No. 105, Malaysia and Singapore took the unusual step of denouncing their ratification, which they are unlikely to reverse.

In sum, excepting the two child labour Conventions, one can expect little further ratification by the current member States of the International Labour Organization. New member States such as Timor-Leste and Vanuatu or others that may join in the future will probably ratify core Conventions in all areas. But the group I called 'extensive recent ratifiers' is a dying breed that will cease to play havoc with the new indicator system.

6.2 Reweighting adherence

Whether in a country's national constitution, domestic law or in its act of ratifying an international Convention, the expression of commitment to certain values is necessary to realize fundamental human rights. But formal *adherence* does not by itself suffice to achieve rights. It has to be followed by concrete *implementation* measures to enforce the law and to give it practical effect. The proof of the human rights pudding lies not in the recipe but in its realization. It follows that the importance of *adherence* in the estimation of CRGs should be downgraded somewhat relative to the importance of *implementation*.

Downgrading happens at the second stage of the *gap* system's construction (see also Box 3.3). It is carried out after completion of the first stage because the weights of reporting on ratified Conventions, the two Declaration indicators and the three *implementation* indicators are expressed as a proportion of the value of ratifying a Convention and had to be introduced in a transparent and easy-to-follow manner.

Following sensitivity tests, the weight of the whole of the *adherence* dimension in calculating CRGs is reduced to one quarter of its first-stage weight. This is reweighting's primary impact.

Reweighting's secondary impact keeps time-lag effects within bounds. By reducing the difference between pre-ratification and post-ratification *adherence* scores, the instant improvement in countries' statistical fortunes associated with ratification is reduced to one quarter of its first-stage size.

That the downgrading of the *adherence* dimension diminishes its impact on CRGs can be illustrated with the help of Pearson product moment correlations. The coefficient of correlation between the 2000–04 CRGs and *adherence gaps*, +0.33, is weak. It is much stronger when the 2000–04 CRGs are correlated with *implementation gaps*, +0.73 (both significant at 1 per cent).

6.3 Normalization

The final finishing touch applied to the new indicator system normalizes the reweighted data. Normalization (or standardization) is a simple technique to render disparate quantities comparable. One method would be to divide aggregate results by the number of countries in the system; but this is inapplicable to individual countries' data. It is preferable to standardize individual countries and aggregates by the same method; and to choose a technique that permits the integration and comparison of different system's indicators that are similarly scaled without incurring stressful interpretation difficulties.[6] UNDP adopted such a method to scale its three-dimensional HDI and the indexes subsequently developed on similar lines (see UNDP, 2003, pp. 340ff); and this technique will be used here with slight simplifications. Normalization of *gaps* amounts to a rescaling of the calculations carried out at the first stage that compresses the reweighted *adherence* data into a scale of 0–0.250 points and the *implementation* data and CRGs into a scale of 0–1 point.

Normalization must be carried out separately for *adherence*, *implementation gaps* and CRGs. For, unlike at the first stage, the normalized CRG is not the sum of the normalized *adherence gap* and the normalized *implementation gap* (summing the two could yield values in excess of 1 point) but has to be calculated separately using the reweighted data.

As regards the formula to be applied, UNDP's normalization method (actual points–minimum points)/(maximum points–minimum points) can be appropriately simplified because *gaps* are more variable in the short term – up and down – than life expectancy, education and economic success on which the HDI is based. Due to both the reporting-cum-CEACR cycles and the volatility of political developments, variations of the minima and maxima would unnecessarily force the *gap* data into different ranges in different years. My simplifications apply to the minimum as well as the maximum. As regards the minimum – the lowest number of points attained by a country – given that 0 *adherence* points, 0 *implementation* points and 0 CRG points are attained by a number of countries in each area, although not always simultaneously, I put all minima at 0, which enables me to drop the minimum altogether and use the intuitively comprehensible formula (actual *gaps*/maximum *gaps*). The actual points are those estimated at the first stage. As regards the maximum – the highest number of points or largest *gaps* – I use the maxima foreseen by the system (summarized in Box 3.3 above). In the case of the overall scores that cover all seven or eight Conventions and the constitutional principles and rights of freedom of association, the first stage maxima were 100 points for *adherence*, 75 for *implementation* and 115 for CRGs.[7] After reweighting, they become 25 for *adherence* and 81.25 for CRGs.[8] *Implementation* is not reweighted, and its maximum of 75 points stays unchanged. The advantage of choosing identical lower and upper limits throughout the new indicator system is that the reference points are always the same. Thus, a country's normalized *gap* data are strictly comparable across all areas and during all years.

6.4 Long-standing ratifiers

The fact that the new indicator system measures quantitatively the extent to which countries give effect to their policies can be exploited analytically in various ways. One possibility is to focus on the *implementation* record of a group of countries I call 'long-standing ratifiers'. In line with the starting date of the *gap* system, I fix the cut-off point of this group at December 1984. Long-standing ratifiers comprise only current member States of the International Labour Organization that *adhered* before 1985 to such core Conventions as were listed as having been ratified by them on 31 December 2004, excluding Convention No. 182. When a country is listed as having ratified before 1985 one or both of the two Conventions in any area, it qualifies as a long-standing ratifier. If it ratified one before 1985 and the other afterwards, it does not qualify as long-standing ratifier (the presentation would otherwise become confusing). Some of this venerable group of countries ratified Convention No. 29 over seven decades ago;[9] some ratified Convention Nos. 87, 98 and 100 during the early 1950s, five decades ago; some ratified Convention Nos. 105 and 111 during the early 1960s, four decades ago; and some ratified Convention No. 138 during the mid-1970s, three decades ago. Long-standing ratifiers do not include new member States and exclude all former member States such as the USSR and the Czech and Slovak Republic that do not form part of the new indicator system (see Box 3.4 above). Long-standing ratifiers are identified in this book's Tables by italicized letters.

There are 28 long-standing ratifiers if one puts all core Conventions together (excluding Convention No. 182 because it entered into force in 2000). High ratifiers such as Costa Rica and Poland form part of them, medium ratifiers such as Canada and Mexico as well as low ratifiers such as Laos and Myanmar. The 'usual suspects' include five Scandinavian or western European countries (Finland, Germany, Italy, Norway and Spain) along with eight African countries (Algeria, Chad, Djibouti, Gabon, Ghana, Guinea-Bissau, Niger and Sierra Leone). Long-standing ratifiers are not a very homogeneous group – except that they should have experienced few or decreasing *implementation* problems during 1985–2004. As regards each pair of core Conventions, again defining long-standing ratifiers as countries that *adhered* before 1985 to such Conventions as were listed as having been ratified by them on 31 December 2004, their number is much higher than when countries have to fulfil the same criterion for up to seven Conventions simultaneously. In the new indicator system, 92 countries are long-standing ratifiers in the case of the two freedom of association Conventions, 97 in the case of the forced labour Conventions, 86 in the case of the non-discrimination Conventions and 28 in the case of Convention No. 138. Since one should assume that long-standing ratifiers' teething problems of applying ratified core Conventions are well behind them, the book examines repeatedly whether that is true.

Long-standing ratifiers constitute an unchanging universe that permits proper trends to be estimated for the 20 years at present covered by the *gap* system. In comparing their scores with the scores of all countries it is also possible to judge whether extensive recent ratifiers introduce distortions that significantly affect aggregate results.

The evolution of scores and trends can move in the 'right' or 'wrong' direction. In the case of *observations*, the movements would point in the right direction if their time paths sloped downward because this would suggest a decreasing number of critical remarks by the CEACR or an increasing number of cases of progress or some combination of desirable developments. If the time paths sloped upward, they would point in the wrong direction because this would suggest that *implementation* problems were on the increase.

The movements of expressions of *satisfaction* are mirror-like in the sense that they point in the right direction if they slope upward, thereby indicating an increasing number of cases of progress in the course of time. If they point downward because the CEACR finds less and less reason to express its *satisfaction*, they move in the wrong direction.

7
Human Rights Achievements – Measuring the Four Freedoms as a Whole

7.1 Introduction

The empirical results generated by the new indicator system can now be illustrated with the help of different table and graphic formats, which will demonstrate the richness and exploitability of the *gap* system. The presentation will start with the broad sweep of global developments and regional distinctions, descend to the level of ranking individual countries and take a more detailed look at the worst *implementers*, the latter with the help of both the full measurement and the proxy. Where comparable other indicators are available, they will be correlated with *adherence, implementation* and CRG data. Chapter 7 presents the overall results, that is, the achievements measured across the four areas. Chapters 8–11 analyse separately freedom of association, freedom from forced labour, freedom from child labour and freedom from discrimination.

It is worth reiterating at the beginning of the interpretation of the results that, because the system is a mixture of annual and biannual data, it makes no sense to look at a single year's results. Although the mix of annual and biannual entries washes out somewhat over the seven or eight core Conventions and their different reporting rhythms, it can incur uncharacteristically high or low scores in a particular year. These are most sensibly trended away or averaged out. Since the general biannual rhythm of reporting on ratified Conventions and the associated *direct requests* or *observations* by the CEACR renders the new indicator system essentially biannual in nature, valid comparison requires as a minimum two sets of two-year averages. This book presents averages covering a period of five years,[1] complemented by long-term trendlines. The ultimate aim of the *gap* system being to determine how countries' human rights achievements change in the course of time – whether they are moving in the right or wrong direction – developments can be expressed in qualitative terms when five-year averages are compared and when the inclination of the slope of long-term trendlines can be determined.

The message conveyed by averages and trendlines can be expressed in different words with similar meanings, which I use interchangeably. When averages increase or trendlines point upward, *gaps* grow, increase, worsen, get bigger or higher – an undesirable development as far as human rights are concerned. When averages decrease or trendlines point downward, *gaps* get smaller, lower or decrease and the achievement of human rights improves. When averages are flat or trendlines are horizontal, there is no change in a country's situation. To assess the implications of averages or trendline movements properly, one should look at the size or level of *gaps*, which can be perceived in Tables 1–5 of the Right Gaps Indicators. A low-level *gap* that stays unchanged or gets a little worse is not as worrisome as a high-level *gap* that stays unchanged or a medium-size *gap* that gets a lot worse.

Different quantitative performance measures can be used for individual countries and aggregates such as regions, the four freedoms and long-standing ratifiers. In the case of individual countries, rates of change of scores could be calculated, but the implied precision might be premature given the time-lags affecting recent ratifiers.[2] When comparing regional aggregates one has to be aware of the different number of countries that make up a region – everything else being equal, Africa's 48 countries will generate more *observations* than the 33 countries of the Americas. One also has to be aware of the fact that aggregates may have different starting positions. For instance, a region that in the past had ratified most Conventions is likely to have small *adherence gaps* at the beginning of the review period, which means that its scope for having many improving *adherence* averages or trendlines is more limited than in the case of a region with large initial *adherence gaps*. Conversely, a region that had large *gaps* to start with should ideally perform better than a region with low initial *gaps*. However, the principal interest lies not in the starting positions of aggregates (or of countries for that matter) but whether their slopes point upward or downward and whether the angle is steep or not. Slopes of *implementation gaps* will be portrayed graphically. Quantitative performance measures that take account of the different number of countries and their starting positions and which will be calculated repeatedly are the ratios of the number of improving to worsening averages or trendlines and similar comparable data.

Of course, as in all indicator systems, the weights influence the size of scores. Had the *gap* system remained at the first-stage weight of equal importance of the *adherence* and *implementation* dimensions, the size of CRGs would generally have been larger, reaching up to twice the size of those shown. Countries' relative positions, however, would change only very marginally; and the direction of the inclination of trendlines would not change at all. In my judgement, the reweighted and normalized data portray more accurately countries' situation in the world today than the first-stage data would.

By December 2004, the numbers and proportions of ratifications of the eight core Conventions were more than sufficiently large to cover – time-lag effects notwithstanding – most countries' *implementation* problems. Of the 159 countries, 99 had ratified all eight, a further 25 had ratified seven and an additional 11 had ratified six of the core Conventions (see the reverse data in Table 6.1). Universal ratification is almost within sight but is unlikely ever to be reached. Of course, the level of ratification was lower at the beginning of the review period in 1985. This does not imply that non-ratifiers are 'advantaged' by the *gap* system. On the contrary, they incur sizeable *adherence gaps* that feed through to CRGs.

7.2   Global and regional evolution

Long-term trendlines covering at least ten years can be established for 154 countries, that is, all countries except Albania, Bosnia-Herzegovina, Kiribati, St. Kitts and Nevis, and Sierra Leone. Table 7.1, which covers every Convention, principle and right, is built on a count of the lines' movements. A general remark is in order about the 'unchanged' trends in this and the later Tables concerning the different areas of freedom. Trends that do not change direction occur mostly under *adherence* and *implementation gaps*; their values tend be close to or at 0 points; but there are exceptions.

At the global level, more than three fifths of the overall CRG trendlines improved, about a third worsened. The ratio of improving to worsening trends is 1.8:1. The regional ratios of improving to worsening CRG lines would rank the Caribbean/Canada/US group (3.3:1) ahead of the 'other' Asian-Pacific countries (3:1), Latin America (1.7:1), Africa (1.6:1), Europe (1.4:1) and the 'favourably inclined' Asian-Pacific countries (1.3:1). When the Table's two sets of subregions are re-aggregated,

Table 7.1   Achievement of basic labour rights as a whole, by region, 1985–2004 (%)

	Worse*	Better**	Unchanged
Global			
CRGs	34	62	5
Adherence gaps	19	73	8
Implementation gaps	64	31	5
Africa			
CRGs	36	60	4
Adherence gaps	26	68	6
Implementation gaps	79	17	4
Asia-Pacific 'favourably inclined'			
CRGs	44	56	0
Adherence gaps	22	78	0
Implementation gaps	44	44	11
Asia-Pacific 'other'			
CRGs	24	72	3
Adherence gaps	10	83	7
Implementation gaps	59	34	7
Caribbean, Canada, US			
CRGs	23	77	0
Adherence gaps	23	69	8
Implementation gaps	46	46	8
Latin America			
CRGs	32	53	16
Adherence gaps	16	74	11
Implementation gaps	53	42	5
Europe			
CRGs	41	57	3
Adherence gaps	16	73	11
Implementation gaps	65	32	3

* When trendlines point upward, gaps grow.
** When trendlines point downward, gaps decrease.
Figures may not add up to 100% due to rounding.

the Asian-Pacific region (ratio 2.4:1) out-performs all others as far as long-term CRG trends are concerned, and the Americas rank second (ratio 2.2:1).

Of the global *adherence* trendlines, almost three quarters improved, thanks mainly to ratifications. The ratio of improving to worsening *adherence* lines is 3.9:1. The fact that nearly one in five worsened is due to the non-ratification of Conventions by countries that came into the system in the course of the review period, non-ratification of Convention No. 182 that was added to the system in 2000, and unsatisfactory reporting to the Committee of Experts on ratified Conventions or to the Declaration Expert-Advisers on unratified Conventions. The movements of regional *adherence* trends are similar to those of CRG trends.

The positive impression conveyed by CRG and *adherence* scores is reversed when one considers how countries got to grips with *implementation* problems during the period 1985–2004. No more than 31 per cent of the trends move in the positive direction, close to two thirds in the negative direction, a ratio of 0.5:1. The negative *implementation* developments call for a more detailed analysis (see Chapter 7.4). As regards regional trendlines, the Caribbean/Canada/US group and the 'favourably inclined' Asian-Pacific countries are identified as the best performers (ratio 1:1); but a little caution is in order when interpreting both subregions' percentages because of the low number of countries involved (the 'favourably inclined' Asian-Pacific countries number nine, the Caribbean/Canada/US group comprises 13 countries). Latin America is the third-best *implementer* (ratio 0.8:1), followed by the 'other' Asian-Pacific countries (0.6:1) and Europe (0.5:1). When the Table's two sets of subregions are re-aggregated, the Americas are better *implementers* (0.9:1) than the Asian-Pacific region (ratio 0.7:1). Africa has the highest proportion of negative trends, 79 per cent, and its ratio of improving to worsening lines is the worst of all regions (0.2:1).

7.3   Overall ranking of countries

All 159 countries' average scores and selected ranks are shown in the Rights Gaps Indicators at the end of this book. Ranking is limited to the 1995–99 CRGs and the 2000–04 *adherence, implementation* and *Core Rights Gaps*. In all Rights Gaps Indicators, countries' ordinal sequence is determined by the most recent CRG average, 2000–04. Ranks start with the best performer; but each of the Rights Gaps Indicators groups countries into high, medium and low or non-ratifiers; and the ranks are distributed across these three groups. For example, Table 1 starts with rank 1 to 19 in the group of high ratifiers and then continues with rank 21 because rank 20 belongs to the first medium ratifier (Turkmenistan) and can be found under that heading.

In interpreting the results one should take account of the time-lag effect of ratifications on *implementation* and CRGs, which lowers *adherence* scores instantly but may not incur *implementation gaps* during four years or more and can yield CRGs that are not up-to-date (see Chapter 6.1). The Tables in this book draw attention to extensive recent ratifiers by capitalizing the concerned countries' names. Given the definitions applied to all basic rights, they number 51 in Table 1 of the Rights Gaps Indicators; in a few years' time there will be much less when the reference period is moved along. Quite a few extensive recent ratifiers advanced strikingly. Examples at the top of Table 1 are Gambia (seven ratifications in 2000, the eighth in 2001), St. Kitts and Nevis (seven ratifications in 2000), South Africa (all three of the outstanding Conventions were ratified in 2000), Namibia (four ratifications in 2000) and the Seychelles (six ratifications in 1999, the remaining two in 2000).

A limitation of rank indicators is that countries can move up or down the scale of 159 positions even though their underlying scores change little because other countries' scores rise or fall significantly. An example in the Table 1 is Tunisia, which had a CRG of 0.178 points that put it on rank 43 in 1995–99, but which dropped to rank 61 in 2000–04 even though its CRG was unchanged. When looking at a country's rank, one should always take account of the actual size of its *gaps*. Countries with identical scores are ranked in alphabetical order.

The categorizations and stylistic identifications of countries in Table 1 help to detect certain general patterns, which will come out stronger later when pairs of core Conventions are examined. One predictable pattern is that capitalized extensive recent ratifiers often have unexpectedly good *implementation* scores and CRGs – at least for a while. Cases in point among high ratifiers are Gambia and St. Kitts and Nevis, among medium ratifiers Turkmenistan and Estonia, among low ratifiers Kiribati and Bahrain, which are all close to the top of their respective categories. Another pattern is that a high degree of ratification does not *ipso facto* saddle a country with high charges on the *implementation* indicators. The first 50 high ratifiers (two fifths of all high ratifiers) have single or double-digit *implementation* ranks in 2000–04. Long-standing ratifiers that are high ratifiers also fall into this pattern. For example, Italy Nicaragua and Poland have respectable CRGs (ranked 3, 7 and 13 in 2000–04) and respectable *implementation* ranks as well (23, 37 and 42). Political determination to ensure that human rights do not merely stay on paper makes the difference. Lack of determination gives rise to the other pattern among high ratifiers that is visible towards the end of this category of countries in Table 1 where high *implementation* ranks and high CRGs go together despite mid-level *adherence* performance.

Examples in 2000–04 are Bangladesh (CRG rank 143, *implementation* rank 147, *adherence* rank 85), Venezuela (CRG rank 152, *implementation* rank 155, *adherence* rank 79), Turkey (CRG rank 156, *implementation* rank 158, *adherence* rank 35) and Guatemala (CRG rank 158, *implementation* rank 159, *adherence* rank 40).

A low degree of ratification naturally ranks countries down on the *adherence* scale. For example, low ratifier India had a score of 0.111 points in 2000–04 (*adherence* rank 143, CRG rank 146), and the worst *adherent* of all countries, Laos (CRG rank 138), a score of 0.217 points that is close to the maximum of 0.250 points. Medium ratifiers' *adherence* scores may be equal to or better than high ratifiers' scores if the latter do not fulfil their reporting obligations well. Thus, medium ratifiers El Salvador, Mexico and Australia have the same 0.055 *adherence* points (CRG ranks 109, 121 and 128 in 2000–04) as high ratifier Bosnia-Herzegovina (CRG rank 108), and their scores are lower than high ratifier Pakistan's at 0.058 points (CRG rank 157). El Salvador, Mexico and Australia have excellent reporting records, the other two countries do not.

When the overall achievement of basic human rights in the labour field is examined according to the data in Table 1 of the Rights Gaps Indicators, the first impression is that they are in a parlous state. In 2000–04, only seven countries had CRGs below the level of 0.100 points (one tenth of the maximum score), and three of them were extensive recent ratifiers. At the other end of the scale, while no country was close to total failure, the worst CRGs exceeded 0.400 points during all periods. The absolutely worst scores were shared by Pakistan and India (0.480 in 1985–89 and 1990–94, respectively), followed by Peru (0.460 in 1990–94). Fifteen years later, Pakistan's CRG had only just dropped to 0.385, India's had moved further down to 0.297 and post-Fujimori's Peru even more to 0.191 (CRG ranks 157, 146 and 75 in 2000–04). Most recently, previously non-functioning Sierra Leone had the worst overall CRG along with Guatemala. Guatemala's evolution is particularly worrying because the country has done reasonably well in terms of *adherence*; but when *implementation* is figured into the equation, its CRGs passes from quite high in 1985–89 (0.255) and 1990–94 (0.247) to even higher scores in 1995–99 (0.392) and 2000–04 (0.413). Bolivia (ranked 154 in 2000–04) has fallen into a similar mould, Mexico, Australia and others as well. As the example of Japan shows (ranked 155) advanced industrialized countries can also be found among the worst overall performers. In Japan's case, *adherence* was not the source of the problem, *implementation* problems were.

If one disregards extensive recent ratifiers, the CRGs of Table 1 identify a number of European countries as the best across-the-board performers in 2000–04, principally smaller countries (San Marino, Ireland, Austria, Portugal, Hungary and Poland) and southern European countries (Italy and Malta in addition to San Marino and Portugal). The latter recalls the finding of the OECD study on employment protection that credited southern European countries with the best laws (OECD, 1999). The usual suspects from Scandinavia are not far behind (Finland ranks 15, Sweden 22 and Norway 62), but Denmark (rank 140) is right down the scale. However, non-European countries that are not extensive recent ratifiers are not by any means absent from the top scorers. Nicaragua and Israel, both long-standing ratifiers, rank 7 and 19 in 2000–04, with Togo, Jordan, Benin and Senegal following on CRG ranks 23, 26, 28 and 30, respectively.

Noticeably worsening overall CRGs are visible in the ranks of, for instance, Uruguay (65 in 2000–04, down from 15 in 1995–99), Australia (128, down from 50), Dominica (133, down from 38), Denmark (140, down from 25) and Venezuela (152, down from 116). The trendlines recorded in the database indicate where their problems stem from, namely, *adherence* in the case of Israel, *implementation* in the case of Denmark,[3] Dominica and Uruguay, and both *adherence* and *implementation* in the case of Australia[4] and Venezuela.

Among the poor overall performers, Turkey, Pakistan and Guatemala stand out in addition to previously non-functioning Sierra Leone, but also low ratifiers Sao Tome and Myanmar and medium ratifiers Uganda and Japan. The US, a low ratifier, is at rank 123 of the 159 CRG scores in 2000–04. Myanmar's low score is a combination of low ratification and *implementation* problems of Convention Nos. 29 and 87. Guatemala has a fairly good ratification record but is afflicted by *implementation* problems across the board. It has been the object of many CEACR' *direct requests* and *observations* as well as of numerable freedom of association cases that were reported on by the CFA.

The scores of eight countries drawn from the four major regions will be illustrated systematically throughout the empirical Chapters. Half are good overall performers with improving CRG trendlines: Ireland (rank 6 in 2000–04), Togo (rank 23), Jordan (26) and Barbados (45). They have good ratification records and do not experience many *implementation* problems. The other four countries are poor overall performers with worsening CRG trendlines: the Czech Republic (rank 144), Uganda (148), Japan (155) and Guatemala (158). Most of these countries' ratification records are quite good, but they battle with a number

(Czech Republic, Uganda and Japan) or large (Guatemala) *implementation* problems. None of the eight is an extensive recent ratifier.

Two poor performers are compared in Figure 7.1 as to the origin of their problems. Guatemala has practically no *adherence* problems. By contrast, its overall *implementation gap* is the largest of all, which heavily depresses Guatemala's CRG. Uganda has sizeable *adherence* problems (rank 150); its *implementation gap* (rank 85) is slightly larger in size than its *adherence gap*, and the two together push the country down the CRG scale to rank 148.

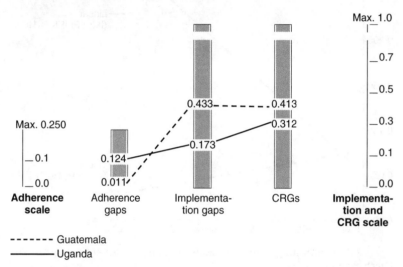

Figure 7.1 Origin of Guatemala's and Uganda's normalized overall CRGs, 2000–04 (approximate scale)

The two reporting indicators have a small but distinct influence on *adherence* and CRG scores. Taking as examples the illustration countries, which have good or fairly good ratification records (except Uganda), their differences stem from indicator 2, that is, the fulfilment of reporting obligations in respect of ratified Conventions where Barbados and Uganda have not performed well, and from indicator 3, that is, reporting obligations on unratified Conventions under the Declaration where Uganda failed to provide one in four reports and Japan one in seven.

Contrasting trendline movements of *adherence* and *implementation gaps* are illustrated in Figure 7.2 with Czech data. The *adherence* trendline points downward – in the right direction – signalling decreasing *adher-*

ence problems. The *implementation* trendline points strongly upward – in the wrong direction – indicating growing *implementation* problems. Graphically speaking, the trendlines form a scissors movement. Ideally, both should point downward.

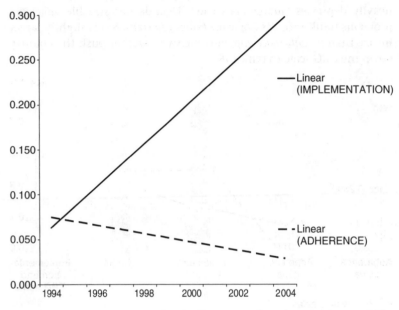

Figure 7.2 Contrasting normalized adherence and implementation gaps: The Czech example

A certain degree of inverse correlation between decreasing *adherence gaps* and increasing *implementation gaps* derives empirically from the inter-linkages built into the system. Without ratification, no *implementation gaps* could be recorded except possibly through the CFA component. With ratification, and after a time lag, negative comments by the CEACR would load the *implementation* dimension with points. Quantitatively, the correlation is weak at the overall level, –0.41, in terms of the Pearson product moment correlation coefficient between the 2000–04 *adherence* and *implementation* figures.

The overall ranking conveyed by Table 1 of the Rights Gaps Indicators may appear to the naked eye to be somewhat volatile. Correlation between the average CRGs of 1995–99 and 2000–04 yields a coefficient of +0.58, significant at 1 per cent. Most of the ups and downs in CRG values are due to three factors, an inherent, a passing and a technical

one. The inherent factor is the fact that human rights data are principally a reflection of political volatility and developments, to a small
extent even of economic misfortunes that feed through to the political
scene. Negative changes, such as governments that decide to clamp
down on workers' organizations or employers who feel that they can act
with impunity towards unionists or desperate job seekers or children,
will quickly come to the notice of the ILO's supervisory or complaints
machinery and inflate the *implementation* indicator. Belarus is an
example, its CRG of 0.134 of the first two period dropped to 0.162 in
1995–99 and 0.203 points in 2000–04. Positive developments usually
have much longer gestation periods. Excepting acts of ratification, which
will instantly reduce *adherence gaps*, new domestic policies must first
be agreed upon among different groups; legislation has to be passed
through a time-consuming process; and it has then to be put into
effect through the mobilization of administrative, financial and other
resources. In other words, the domestic *implementation* of any of the four
freedoms may be slow, imperfect, ineffective and not result in rapid,
definite or dramatic improvements of basic human rights. An example in
Table 1 of the Rights Gap Indicators is Peru (rank 75 in 2000–04). At any
rate, average CRGs are inherently more variable in the short- and
medium-run than, say, a country's adult literacy rate or its population's
life expectancy at birth.

The passing factor that is responsible for the apparent volatility
of CRGs in Table 1 of the Rights Gaps Indicators is the time-lag
effect of new ratifications on *implementation* and CRG scores (see
Chapter 6.1). The rate of new ratifications has now tapered off and
is unlikely to go through another spurt. Recent member States still
have a long way to go, as do countries such as China and the
United States, which have ratified few Conventions.[5] This determinant of the volatility of *adherence* and CRG scores will have less
influence in years ahead; and one may confidently anticipate a high
degree of correlation between the 2000–04 and the future 2005–09
averages. This hypothesis can be tested approximately through a
re-run of the aforementioned correlations by excluding from the
data in Table 1 all countries that ratified Conventions during
1985–2004. When only the 28 long-standing ratifiers are retained,
the coefficient increases from 0.58 to 0.67. Given the limited
number of countries involved and the volatility of politics, one
should not expect a perfect cross-period correlation.

The third and technical factor that entails changes in countries' ranks
was already alluded to: A change in one or several countries' scores can

entail changes in many or most countries' positions simply because, if one country moves up, others move down, and *vice versa*.

7.4 Focus on implementation

7.4.1 Full measurement

The analysis of *implementation gaps* will first put to use the full measure (indicators 5–7) and then exploit the versatility of the proxy (simplified indicator 6). To that end, this book categorizes countries' performance by grouping them into 'good', 'medium' and 'poor' performers. Given that *gaps* represent non-achievements, 'good', 'medium' and 'poor' performers are separated by cut-off points of less than 25 per cent, 25–50 per cent and more than 50 per cent of the maximum score. Taking Guatemala's 0.433 points as the reference point, only 37 countries (23 per cent) turn out to have been good *implementers*, 86 (54 per cent) are medium performers and 36 (23 per cent) are poor performers. This is a fairly normal distribution for these kinds of static comparisons.

A dynamic comparison is more informative and more relevant for advocacy and technical assistance purposes. Table 7.2 illustrates it by selecting the 20 bottom-ranked implementers and comparing their scores across the four five-year periods. The bottom of the Table provides summary data in two forms, averages and ratios. The averages have crept up since the early 1990s, and the ratios have gone from marginally positive to strongly negative. At the beginning of the 21st century, almost three times as many poor implementers regressed than progressed, including the extensive recent ratifiers that may be advantaged by the system temporarily and whose future scores might be anticipated with a degree of trepidation. Four countries had deteriorating implementation scores throughout the four periods, namely, the Philippines, Indonesia, Bolivia and Guatemala. The absolutely worst scores, which can go up to 1 point, are attributed by the gap system to Guatemala, 0.433 points in 2000–04 and 0.425 points in 1995–99. Other countries with scores in the vicinity of 0.400 points are the Central African Republic in 1985–89 and Pakistan during the same period. Only one country, Pakistan, had improving scores across the four averages, though the ameliorations were small and did not save it from being the fourth-worst performer in 2000–04.

In the light of these various comparisons, the conclusion is quite startling as far as the realization of fundamental human rights in the labour field is concerned: On balance, things tend to get worse, much worse, rather than better.

Table 7.2 The 20 worst overall implementers in 2000–04 and short-term trends

Country	1985–99	1990–94	1995–99	2000–04	Rank	Country	Changes in gaps		
	1	2	3	4			2/1	3/2	4/3
TRINIDAD & T.	0.244	0.229	0.229	0.260	140	TRINIDAD & T.	Smaller	Same	Larger
Philippines	0.183	0.221	0.251	0.260	141	Philippines	Larger	Larger	Larger
INDONESIA	0.107	0.137	0.152	0.267	142	INDONESIA	Larger	Larger	Larger
Dominica	0.099	0.229	0.175	0.267	143	*Dominica*	Larger	Smaller	Larger
C. African Rep.	0.396	0.301	0.185	0.267	144	C. African Rep.	Smaller	Smaller	Larger
Paraguay	0.274	0.312	0.328	0.267	145	Paraguay	Larger	Larger	Smaller
Cameroon	0.236	0.251	0.366	0.267	146	Cameroon	Larger	Larger	Smaller
Bangladesh	0.297	0.183	0.259	0.273	147	Bangladesh	Smaller	Larger	Larger
Denmark	0.183	0.160	0.145	0.280	148	Denmark	Smaller	Smaller	Larger
MAURITANIA	0.152	0.221	0.183	0.280	149	MAURITANIA	Larger	Smaller	Larger
Algeria	0.267	0.267	0.297	0.280	150	*Algeria*	Same	Larger	Smaller
Guinea	0.305	0.198	0.350	0.287	151	Guinea	Smaller	Larger	Smaller
Dominican Rep.	0.320	0.259	0.190	0.293	152	Dominican Rep.	Smaller	Smaller	Larger
Japan	0.190	0.137	0.198	0.293	153	Japan	Smaller	Larger	Larger
Bolivia	0.084	0.145	0.244	0.293	154	Bolivia	Larger	Larger	Larger
Venezuela	0.221	0.168	0.305	0.320	155	Venezuela	Smaller	Larger	Larger
Pakistan	0.404	0.381	0.357	0.340	156	Pakistan	Smaller	Smaller	Smaller
Sierra Leone	–	–	–	0.367	157	*Sierra Leone*	–	–	–
TURKEY	0.168	0.145	0.236	0.373	158	TURKEY	Smaller	Larger	Larger
Guatemala	0.190	0.244	0.425	0.433	159	Guatemala	Larger	Larger	Larger
Average						Ratio			
Score	0.227	0.220	0.244	0.298	–	larger:smaller	0.8:1	2:1	2.8:1

– Not applicable.
Capitalized countries are extensive recent ratifiers, italicized countries are long-standing ratifiers.

7.4.2 Proxy measurement

A shortcut to the representation of *implementation gaps* was introduced in Chapter 5.4. It is composed of the CEACR's *observations* and expressions of *satisfaction*. 'Negative' *observations* are given a value of 1, expressions of *satisfaction* a value of 0, and 'mixed' *observations* that contain both negative remarks and positive *satisfaction* are given a value of 0.5. The *implementation* proxy has a triple advantage. First, scoring is simple. Second, when aggregated at the regional level or for individual areas of freedom, it nets out improving, unchanging and worsening country scores, thereby conveying the dominant tendency. The third advantage is the distinct measurement of *satisfaction*, which permits the reality of the achievement of rights to be explored from another angle.

The fact that the proxy variable is a valid shortcut to the *gap* system's *implementation* dimension can be verified by simple correlation. At the level of all core Conventions, principles and rights, the coefficient comes to +0.88 between the 2000–04 proxy and the corresponding full *implementation* data, significant at the 1 per cent level. This is a fairly high degree of correlation that legitimizes the use of the shortcut.

Figure 7.3 presents the overall evolution of the four major regions. This and the subsequent Figures of the same construction reveal graphically the regions' different starting positions to which reference was made at the beginning of this Chapter. The principal interest, however, lies in the inclination and steepness of the trendlines' slopes. While the number of *observations* during the last years could be slightly inflated for the Asian-Pacific and the European regions because more countries formed part of them at the end of the review period than at the beginning (10 in Asia-Pacific, 11 in Europe, compared with two in Africa and one in the Americas), it is certain that this factor does not account for the uncomfortable message conveyed by Figure 7.3, that is, all major region's *implementation gaps* were significantly higher at the end than

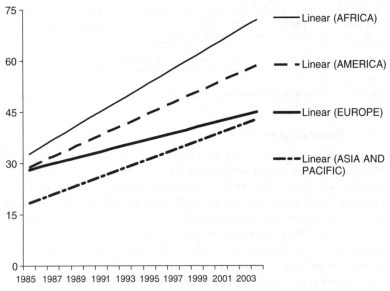

Figure 7.3   Trends in regional observations, 1985–2004

at the beginning of the period.[6] If the summary global trendline had been included it would be positioned way above the others, and its slope would be very steep indeed.

One may wonder whether Weisband's warning has come true that he put in the following words: 'The risk of state defection, the risk that any state might opportunistically depart from its regime obligations, thus generating incentives for a collective race to the bottom, permeates the relationship that member states are destined to have with many regimes' (Weisband, 2000, p. 645). I personally do not think that voluntaristic or imitative behaviour of States is the reason for the worsening *implementation* problems revealed by the *gap* system. It seems to me that numerous individual circumstances, many of which are linked to the pressures of contemporary globalization, are to blame, as elaborated in the later conclusions.

The picture of regional performances conveyed by the *implementation* proxy in Figure 7.3 is similar to the picture suggested by the count of improving to worsening *implementation* trendlines in Table 7.1. Africa performs worst in both the Figure and the Table. It has had the largest number of *observations* to start with and accumulated a great many more during the 20 years under review. The Asian-Pacific region, despite an increase in membership, performs relatively well, perhaps because of its historically low degree of ratification, though its *implementation gaps* worsened quite a bit as time went by. Each measure of performance has a distinct scope and is valid on its own.

Figure 7.4 presents the *implementation* proxies of the four freedoms, where the summary trendline of global evolution is included. Three of the four slopes are decidedly unsatisfactory in that they point strongly upwards, namely, the slopes of the broken trendlines for freedom of association, non-discrimination and child labour. In the case of forced labour, the trendline for *observations-cum-satisfaction* is almost horizontal, but it is not actually pointing downward – as it should. It is worth underlining that the inclusion of Convention No. 182 in the new indicator system starting in the year 2000 is not at the heart of the upward-sloping global trendline of *observations*. As can be seen from the following numbers of *observation* recorded in the *gap* system during 2000–04 for Convention Nos. 138 and 182, respectively – 15 and 4 in Africa, 25.5 and 10 in the Americas, 8 and 7 in the Asia-Pacific region, and 8.5 and 3 in Europe or a total of 57 and 24 – it is not even the main factor behind the upward-sloping line for child labour itself. The impact of Convention No. 182 on trendlines may change in the future, but for the time being the measurement of *implementation* problems, as anticipated in Box 3.2, has not been influenced disproportionately.

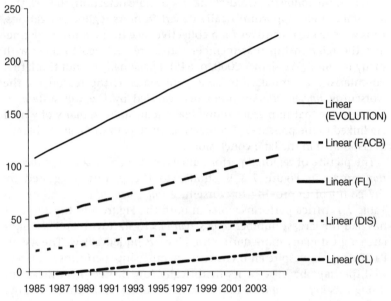

FACB = Freedom of association and collective bargaining, FL = Forced labour, DIS = Non-discrimination, CL = Child labour

Figure 7.4   Trends in observations in the different areas of freedom, 1985–2004

It may be contended that the upward sloping *implementation* lines are due to the substitution of *direct requests* by *observations*. Has the Committee of Experts adopted a 'tougher' line during recent years? This is a valid interrogation. However, nothing in the history of the CEACR suggests that a 'tougher' approach could be or has been adopted (see Chapter 5). The *direct requests* data, which are not displayed here for reasons of space, do not support the substitution hypothesis. With the exception of the slightly downward-sloping trendline for forced labour, all lines for *direct requests* point in the same undesirable direction as the lines for *observations* – upward.

Are the growing *implementation* problems mirrored in lack of expressions of *satisfaction*? Figure 7.5 presents the relevant long-term trendlines. The first thing that needs to be made clear about Figure 7.5 is that its scale is one twentieth of the scale of Figure 7.4! If the data of Figures 7.4 and 7.5 were put on the same scale, the lines for *satisfaction* would be crouching indistinguishably at the bottom.

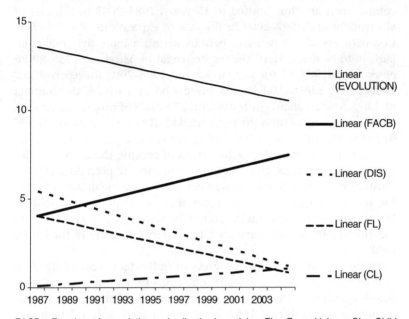

FACB = Freedom of association and collective bargaining, FL = Forced labour, CL = Child labour, DIS = Non-discrimination

Figure 7.5 Evolution of cases of progress in the different areas of freedom, 1987–2004

The sum of the four areas' data – the line at the top of Figure 7.5 – visibly recalls the previous finding that *implementation* problems have gotten worse in that the trendline of cases of progress slopes significantly downward. The areas of non-discrimination and forced labour are responsible for the overall slope. Fortunately, the picture is more reassuring in the other two areas, freedom of association and child labour, where the slopes point in the right direction, though the number of cases involved is excruciatingly low for child labour – one on average during the last five years.

Changing the approach from visualization to quantification, one can compare the incidence of *observations* with expressions of *satisfaction* to see whether the ratio between the two is close to 1:1, in the long run if not in the short run. If it were, this would indicate that *implementation* problems get resolved sooner or later. The data have to be time-lagged because expressions of *satisfaction* relate to previous years' *observations*. According to Chapter 5, a two-year time lag is appropriate. Long-term comparisons are thus limited to 18 years, 1985–2002 in the case of *observations* and 1987–2004 in the case of expressions of *satisfaction*. Comparisons of the two end periods permit a more dynamic comparison to be made. Here, the respective ratios pertain to 1985–89 for *observations*/1987–91 for *satisfaction* and 1998–2002 for *observations*/ 2000–04 for *satisfaction*. Across the period as a whole, the number of 2,825.5 *observations* contrasts with 224 cases of progress, a ratio of 12.6:1, which is far from the postulated ideal of 1:1. During the initial five years the ratio was 8.7:1, during the last five years 18.6:1, which means that it worsened greatly instead of coming closer to 1:1. This performance measure gives more precision to the preceding graphic illustrations. Not only was the number of *observations* (already adjusted for *satisfaction*) many times higher than it should be, it doubled between the beginning and the end of the review period. This is a terrible indictment of contemporary human rights practices in the labour field!

If one considers cases of progress in individual areas of freedom and annualizes the calculations, one finds that in the case of non-discrimination there were an average of five expressions of *satisfaction* each year during 1987–91, but there were only 1.7 each year during 2000–04, and this despite the growth in the number of countries during the intervening years. There has been no case of progress in the Asian-Pacific region since 1997; there was only one in Africa after 1998 and one in the Americas after 1999. The picture is similar in the area of forced labour, where close to four expressions of *satisfaction* during each of the initial five years contrast with no more than 1.5 each year during the final period. In 2004, the *gap* system entered only a single case of progress in the area of forced labour (New Zealand). The more reassuring picture for freedom of association and child labour is naturally also reflected in the quantification. In the case of freedom of association, there were in excess of four expressions of *satisfaction* during each of the initial five years and of seven during each of the final years. In the case of child labour, there were 0.4 expressions of *satisfaction* during each of the initial five years and one during each of the final years. However, a look at the major regions' achievements in the area of child labour shows that the *gap* system registered not a single case of progress in Africa during the 18 years covered, only 'half' a case in the Americas and only one in the Asia-Pacific region. The explanation for this sorry state of progress in the area of child labour lies to a small extent in the low level of ratification of Convention No. 138 and the late addition of Convention No. 182 to the new indicator system. Judging by the past, however, the CEACR's supervision of the latter Convention will likely generate many *observations* and few cases of progress in future years.

The presentation of the overall *implementation gaps* suggests three sobering conclusions. First, countries appear to grapple less with low-level and easy-to-resolve problems today than with more important problems that require sustained political commitment and greater mobilization of resources. Resources, of course, are a function of political commitment – you can't have one without the other. Second, the worst *implementers*, which comprise long-standing and extensive recent ratifiers, have generally experienced more rather than less *implementation* problems. Third, the long-standing ratifiers themselves experienced more rather than less problems since the mid-1980s. Of all countries, they should have been able to perform fairly faultlessly during recent years! That is not the case for most of them and suggests that core labour standards are in serious trouble – not at the level of *adherence* in principle but at the level of *implementation* in practice.

To the extent that poor implementers need help and are willing to accept it, bilateral donors, regional organizations (for example, the European Union) or the international community (for example, the ILO) should focus their assistance with priority on the worst overall performers listed in Table 7.2. Nothing could be more urgent than to help those who need help most.

7.5 Correlations?

The starting point about correlation of *gaps* with other indicators is that – contrary to normal practice – the correlation with existing indicators should at best be weak (<0.50) or modest (0.50–0.75). Why should this be so? Does it not call into question the new indicator system? Not in the least! *Gaps* are a unique new measurement in a barren field where most of the few existing indicators or proxies that are meant to capture the essence of labour rights do not come near to fulfilling one or the other or several of the requirements of human rights indicators (see Chapter 2.3). In particular, a serious lack of objectivity renders several pretenders' results spurious. If there were credible and good indicators of the achievement human rights achievements in the labour field, there would be no need for a new indicator system!

The *gap* data for 1995–99 and 2000–04 probably contribute at present to a small extent to weak correlations with *implementation gaps* and CRGs because some countries' figures may temporarily be out of kilter due to the time-lag effects of extensive recent ratification. To minimize these effects and to demonstrate that it is not the time-lag effects that are at the origin of weak correlations, I shall re-run the correlations with long-standing ratifiers' data; but, in the light of what has been postulated in the preceding paragraph, one should not expect dramatic improvements in the coefficients; and the low number of long-standing ratifiers across the seven 'old' core Conventions, 28, does not enable valid correlations to be made with several sources (there would, for instance, be only three countries relative to Verité's data and 16 relative to ILO's aggregate indexes). Higher correlations can only be expected when future averages are correlated with better indicators or proxies elaborated by other authors.

What do the data show? Table 7.3 includes available labour rights, political, economic and development indicators that are correlated with CRGs, *adherence* and *implementation gaps* (Pearson coefficients). Such correlations as may be hypothesized to exist should be inverse (negative): The higher the non-achievement of basic labour rights, the lower should be the values of the other indicators.[7] The Gini index, however, should correlate positively.

Basic labour rights are represented by three sets of indicators. The first uses the data of a US-based private social auditing company that assesses labour conditions in selected emerging markets for institutional investors such as the California Public Employees Retirement System (Verité, 2000 and 2004). Its methodology involves dozens of grading decisions covering ratification (10 per cent of a country's final score), laws and legal systems (25 per cent), institutional capacity (15 per cent) and implementation effectiveness (50 per cent). Verité's scope of assessments extends to working conditions and the treatment of non-national workers, which can be taken out of the constituent components except for countries' aggregate scores. Presumably limited to the formal economy, the assessments derive partly from desk research and partly from interviews and factory audits. On the down side, only 27 countries are covered,[8] replication by outsiders is impossible, and it is doubtful that this labour-intensive and costly exercise can be sustained. What should one expect? Verité's ratification indicator should correlate well (inversely) with *adherence gaps*, which it does. Its laws and legal system indicator aims to determine whether countries'

Table 7.3 Correlations of countries' overall gaps with other indicators

	CRGs			CRGs	Adh.	Imp.
	1985–89	1990–94	1995–99	2000–04		
Basic labour rights indicators						
Verité (beginning 21st century)[1]						
Ratification	–	–	–0.22	–0.14	–0.98	0.47
Laws and legal system	–	–	–0.52	–0.33	–0.20	–0.18
Institutional capacity	–	–	–0.22	–0.18	–0.16	–0.07
Implementation effectiveness	–	–	–0.57	–0.50	–0.36	–0.24
Aggregate score	–	–	–0.54	–0.45	–0.42	–0.16
CIRI (avg. 1995–99 or 2000–03)[2]	–					
Workers' rights	–	–0.32	–0.38	–0.28	–0.34	–0.02
ILO Workers' participation (in or before 1999)[3]						
Input indicator	–	–0.31	–0.37	–0.23	–0.47	–0.08
Process indicator	–	–0.41	–0.48	–0.22	–0.31	–0.01
Output indicator	–	–0.31	–0.47	–0.34	–0.11	–0.26
Representation Security Index	–	–0.42	–0.55	–0.35	–0.34	–0.12
Political proxies						
Freedom House scale (avg. 1993–97)[4]	–0.35	–0.33	–0.40	–0.26	–0.36	0.02
Polity IV democracy scale (avg. 2000–02)[5]	–	–	–0.38	–0.15	–0.09	–0.08
Economic proxies						
FDI inflows (avg. 1993–99)[6]	0.02	0.04	0.01	0.02	0.24	–0.16
Value added per worker (1990–04)[7]	–0.22	–0.24	–0.19	–	–	–
Gini coefficients[8]	0.28	0.34	0.26	0.12	–0.01	0.12
Development proxies						
UNDP (2000)[9]						
Human Development Index	–0.31	–0.33	–0.43	–0.27	–0.07	–0.20
ILO aggregate indexes (in or before 1999)[10]						
Input indexes	–	–0.52	–0.50	–0.36	–0.59	–0.04
Process indexes	–	–0.45	–0.62	–0.38	–0.16	–0.28
Output indexes	–	–0.42	–0.59	–0.38	–0.12	–0.30
Economic Security Index	–	–0.48	–0.61	–0.40	–0.24	–0.25

– = Not applicable or not available. Adh. = adherence gap. Imp. = implementation gap. Avg. = average. The number of countries given in the notes hereunder relates to the 2000–04 averages. Preceding periods' averages are lower because they exclude States that were not members at the time or were non-functioning or non-independent States.
[1] Verité, 2004, scores pertain to the eight core Conventions of the International Labour Organization except the aggregate score, which is much broader in scope. 25 countries.

Table 7.3 Correlations of countries' overall gaps with other indicators –
continued

	CRGs			CRGs	Adh.	Imp.
	1985–89	1990–94	1995–99	2000–04		

[2] CIRI, n.d., scores averaged for 1995–99 and 2000–03. Those for 1995–99 were correlated with the Table's CRGs for 1990–94 and 1995–99 (135 countries); those for 2000–03 were correlated with the last three columns that show averages for 2000–04 (159 countries).
[3] ILO, 2004d, pp. 417–419. 91 countries.
[4] Average of Freedom House's civil liberties and political rights scores, reversed scaling. Data kindly made available by David Kucera. 150 countries.
[5] Average of last three scores of Polity IV. 138 countries.
[6] Percentage shares of total world inflows of FDI per country, kindly made available by David Kucera. 129 countries.
[7] Value added in industry. Figures drawn from the Rama datafile of the database set up for the World Bank (Rama and Artecona, 2002). Source kindly made available by Patrick Belser. 69 countries.
[8] World Bank data as presented by UNDP, 2003. 117 countries.
[9] UNDP, 2002. 148 countries.
[10] ILO, 2004, pp. 425–427. 83 countries.

national labour laws accord with the stipulations of Conventions. It does not correlate well *gaps*.[9] Verité's indicator of institutional capacity mixes the assessed effectiveness of governmental capacity to develop, monitor, correct and implement labour laws with the lack of restrictions on involvement of NGOs in social issues. It has no direct counterpart in the *gap* system, which is reflected in the lack of correlations. Verité's implementation effectiveness indicator grades on-the-ground outcomes such as the per capita scale of child labour and the scale of unequal remuneration between men and women. It is similar in conception to *implementation* indicators 5 and 6 of the *gap* system, though it has a broader scope and a focus on subjects of interest to US private investors. Although it correlates modestly with 1995–99 and 2000–04 CRGs, it does not correlate with 2000–04 *implementation gaps*. Verité's aggregate score adds together the points countries obtain under each of the four constituent indicators. Given the components' low correlations with CRGs, it is not surprising that these aggregates do not correlate highly with *gaps*. Not only are Verité's constituent elements not equivalent to those of the new indicator system, but the aggregate scores also contain Verité's assessments of health and safety questions, wages and hours of work, the status of foreign contract labour and the impact of Export-Processing Zones on labour conditions, which cannot be parcelled out. In toto, therefore, Verité's five indicators are no substitute for the *gap* system.

The second basic labour rights indicator is drawn from the Cingranelli-Richards human rights database (CIRI, n.d.). According to the coder manual, these indicators measure human rights practices by governments and use as their principal source the US State Department's *Country Reports on Human Rights Practices* or, where these do not cover a particular country (such as the US), Amnesty International *Annual Reports*. CIRI distinguishes a wide range of rights, among them workers' rights and women's economic rights. (The latter will be correlated with non-discrimination *gaps* in Chapter 11.5.) Workers' rights are graded on a three-point scale where two points correspond to fully protected, one point to somewhat restricted and 0 to severely restricted. Unfortunately, CIRI's scale is heterogeneous. Two points are accorded when governments protect the right to freedom of association and no problems regarding other rights of workers are mentioned in the source(s); one point is given to countries when there is evidence of problems in respect of freedom of association or forced labour or child labour or discrimination in hiring or treatment at work other than gender-based discrimination, or when there is no minimum wage; zero points identify countries whose governments fail to protect the rights of almost all workers to freedom of association or to bargain collectively. This is a hotchpotch of items and reference points that are not defined uniformly across the scale, which renders CIRI's human rights dataset questionable. On top comes the fact – it is possibly at the origin of the coding decisions – that the principal source used is US State Department reports, where the questions that embassy officials are asked to answer range from factual to interpretative and judgemental, and where local superiors and headquarters' committees can put their own gloss on country reports. The interplay of the source material and of the coding decisions gives rise to a number of – to put it mildly – curious scores such as the Czech Republic being scored 1 in 2000, 2 in 2001, 2 in 2002 and 0 in 2003; Suharto's Indonesia being scored 1 in 1995 but the democratic Indonesia, after great strides to legislative and practical reforms had been undertaken, being scored 0 in 2003; and the United Kingdom finding itself in 1995 at the same level as Suharto's Indonesia before graduating by one point in 1999 and by another in 2000. At any rate, CIRI's human rights indicators are seriously flawed, and one should not expect them to correlate with my *gap* data. Table 7.3 shows clearly that they don't. When the correlations are re-run for 24 (1995–99) and 28 (2000–04) long-standing ratifiers (details not shown here), only the coefficient with 2000–04 *adherence gaps* improves somewhat to –0.51.

The third labour rights indicator measures the extent to which workers have a collective voice in national and enterprise-level decisions concerning them. While this subject will be looked at in greater detail in the next Chapter, ILO's Representation Security Index is correlated in Table 7.3 with overall *gaps* that comprise all four areas of freedoms, on the assumption that freedom of association is the most powerful and most enabling right of workers to defend any and all of their rights. The data were put together by Guy Standing's group and published in final form in ILO 2004d. They are based on both objective facts such as ratifications and on local responses to a large-scale questionnaire, requiring intensive work to come up with credible figures. The input-process-output distinctions made by Guy Standing's group (see also Chapter 2.3) give rise to five input indicators such as the ratification of Convention Nos. 87 and 98 and of another ILO Convention, four process indicators such as the existence of national tripartite bodies and a scale of workers covered by collective bargaining agreements, and four outcome indicators such as unionization rates and Freedom House scores. I already suggested in Chapter 2.1 that union density is an invalid measure of freedom of association and that it is unclear what a certain degree of this or that form of coverage of collective bargaining actually represents in terms of the achievement of basic rights in the labour field. It is not surprising, therefore, that the correlation coefficients of this imperfect proxy with CRGs and *adherence* are low relative to their closest counterpart, 1995–99 data, and this despite the fact that the two data sets are very slightly auto-correlated because the workers' participation index includes ratification of core Conventions of the International Labour Organization. More mature *gap* data might provide slightly higher correlations. The sign of the coefficients suggests that the effective participation of workers in their countries' affairs and the achievement of basic labour rights go together. Of course, free workers' organizations and democracies also go together, which explains the similar size of and variations in most coefficients pertaining to political indicators in Table 7.3. When the correlations are re-run for 18 long-standing ratifiers, the coefficients do not change much.

All the other data sets in Table 7.3 are, in some distant way, proxies of fundamental human rights. Two political indicators are included.

If one takes for granted that populations of democracies enjoy higher levels of human rights than populations of other regimes, one should expect there to be a fair degree of correlation with *gaps*. For the labour field, however, that assumption may not hold as much as for inter-relations between, say, free elections and multi-party systems. It also presupposes that the political indicators are not culture specific but objectively constructed. That is evidently not the case for the evaluations of civil liberties and political rights by Freedom House, which are carried out by people who share the same geopolitical background and whose scoring decisions are not open to public scrutiny. The actual scale, slightly oddly, ranges from a value of 1 for strongest rights to 7 for weakest rights (see, for example, Freedom House, 1999). Geopolitical limitations also influence Polity IV (n.d.), which are not free from other problems either (see Munck and Verkuilen, 2002). Polity's assessors range countries along a democracy-authoritarianism scale from +10 to –10 points. Emphasis appears to be put on institutional characteristics rather than on actual outcomes of procedures and institutions, which has the effect of bunching countries at the top end of the democracy scale. Polity IV contains slightly counterintuitive results for at least two countries with which I have some experience, Papua New Guinea (which is credited with a maximum score of 10 from 1975 onwards) and France (which has a score of 8 in 1985 and of 9 thereafter). Table 7.3 contains the expected rather weak correlations of both Freedom House and Polity data with CRGs and *adherence gaps*. The fact that they are inverse supports the underlying hypothesis. The fact that they are weak puts a question mark over simplistic or one-to-one relationships. Future correlations with mature *gap* data might raise the level of coefficients somewhat, though one should not expect it to be very high because the proxy relationships are diluted by the differences in objectivity and scope of the data. As regards *implementation gaps*, they are either not at all or wrongly correlated with the democracy ratings. This may imply that the assessments by Freedom House and Polity put primary emphasis on the formal components of democracies rather than actual outcomes or that there is a more conflictual relationship between fully-fledged democracies and basic labour rights in recent years than is generally acknowledged. The latter is suggested by the *gap* system's results more than once. When the correlations are re-run for the 28 overall long-standing ratifiers, most coefficients increase from the level of weak to the level of modest correlations but not enough to change the conclusions.

Three economic variables are shown in Table 7.3. They measure outputs of economic development rather than inputs into the kind of political processes that are concerned with the achievement of human rights, but they are included here because economists are wont to attribute virtues of democratization and human rights advances to economic advances. Chapter 2.2 already debunked these claims analytically. Table 7.3 contains coefficients to underpin the argument empirically in that there is a total lack of correlation. In abstract, one might postulate an indirect link between FDI and *gaps* on the assumption that foreign investors, everything else being equal, prefer to put their money into countries characterized by good governance where legislation has a high value and is applied strictly in practice; basic labour rights being part of governance, good governance should be reflected in low *gaps* that, in turn, should be associated with high FDI inflows. Nothing of the sort is revealed by the coefficients. Non-correlation might be explained by factors on which investors place greater emphasis such as property, company and copyright laws, wages levels or the size and anticipated growth of markets. Furthermore, the bulk of FDI flows takes place between a limited number of countries, chiefly advanced market economy countries. It is probably a combination of all these factors, including labour law and practices, that determines investors' preferences and accounts for the empirical results in Table 7.3. It is interesting that my results are similar to those of Kucera who tested whether foreign investors favour countries with low freedom of association rights and found 'an accumulated lack of evidence, a sort of non-result' (Kucera, 2002, p. 59). He likewise found 'no evidence...that countries with more child labour and greater gender inequality have a comparative advantage in attracting FDI inflows, indeed all evidence of statistical significance suggests rather the opposite' (*ibid.*, p. 63). Kucera did not measure freedom from forced labour and was thus unable to construct a comprehensive core rights indicator.

In the case of value added per worker, which measures how productive different nations are, the correlation coefficients are marginal. For the Gini index, positive correlations should be expected if one assumes that higher *gaps* are associated with societies that have more unequal income distributions. Most coefficients in Table 7.3 have the right sign but are too small to attach any significance to this fact. When the correlations are re-run with varying numbers of long-standing ratifiers, the coefficients stay at about the same level as for all countries taken together.

Several conclusions could be drawn from the lack of relationships between economic variables and the *gap* system's overall indicators. The most uncontroversial would be that, in today's world, countries *adhere* to and *implement* basic human rights in the labour field irrespective of how well their economies perform – which is how it should be! Another conclusion is that the jury is still out on the link between equality and fundamental human rights.

Two development indicators, UNDP's HDI and ILO's composite Economic Security Index, are presented to test whether they predict the degree of realization of fundamental human rights. The HDI estimates the average achievement of a country's population in attaining basic human capabilities as measured by life expectancy, adult literacy, school enrolment and GDP per capita. This has nothing directly to do with human rights – they should be realized by any country irrespective of how long its people live, how literate they are and what living standards they enjoy – but it may be indicative of countries' administrative capacity to give practical effect to human rights and enforce them on the ground. Table 7.3 simply correlates the turn of the century HDI values (UNDP, 2002) with *gaps* across the system's five-year averages. My new indicator system deals with countries' administrative capacities or their general capabilities by excluding the most stricken countries such as Afghanistan and Somalia, which form part of the group of non-functioning States (Chapter 3.2). This still leaves an enormous range of countries that are covered by it, some of which are incredibly weak administratively and face tremendous problems *implementing* ratified core Conventions. They are bound to incur criticism by the CEACR. The coefficients, however, suggest that there are at best weak correlations between *gaps* and countries' capabilities. When they are re-run for 26 long-standing ratifiers, the coefficients increase slightly (for example, the coefficient between 2000–04 CRGs and the turn of the century HDI is –0.56) but not enough to call into question the reasoning presented in this Chapter. The lack of stronger correlation between *gaps* and the HDI actually underlines the autonomous nature of the new indicator system. The all-purpose HDI is no proxy for *gaps*, which is unsurprising because it really measures something else.

The Economic Security Index (ILO, 2004d), initially called Decent Work Index, combines the seven individual indexes of peoples' social and economic security elaborated by Guy Standing and his colleagues, including the above-mentioned Representation Security Index. It contains ratification data concerning many Conventions but gives them a relatively low weight, which entails a very minor auto-correlation with *gap* data. The ILO's Economic Security Index indirectly measures capacity and correlates strongly with UNDP's HDI. Its correlation with *gaps* yields coefficients that are a little larger in size than those of the HDI. But the Economic Security Index can also be looked at for what it stands directly, that is, a measure of the achievement of several forms of security or decent work. *Adherence* to and *implementation* of core labour standards form part of economic security because no country can attain high levels of economic security if there is no freedom of association and if there is forced labour, child labour and discrimination. One would not go wrong in assuming that countries which care more than others about putting their mind to realizing economic security or decent work also care more than others about fundamental human rights in the labour field. Table 7.3 confirms the existence of a modest degree of correlation with CRGs in 1995–99, the closest reference period. That the coefficients are not higher derives undoubtedly from the fact that the Economic Security Index encompasses, besides rights, a very wide range of subject matters in terms of economic, social and institutional developments, employment and social security. When the correlations are re-run for 16 long-standing ratifiers, more of the coefficients fall into the modest range (0.50–0.75), even for *implementation gaps*, but the low number of data being compared casts doubt on the strength of the improvements.

Across the board, the correlation coefficients confirm the expectation put forward at the beginning of this section that, because the new indicator system is *sui generis*, there would be only weak-to-modest correlations with existing indicators of fundamental labour rights or those one might be tempted to take as proxies. None of them matches the *gap* system's combination of validity, transparency, replicability, non-truncation, objectivity and the fact that its data are easy and cost-effective to collect and process.

7.6 Conclusions regarding overall gaps

The overall *gap* indicators perform credibly. Resting on sound theoretical foundations, the system produces intuitively obvious empirical results except for a number of time-lagged countries. The results are consistent across differing data sets that can be extracted from it. The fact that *gaps* do not really correlate with other indicators confirms the *sui generis* nature of the new system – there are none that cover the same ground or which could be taken as proxies.

As regards the extent of and changes in the achievement of fundamental labour rights, several general conclusions can be drawn from
the picture painted on the preceding pages. The first is that countries
have increasingly *adhered* to the values embodied in core labour standards and the Declaration's principles and rights. The second is that
they face growing problems of giving effect to them in practice. In
effect, there is a yawning gap between the values that countries have
embraced and the realities on the ground.[10] *Implementation* problems
not only abound but, on balance, worsen as time goes by. What is
perhaps most worrying is the fact that long-standing ratifiers' *implementation* problems increase in the course of time. Basic human rights
in the labour field are clearly in crisis today!

Implementation presupposes *adherence*, and this inter-relationship is
built into the *gap* system. Logically, lack of *implementation* can only
be a more-or-less-large proportion of the value of ratifying a core
Convention. It so happens that, due to the delays associated with
reporting on a newly ratified Convention and the working habits of
the CEACR, to which attention was drawn in Chapter 6.1, extensive
recent ratifiers' *implementation* problems may not show up in the
system for a number of years. This is visible in the overall CRGs.
Given the already high levels of ratification of most core Conventions, which will barely increase in the coming years, the time
lag between ratifications and the detection of *implementation gaps*
and CRG scores will dissipate in the course of the next few years.
The more annual data are fed into the *gap* system in years ahead, the
more up-to-date and informative become its *implementation* dimension and CRGs. The system will reach maturity when *gaps* can be
estimated for the period 2005–09.

While leaving the more detailed analysis to each area of basic labour
rights, some general pointers can be given here as to possible explana-
tions for this worrisome state of affairs. One has to do with the different role of the State in the economic and social spheres that is
associated with contemporary globalization. In Deepak Nayyar's
succinct phrase, the State has shifted from pursuing 'equity to
efficiency and from development to growth' (Nayyar, 2003, p. 17).
It has in practice diluted the social contract that, at least in European
political philosophy, pitted it in the role of a protector of the weaker
side in the marketplace, workers. Governments today are mesmerized
by the need to promote investment in an ever more competitive global
market, which makes them pamper the stronger side, employers, in
advanced countries as much as in transition economies or developing

countries (Bhaduri, 2002). 'Whereas many civil and political rights resonate with the globalization trajectory, workers' rights contradict its neoliberal form and engender greater resistance' (O'Brien, 2004, p. 203). The pendulum has swung against workers. Their basic human rights are under threat of being eroded when they are – falsely – perceived to stand in the way of the market, investment and the golden eggs promised.

Another factor that comes into play, probably unrelated to the policies of globalization, is encapsulated in UNDP's finding that 'the spread of democratisation appears to have stalled, with many countries failing to consolidate and deepen the first steps towards democracy and several slipping back to authoritarianism' (UNDP, 2002, p. 13).[11] It would be surprising if such 'stalling' and 'slipping back' had not entailed some calling into question of existing basic workers' rights in some countries, which the CEACR would surely have noticed and commented upon.

8
Achievements in the Area of Freedom of Association

8.1 Introduction

The *gap* system's methodology will now be applied to each of the four subject matters, starting with the most important and political of human rights in the labour field, freedom of association. In this area, thanks to the CFA component all three *implementation* indicators (5, 6 and 7) will be put through the mill. In the other areas, where assessment of *implementation* presupposes ratification of the relevant Conventions, only indicators 5 and 6 provide the data on the basis of comments by the CEACR.

Freedom of association is largely accepted in established democracies, albeit sometimes with unjustified limitations, especially in the public sector. Totalitarian, dictatorial, authoritarian and even transition regimes continue to repress trade unions to varying degrees. Workers in agriculture, Export-Processing Zones, civil servants, migrant and domestic workers face most difficulties in law or in practice when they want to organize in the defence of their interests and to bargain with public or private employers (ILO, 2000c and 2004b). Although the principles and rights of freedom of association cover employers just as much as workers, for all practical purposes they benefit essentially trade unions. The ILO's supervisory and complaints bodies have, over many decades, elaborated detailed jurisprudence on this most enabling of all the rights of workers (ILO, 1996).

By December 2004, the numbers and proportions of ratification of the two freedom of association Conventions were sufficiently high to cover most countries' *implementation* problems. Of the 159 countries, 133 (84 per cent) had ratified Convention No. 87 and 141 (87 per cent) Convention No. 98. Some of the non-ratifiers' *implementation* problems are captured thanks to the CFA component, as in the case of China and the US, for example.

The time-lag effects of recent ratifications on *implementation* scores and CRGs are somewhat attenuated in the area of freedom of association for two reasons. First, a comparatively small number of countries, only 31, ratified one or both of the freedom of association Conventions between January 1996 and December 2004. Second, CFA *interim* reports can charge the *implementation* dimension of this area at any time before or after ratification.

To normalize the freedom of association data, the first-stage maxima[1] are reweighted in the case of *adherence* to 7.1 points up to 1999 and 6.3 afterwards, and in the case of CRGs to 33.9 points up to 1999 and 31.6 afterwards. *Implementation's* values are not affected by reweighting and stay unchanged at 32.1 and 30 points, respectively.

8.2   Global and regional evolution

The long-term trendlines covering at least ten years that can be established for 154 countries were counted and regionalized in percentage terms in Table 8.1 for the area of freedom of association. At the global level, only 45 per cent of the CRG trends improved, 17 per cent less than in Table 7.1 for all basic labour rights taken together, which reflects the slow pace of change in the area of freedom of association. In fact, change is going in the wrong direction! More than half of the global CRG lines worsened in the course of the last 20 years. In regional terms, taking the ratio of improving to worsening CRG trendlines as a performance measure, the ratio of 3:1 of 'other' Asian-Pacific countries ranks them first, followed by the Caribbean/Canada/US group (ratio 1.4:1), Africa (1:1), the 'favourably inclined' Asian-Pacific countries (0.6:1), Europe (0.5:1) and Latin America (0.3:1). If the Table's two sets of subregions are re-aggregated, the Asian-Pacific region (2:1) is ahead of Africa, the Americas (0.6:1) and Europe in terms of improving to worsening CRG trends.

Of the global *adherence* trendlines, more than half improved, chiefly due to ratifications. Nearly a quarter worsened as a result of poor reporting on ratified or unratified Conventions. The ratio of improving to worsening trends is 2.3:1. The explanation for the lower level of improving long-term *adherence* scores in the freedom of association Table 8.1 compared with the overall Table 7.1 derives from two factors. One is that ratifications since the mid-1990s did not surge as much in the area of freedom of association as in the

Table 8.1 Achievement of freedom of association rights, by region, 1985–2004 (%)

	Worse*	Better**	Unchanged
Global			
CRGs	53	45	3
Adherence gaps	23	53	25
Implementation gaps	68	25	7
Africa			
CRGs	47	49	4
Adherence gaps	36	57	6
Implementation gaps	77	21	2
Asia-Pacific 'favourably inclined'			
CRGs	67	33	0
Adherence gaps	11	33	56
Implementation gaps	67	33	0
Asia-Pacific 'other'			
CRGs	24	72	3
Adherence gaps	14	79	7
Implementation gaps	45	28	28
Caribbean, Canada, US			
CRGs	38	54	8
Adherence gaps	15	62	23
Implementation gaps	62	31	8
Latin America			
CRGs	79	21	0
Adherence gaps	16	42	42
Implementation gaps	79	21	0
Europe			
CRGs	70	30	0
Adherence gaps	22	32	46
Implementation gaps	73	24	3

Annotations same as for Table 7.1.

other areas, which is also reflected in the high proportions of unchanged *adherence* trendlines. The other explanation is that countries seem to have fulfilled their reporting obligations on both ratified and unratified Conventions (indicators 2 and 3) less satisfactorily in this area than in others, possibly because reporting might be more revealing of governments' basic policies than reporting on forced labour, child labour or non-discrimination.

The *implementation* data convey the most telling information regarding the evolution of freedom of association in the last 20 years. Globally, two thirds of the trends moved in the wrong direction; only one in four moved in the right direction; the ratio between improving and worsening lines is negative, 0.4:1. When one considers regional variations, the mid-1980s' starting positions have to be taken into account that are approximated by the data in Figure 8.2, where the Asia-Pacific region comes in lowest and would seem predestined for rather more critical comments than the other regions. Not so! The count at the basis of Table 8.2 that permits the calculation of improving to worsening lines puts 'other' Asian-Pacific countries' ratio (0.7:1) ahead of 'favourably inclined' Asian-Pacific countries' and the Caribbean/Canada/US group's (both 0.5:1), followed by Europe, Africa and Latin America (all 0.3:1). All ratios are negative, which means that the dominant tendency of all regions is that *implementation* worsened during the last 20 years or so in the area of freedom of association.

8.3   Ranking of countries

Table 2 of the Rights Gaps Indicators contains the ranks of countries sorted according to their 2000–04 average CRG score and distributed by category of 'high', 'medium' and 'non-ratifiers'. As each area of freedom comprises only two core Conventions, the definitions have to be adapted from the overall level where they concern eight Conventions. In the area of freedom of association, 'high' ratifiers are defined as having adopted both Convention Nos. 87 and 98, and 'medium' ratifiers as having adopted one or the other Convention, by 31 December 2004.

The size of the correlation coefficient between the average CRGs of all countries in 1995–99 and 2000–04 is about the same for freedom of association (+0.60) as for overall CRGs in Table 1 of the Rights Gap Indicators (+0.58). When only long-standing ratifiers are included, it climbs to +67 (all significant at 1 per cent), the same level as for all four areas taken together. One reason for the similarity of the coefficients is the enormous weight of the freedom of association component in the new indicator system, where 48 per cent of the total number of 3,268.5 *observations-cum-satisfaction* are generated by it (compared with 28 per cent by forced labour, 4 per cent by child labour and 20 per cent by non-discrimination). Another reason is that the variations in countries' achievements of freedom of association have been comparatively limited in the last ten years or so.

The categorizations and stylistic identifications at the level of two Conventions render certain general patterns more easily visible than in

Table 1. In the freedom of association Table 2, capitalized extensive recent ratifiers tend to be closer to the top of the group of high ratifiers when ranked according to 2000–04 averages, which has to do with the time-lag effects that may make them benefit temporarily from unexpectedly low *implementation* scores and CRGs. Cases in point are Surinam, Kiribati and St. Kitts and Nevis. Among medium ratifiers, New Zealand is the only capitalized country. Long-standing ratifiers tend to be closer to the bottom of the group of high ratifiers, which suggests that they face disproportionately large *implementation* problems. A general pattern already found across all Conventions, principles and rights that comes out more strongly in individual areas is that a high degree of ratification does not *ipso facto* entail high *implementation* points. The first 60 high ratifiers (47 per cent of this group) have single or double-digit *implementation* ranks. Some long-standing ratifiers that are high ratifiers also show positive patterns. For example, Ireland, Italy and Sweden rank 1, 5 and 7 on the scale of freedom of association CRGs in 2000–04 (leaving aside extensive recent ratifiers) and also occupy top ranks on the *implementation* scale (4, 20 and 29, respectively). Ireland, which has a perfect score of 0 points, adopted an exemplary policy of respect for trade unions and pulling them into national policy-making in the mid-1980s and has reaped the benefits in the form of sustained high economic growth. Rather different policies have given rise to the other pattern among high ratifiers that is visible towards the end of this group of countries in Table 2 where high *implementation* ranks and high CRGs go together, and this despite perfect *adherence* scores of 0 points. Examples are Australia (CRG rank 145, *implementation* rank 146), Peru (CRG rank 146, *implementation* rank 147), Belarus (CRG rank 147, *implementation* rank 149) and Bangladesh (CRG rank 148, *implementation* rank 148).

If one applies the standard cut-off points (<25 per cent, 25–50 per cent and >50 per cent of the maximum score) to the 2000–04 averages, 39 countries (25 per cent) are good achievers, 82 countries (52 per cent) are medium performers and 38 countries (24 per cent) are poor performers in terms of CRGs.

It is no surprise to find European countries – Ireland, San Marino, Italy, Sweden, Hungary, France, Finland – bunched at the top of the 2000–04 CRG scale in Table 2 if extensive recent ratifiers are disregarded. Israel, St. Lucia and Grenada are the best-ranked non-European countries. At the other end of the scale, two Asian countries (Japan and Pakistan, ranked 153 and 158 in 2000–04), one European and African country each (Turkey and Ethiopia, ranked 154 and 155) and three Latin American countries (Paraguay, Guatemala and Venezuela, ranked

156, 157 and 159) turn out to be the worst achievers. The highest non-achievement score ever is associated with Fujimori's regime in Peru, 0.609 points in 1990–94, which has since fallen by half (CRG rank 146 in 2000–04). The most recent worst average was Venezuela's at 0.459 points, which was entirely due to *implementation* problems.

Seven of the non-ratifiers are Asian countries narrowly defined, five are Arab States, the others are the US and El Salvador. The bottom *adherence* ranks are occupied by Saudi Arabia, Vietnam and Laos. None of them has been the object of a CFA *interim* report during 2000–04, which means that they were without *implementation* points and, due to the *gap* system's inter-linkages, had mid-level CRGs (ranked 88, 91 and 94). The same holds true for countries such as Thailand, the US and China. El Salvador, India and the Republic of Korea (ranked 95, 107 and 128) have had respectively one, two and four *interim* reports addressed to their governments during 2000–04.

Among the illustration countries, Ireland, which is a long-standing ratifier of Convention Nos. 87 and 98, has a perfect score in this area in both 1995–99 and 2000–04. The country is credited with the full achievement of freedom of association – no *adherence gap*, no *implementation gap* and therefore no *Core Rights Gap*. Togo has reasonably low averages during both periods (CRG rank 27 in 2000–04). The country, which has ratified the relevant Conventions, experienced some minor reporting problems in the past and received a number of CEACR *observations* on Convention No. 87, six during the last ten years. Barbados' record (rank 65) is slightly worse in that it experienced reporting problems repeatedly, was the object of both *direct requests* and *observations*, and of an *interim* report addressed to it in 1997. The Czech Republic (rank 120) does not have a good reporting record on the two ratified Conventions, and the CEACR has queried the *implementation* of Convention No. 87 at the level of *direct requests* and of Convention No. 98 at the level of *observations* (four since 2001). Together, *adherence* and *implementation* problems made the country drop to CRG rank 120 in 2000–04. Uganda's score (rank 122) is a combination of *non-adherence* to Convention No. 87, reporting problems on Convention No. 98 and a string of *observations* on that Convention.

Figure 8.1 compares the contrasting origins of Jordan's and Japan's CRGs (ranked 63 and 153 in 2000–04). Jordan has a freedom of association CRG in the medium range. A sizeable part of its CRG derives from an *adherence gap* (Convention No. 87 not ratified); a smaller part is due to *implementation* problems that have been detected on a number of occasions by the CEACR. Japan, which has no *adherence* problem as here defined, has repeatedly been the object of CEACR comments on both freedom of association Conventions as well as of four CFA *interim* reports in 2000–04, which explains its poor *implementation* and CRG scores in the area of freedom of association. Japan's scores in Table 2 of the Rights Gaps Indicators and Figure 8.1 highlight the fact that sizeable *implementation* problems exert a strong influence on CRGs.

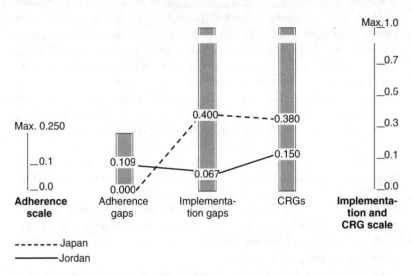

Figure 8.1   Origin of Japan's and Jordan's normalized freedom of association CRGs, 1985–2004 (approximate scale)

The fact that a certain degree of correlation exists between decreasing *adherence gaps* and increasing *implementation gaps* due to the inter-linkages built into the system can also seen in the area of freedom of association. For 2000–04, the coefficient is –0.47, but a little weaker if only long-standing ratifiers' scores are correlated (–0.27).

8.4   Focus on implementation

8.4.1   Full measurement

Distinguishing 'good' from 'medium' and 'poor' performers by application of the standard cut-off points (<25 per cent, 25–50 per cent and >50 per cent of the maximum score) to countries' *implementation* data in 2000–04 designates 69 countries (43 per cent) as good achievers,

63 countries (40 per cent) as medium achievers and 27 countries (17 per cent) as poor achievers in the area of freedom of association. The distribution assigns relatively few countries to the worst achievers because of Venezuela's rather high score, 0.483 points. If the second-worst scores of Guatemala and Pakistan were taken as a yardstick (0.417 points), 38 per cent would be good achievers, 35 per cent medium achievers and 26 per cent poor achievers.

Table 8.2 enables a dynamic comparison to be made of the 20 worst *implementers'* performance by identifying the direction of short-term trends' changes. The worst freedom of association *implementation* score in the indicator system is attributed to Fujimori's Peru in 1990–94, 0.627 points, and the second worst to Guatemala in 1995–99, 0.547 points. The average scores of the 20 countries worsened with every period. Sixteen are long-standing ratifiers for the Conventions they adopted. Four countries actually had worse scores during each subsequent period: Australia, Macedonia, Kyrgyzstan and Turkey. Not a single country had continuously improving scores.

Workers' organizations have clearly been afflicted by growing problems since globalization took hold. When the freedom of association averages of 1985–89 in Table 8.2 are compared with the overall averages in Table 7.2, a miniscule difference of 0.009 points appears, By 2000–04, however, the freedom of association averages were larger by 0.067 points, which implies that this area has been afflicted by disproportionate problems.

Two sets of CFA data throw further light on developments in the area of freedom of association. One is the number of allegations submitted to the ILO and declared to be receivable by the CFA, which was included for reference purposes in Table 5.2. This variable covers not only ratifiers but also non-ratifiers since the CFA can receive complaints even in the absence of ratification of Convention Nos. 87 and/or 98. Putting a trend through this variable (see Böhning, 2003b, p. 36) reveals a rather steep rise in complaints, which implies that *implementation* problems, instead of withering away, have grown as time went by. Indeed, complaints have risen from about 40 per year in the second half of the 1980s to around 60 during the first years of the 21st century. There are pronounced regional differences. The American region is the main source of complaints and accounts for much of the steep global upward slope. Africa, which started out with the lowest number of complaints, has seen a notable rise, reaching European levels today. Europe itself exhibits a slightly upward slope, which is possibly a result of the growth in the number of countries in that

Table 8.2 The 20 worst freedom of association implementers in 2000–04 and short-term trends

Country	1985–99	1990–94	1995–99	2000–04	Rank	Country	Changes in gaps		
	1	2	3	4			2/1	3/2	4/3
INDONESIA	0.107	0.213	0.213	0.267	140	INDONESIA	Larger	Same	Larger
Panama	0.213	0.302	0.320	0.267	141	Panama	Larger	Larger	Smaller
Philippines	0.267	0.284	0.213	0.267	142	Philippines	Larger	Smaller	Larger
Swaziland	0.178	0.231	0.320	0.267	143	Swaziland	Larger	Larger	Smaller
Egypt	0.160	0.284	0.213	0.283	144	Egypt	Larger	Smaller	Larger
Macedonia	–	0.000	0.089	0.283	145	Macedonia	–	Larger	Larger
Australia	0.036	0.071	0.231	0.317	146	Australia	Larger	Larger	Larger
Peru	0.213	0.627	0.480	0.317	147	Peru	Larger	Smaller	Smaller
Bangladesh	0.231	0.231	0.196	0.333	148	Bangladesh	Same	Smaller	Larger
Belarus	0.107	0.071	0.178	0.333	149	Belarus	Smaller	Larger	Larger
Kyrgyzstan	–	0.000	0.160	0.333	150	Kyrgyzstan	–	Larger	Larger
Denmark	0.178	0.178	0.196	0.350	151	Denmark	Same	Larger	Larger
Ecuador	0.302	0.338	0.302	0.367	152	Ecuador	Larger	Smaller	Larger
Ethiopia	0.196	0.213	0.409	0.383	153	Ethiopia	Larger	Larger	Smaller
Paraguay	0.373	0.338	0.373	0.383	154	Paraguay	Smaller	Larger	Larger
Japan	0.284	0.142	0.249	0.400	155	Japan	Smaller	Larger	Larger
Turkey	0.142	0.178	0.320	0.400	156	Turkey	Larger	Larger	Larger
Guatemala	0.213	0.284	0.547	0.417	157	Guatemala	Larger	Larger	Smaller
Pakistan	0.231	0.356	0.320	0.417	158	Pakistan	Larger	Smaller	Larger
Venezuela	0.284	0.213	0.480	0.483	159	Venezuela	Smaller	Larger	Larger
Average score	0.218	0.250	0.317	0.365	–	Ratio larger: smaller	3:1	2.2:1	3:1

– Not applicable. Annotations same as for Table 7.2.

region. The Asian-Pacific region is the only region where the trendline points downwards, albeit only marginally so.

The other set of data categorizes the kinds of *implementation* problems that are alleged to occur. The data in Table 8.3 cover the 1995–99 period of the *gap* system completely and the 2000–04 period in large measure, which permits short-term comparisons to be made. Globally speaking, there has been a shift away from the gravest violations represented by civil liberty cases (down from 30 to 10 per cent) towards cases involving the exercise of trade union rights and activities (right to strike, acts of anti-union discrimination, other forms of interference and, especially, collective bargaining). In regional terms, Africa is still afflicted by a high proportion of civil liberty cases. A number of

European countries continue to battle with restrictive legislation at the beginning of the 21ˢᵗ century (19 per cent) and with collective bargaining rights (22 per cent). The Americas (33 per cent) as well as Asia and the Pacific region (31 per cent) have experienced a high proportion of acts of anti-union discrimination (dismissals or other sanctions inflicted on office holders or union members). The Americas also witnessed many collective bargaining cases.

Table 8.3   Type of problems evoked in the allegations examined by the CFA since the mid-1990s (%)

	Denial of civil liberties	Restrictive legislation	By-laws, elections and activities	Establishment of organizations	Right to strike	Acts of anti-union discrimination	Interference	Collective bargaining
1995 (March)–								
1999 (November)	30	6	8	9	9	23	4	11
2000	14	7	13	10	14	22	6	14
2001	6	9	5	9	16	27	5	22
2002	10	5	6	15	13	24	6	20
2003 March–May	9	12	11	5	6	33	6	18
2000 (March)–								
2003 (May)	10	8	9	10	13	26	6	19
of which Africa	28	4	6	6	19	17	9	11
Americas	8	6	9	9	11	33	5	20
Asia-Pacific	11	6	3	8	17	31	8	17
Europe	1	19	12	16	13	10	6	22

Source: Böhning, 2003b, p. 36.
Rounding can result in Figures not adding up to 100%.

8.4.2   Proxy measurement

To test whether the freedom of association *implementation* proxy is a valid shortcut of the full *implementation* dimension, simple correlation coefficients were calculated, which come to +0.90 between the proxy and the corresponding full *implementation* data in 1995–99 as well as in 2000–04, both significant at the 1 per cent level. This is a high degree of correlation, and the proxy can therefore be considered a valid shortcut to the measurement of *implementation* scores in the area of freedom of association. The fact that the coefficients in this area are as large as the overall coefficients (+0.88) also legitimizes once more the CFA component, which has not introduced an extraneous element into the new indicator system.

The *implementation* proxy that portrays the dominant tendency and which is shown in Figure 8.2 includes the four major regions and, for comparative purposes, the global trendline of expressions of *satisfaction*. The global trendline of *observations* is not shown because it would appear way above the regional slopes and point sharply upward. The regional distinctions for freedom of association are the same as for the above overall data (Figure 7.3) in that Africa has the highest number of *observations* corrected for expressions of *satisfaction*, the Americas have the second highest, Europe and the Asia-Pacific region come in third and fourth, respectively, in terms of the level of *observations*.[2]

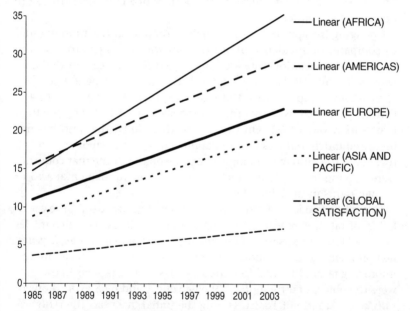

Figure 8.2   Trends in regional observations and global satisfaction in the area of freedom of association, 1985–2004

Critical *observations* by the CEACR are plentiful and have increased strongly, but the number of expressions of *satisfaction* is low and increased only very little. The fact that it has increased at all is a good sign but small comfort. For, the rate of increase of *observations* far outpaces the rate of increase of expressions of *satisfaction*, which means that the absolute distance between the two is getting larger rather than smaller. The absolute distance can be calculated as the number of *observations* minus the number of expressions of *satisfaction* during, for example, the time-lagged initial and the final five years. The figures are 358 for the initial and 466 for the final period, an increase of nearly 22 data entries per year. The differential rates of growth have the effect of opening up a scissors movement between *observations* and *satisfaction*, which is visible to the naked eye when the slopes of the four regions' trendlines are compared with the slope of the global *satisfaction* trendline. The problem with the problems in the area of freedom of association is that they keep growing.

The regional slopes of expressions of *satisfaction* (data not shown here) point in the desirable upward for all major regions. The slopes are not very steep; the Asian-Pacific slope climbs more than the others. The global line, which appears at the bottom of Figure 8.2, is therefore not very steep, either.

Changing the approach from visualization to quantification in order to compare the incidence of *observations* with cases of progress, the freedom of association data are time-lagged by two years in the same way as the overall data in Chapter 7. For the whole period, 1,367.5 *observations* compare with 102 cases of progress, a ratio of 13.4:1. During the initial five years the ratio was also 13.4:1, during the final five years it was 14.6:1. On this count, thankfully, the ratio has not increased much, but it is far from approaching the ideal of 1:1. Only a reversal of the ratio over a longish period would indicate that countries were moving in the right direction in this most fundamental area of human rights in the labour field.

To explore freedom of association realities at greater depth, the calculation of ratios is repeated for long-standing ratifiers. These countries have had tens of years to sort out any legislative or practical *implementation* problems, and one should therefore expect them to have low and improving ratios. In actual fact, the 92 long-standing ratifiers in this area were the object of a total of 1,129 *observations* and 69.5 expressions of *satisfaction*, a ratio of 16.2:1. During the initial five years the ratio was 12:1, during the last five years 22.4:1. Contrary to expectations, the long-standing ratifiers were not only responsible for a disproportionately large number of *observations*, but their ratio of *observations* to *satisfaction* for the whole period exceeded that of all countries, and their final years' ratio was almost double the initial years' ratio. This finding suggests that long-standing ratifiers face deep-seated or new *implementation* problems.[3] The fact that the long-standing ratifiers' ratio has strongly gone in the wrong direction in the course of the last 20 years aptly describes the reality of freedom of association rights in today's world.

Are the upward sloping *implementation* trendlines due to a substitution of *direct requests* by *observations* in the case of freedom of association? Not at all, neither for the subject matter as a whole nor for three of the four regions. *Direct requests* trendlines point upwards in the same way as the lines for *observations* do in Figure 8.2. Only the trendline for the Americas points slightly downwards. However, this is more a reflection of the seriousness of freedom of association *implementation* problems in that region than of a tougher attitude by the CEACR in recent years. The CEACR does not modify the yardsticks it uses to measure the achievement of rights (see Chapter 5).

The conclusions regarding *implementation* problems in the area of freedom of association are similar to those for all basic labour rights. The worst *implementers* have, on balance, experienced more rather than fewer problems recently. The fact that 16 of the 20 countries in the Table of worst freedom of association *implementers* are long-standing ratifiers for the Conventions they adopted bodes ill for this fundamental human right in the years ahead.

8.5   Correlations?

The new measure of freedom of association rights presented in this book respects the demanding criteria that must be observed in the construction of indicators in the human rights field (Chapter 2.3), notably objectivity. As this is not always the case for existing indicators, one should expect at best a mixed bag of correlations of *gaps* with other indicators and proxies. Those that can be assumed to measure the fundamental human right of freedom of association are represented in Table 8.4. The centrality of this right in securing advances for workers has given rise to a wider array of indicators, six different sets, than for core labour standards as a whole. Again, such correlations as may be hypothesized to exist with freedom of association CRGs, *adherence* and *implementation gaps* should, except for strikes, be inverse. The higher the non-achievement of basic labour rights, the lower should be the values of the other indicators. Here, too, the time-lag effects of extensive recent ratifications on *implementation* and CRG scores may marginally weaken correlations pertaining to 1995–99 and 2000–04. To demonstrate the validity of the assumption that no more than weak (<0.50) or modest (0.50–0.75) coefficients can be expected, I shall re-run the correlations for long-standing ratifiers, which comprises a sufficiently large number of countries in this area (92) to permit proper correlations to be carried out.

Table 8.4   Correlations of freedom of association gaps with other indicators

	CRGs				CRGs	Adh.	Imp.
	1985–89	1990–94	1995–99	2000–04			
Basic labour rights indicators							
Verité (beginning 21st century)[1]							
Laws and legal system	–	–	–0.44	–0.59	–0.28	–0.34	
Implementation effectiveness	–	–	–0.31	–0.38	–0.33	–0.14	
CIRI (avg. 1995–99 or 2000–03)[2]							
Workers' rights	–	–0.30	–0.34	–0.23	–0.34	–0.02	
ILO Workers' participation (in or before 1999)[3]							
Input indicator	–	–0.22	–0.35	–0.19	–0.41	0.00	
Process indicator	–	–0.36	–0.31	–0.15	–0.14	–0.07	
Output indicator	–	–0.26	–0.33	–0.35	–0.05	–0.28	
Representation Security Index	–	–0.34	–0.41	–0.31	–0.23	–0.18	
Kucera (1993–97)[4]							
Violations of union rights, unweighted	–	–0.39	–0.46	–0.46	–0.33	–0.21	
Violations of union rights, weighted	–	–0.38	–0.46	–0.45	–0.33	–0.21	
Cuyvers and van den Bulcke (1999 or later)[5]							
Formal freedom of association index	–	–0.22	–0.16	–0.04	–0.98	0.53	
Real freedom of association index	–	0.23	0.13	0.07	0.57	–0.27	
Freedom of association index	–	–0.03	–0.06	0.03	–0.59	0.37	
Botero *et al.* (1997)[6]							
Subindex collective bargaining	–	–0.08	0.00	0.00	–0.31	0.16	
Subindex participation in management	–	–0.06	–0.08	-0.08	0.05	–0.10	
Subindex collective disputes	–	0.10	0.15	0.02	–0.14	0.09	
Summary industrial relations laws index	–	–0.04	0.01	–0.04	–0.21	0.07	

Table 8.4 Correlations of freedom of association gaps with other indicators – *continued*

	CRGs				CRGs	Adh.	Imp.
	1985–89	1990–94	1995–99	2000–04			
Political proxies							
Freedom House scale							
(avg. 1993–97)[7]	–0.28	–0.27	–0.28	–0.18	–0.34		0.03
Polity IV democracy scale							
(avg. 2000–02)[8]	–	–	–0.20	–0.13	0.01		–0.12
Economic proxies							
FDI inflows (avg. 1993–99)[9]	0.01	0.04	0.00	–0.05	0.27		–0.19
Number of strikes per year							
(1990–2004)[10]	–0.22	–0.10	–0.14	–	–		–

Annotations same as for Table 7.3.
[1] Verité (2004) scores pertaining to Convention Nos. 87 and 98. 25 countries.
[2, 3, 7, 8 and 9] Same as notes 2, 3, 4, 5 and 6 of Table 7.3.
[4] Kucera, forthcoming. 141 countries.
[5] Cuyvers and van den Bulcke, forthcoming. 38 countries.
[6] Botero *et al.*, 2003. 80 countries.
[10] Strike figures drawn from the Rama datafile for the database set up for the World Bank (Rama and Artecona, 2002). 56 countries.

Table 8.4 starts with Verité's data. The source material permits the parcelling out of two indicators in the area of freedom of association, that is, laws/legal systems and implementation effectiveness (see also Chapter 7.5). The correlation coefficients are as low as expected. When the correlations are re-run for long-standing ratifiers, some coefficients are a little larger but stay at a weak-modest level.

As regards the CIRI scale, although it appears to give pride of place to freedom of association and collective bargaining subject matters, it mixes apples and oranges, and it is flawed in other respects (see Chapter 7.5). When the CIRI data of workers' rights that were correlated with overall fundamental rights in the preceding Chapter are now correlated with freedom of association rights, the result is the same in that the coefficients are predictably weak. When the correlations are re-run for long-standing ratifiers, they remain weak.

ILO's Representation Security Index, which was correlated in Table 7.3 with overall *gaps*, is correlated in Table 8.4 with its direct counterpart, freedom of association *gaps*; but this does not make any difference to the level of coefficients, which are all weak. Factors without a scalable link to freedom of association rights, such as union density and collective bargaining coverage, appear to be interfering on the side of the Representation Security Index. When the correlations are re-run for long-standing ratifiers, most coefficients are marginally stronger but stay at a low level.

David Kucera coded sources containing *de jure* and *de facto* violations of freedom of association rights described in three publications, the ICFTU's *Annual Survey of Violations of Trade Union Rights*, the US State Department's *Country Reports on Human Rights Practices* and the various reports of the ILO's CFA (Kucera, forthcoming). Coding is equivalent to interpreting, which in the case of CFA reports was carried out by a single person. The *gap* system abstains from applying personal judgements and mirrors what the collective CFA itself identifies as grave violations when it issues *interim* reports as opposed to other reports. Kucera's 'unweighted' indicator gives equal weight to all forms of violation, his 'weighted' indicator purports to reflect the severity of violations. Surprisingly, there is no real difference between the two, which is presumably due to the fact that the ICFTU and State Department sources tend to highlight more of the grave than of the low-level violations of freedom of association. These two sources and the subjective coding of CFA reports pull Kucera's data away from mine and make me assume that there would be little correlation between them. Indeed, there is none worth speaking of. When the correlations are re-run for long-standing ratifiers, several coefficients are a little higher, notably those concerning *implementation*, but not high enough to call into question the arguments puts forward here.

Cuyvers and van den Bulcke constructed indicators that, in some respects, resemble those of the *gap* system. Their 'Formal freedom of association index' comprises a ratification and a reporting component on Convention Nos. 87 and 98, though its objectivity is undermined when they take into consideration the 'compatibility' of a country's legislation with the 'substance' of a Convention 'to substitute for the lack of ratification' (Cuyvers and van den Bulcke, forthcoming, p. 4), which must involve rather subjective judgements. Their 'Real freedom of association index' is made up of three components. The first tallies the number of murders, woundings, arrests and dismissals as reported in the ICFTU's *Annual Survey of Violations of Trade Union Rights* and the

US State Department's *Country Reports on Human Rights Practices*; the second assesses governmental interference in freedom of association rights; the third evaluates legal restrictions. The authors admit that 'this introduces a substantial degree of arbitrariness, especially in cases where no information is available. In such cases it was decided to opt for a 'fine' (read 'score') equal to 0.3, compared to a maximum 'fine' of 1. The lack of information is therefore considered to be equivalent in most cases to information withheld for further scrutiny. The degree of arbitrariness is the price to be paid for quantification' (*ibid.*, p. 8). In addition, the 'Formal' and the 'Real' index are constructed by a procedure that, according to their own admission, 'often becomes very tedious and complicated' (*ibid.*, p. 4). The 'Freedom of association index' itself simply adds the two components together. One can antici-pate, therefore, that the 'Formal freedom of association index' corre-lates highly with my *adherence* dimension, which it does, and that the 'Real freedom of association index' correlates at best weakly with the *implementation* dimension, which is the case. CRGs do not correlate at all with the Cuyvers and van den Bulcke indexes. When the cor-relations are re-run for long-standing ratifiers, the coefficients remain basically in the same mould.

The indexes elaborated in a NBER working paper are included here because they may appear at first sight to bear some relationship to the new system's freedom of association *gaps*. The subindex on collective bargaining scores, *inter alia*, whether employers have to bargain with unions, whether collective contract are extended to third parties by law and whether there is a right to unionization in countries' constitu-tions. The subindex on workers' participation in management scores, *inter alia*, whether workers and/or unions have a right to appoint members to the boards of directors and whether countries' constitu-tions contain a right to participation in management. The subindex on collective disputes scores, *inter alia*, whether wildcat strikes are legal and whether countries' laws mandate conciliation procedures before a strike. All three subindexes code whether or not the specified items are enshrined in countries' laws or constitution. The summary index is appropriately called an industrial relations law index (Botero *et al.*, 2003). In the terminology of the *gap* system, these are measures of *adherence* (indicator 1). However, they should not really correlate with any *gaps* because they cover rather different subject matters. Further-more, Botero's group totally disregards how national laws are applied in practice, which this book has demonstrated to be exceedingly important when one considers complex human rights in the labour field.[4] Table 8.4 confirms this judgement in that correlations are absent. Only the freedom of association *adherence gap* is very weakly correlated with the subindex on collective bargaining, no doubt due to the fact that formal commitments are embodied in both data sets. When the correlations are re-run for long-standing ratifiers, there is no change in the size of the coefficients.

As regards political proxies of freedom of association, the Freedom House and Polity data are once more pressed into service. The coefficients are of a level similar to those of overall correlations in Table 7.3 and confirm my judgement about the inappropriateness of using them as indicators or even as proxies of fundamental human rights in the labour field. When re-run for long-standing ratifiers, some of the correlation coefficients creep up slightly.

As regards economic proxies, the first picks up the FDI data from the overall Table 7.3 and correlates them here with freedom of association scores. The result is the same – no correlation. The second economic indicator, the average number of strikes during the early 1990s, captures political as well as much lower-level forms of strikes, and there are inherent data problems (see Rama and Artecona, 2002). Unsurprisingly, strikes in 1990–94 are unrelated to inter-country variations of *gaps*. A re-run for long-standing ratifiers yields marginally higher coefficients.

The fact that the correlation coefficients in respect of freedom of association are at best modest confirms once more the *sui generis* nature of the *gap* system. It measures the achievement of the fundamental human right of freedom of association with a combination of validity, transparency, replicability, non-truncation and objectivity that is unmatched by other attempts in this area. Unlike some other data sets, *gaps* are easy and cost-effective to collect and process.

8.6 Conclusions regarding freedom of association

The new indicator system performs credibly at the level of the two Conventions, principles and rights concerning freedom of association. The CFA component adds more depth and spread in respect of *implementation* but does not distort the picture or bias the results. There are no other indicators that cover the same area or which could be taken as a proxy.

In terms of the extent of and changes in realizing freedom of association, the conclusions in this area are not greatly different from the overall conclusions in Chapter 7. Countries have increasingly *adhered* to the values embodied in Convention Nos. 87 and 97 and the Declaration's principles and rights. But workers and their organizations have run into increasing problems of securing them in practice. *Implementation* problems abound, especially for long-standing ratifiers, and have gotten worse as time went by. The very slowly rising trend in the number of expressions of *satisfaction* is a small ray of hope that solutions can eventually be found. But while solutions are found to some of the problems, large numbers of old problems remain unresolved, new problems emerge to darken the horizon and the differential rate of growth between problems and solutions widens the gap between them. There is a definite rise in the failure to achieve freedom of association rights satisfactorily or fully.

What factors might explain the growing number of *observations* by the CEACR and of complaints submitted to the CFA? One paradoxical factor appears to be the democratization of regimes in the 1980s – notably in Latin America and Africa, followed by central-eastern Europe and the Balkans in the 1990s – reinforced by contemporary globalization. Democratization is likely to have emboldened trade unions to act with less apprehension, nationally and internationally. Another factor is that globalization-induced deregulation of labour markets and privatization of a range of public services has tended to sap the power that workers wield through their organizations, and this in both old and new democracies. Many private-sector unions have fought deregulation; many public-sector unions have gone on strike against privatization. Some private employers have recently given unions short shrift more often than in the days when the Soviet Union existed, going as far as boasting that they are 'union-free'. Governments are, at the best of times, reluctant to see workers' organizations throw their weight about in the public sector and may not have shelved privatization plans when workers threatened to strike. In these contexts, national or international trade unions might have let the Committee of Experts know of their misgivings by questioning governments' reports on Convention Nos. 87 and/or 98 more often than in the past or by submitting more complaints to the CFA, which would likely have entailed an increasing number of *observations* and *interim* reports.[5]

A further explanation for rising trends may well derive from the fact that national and international workers' organizations have become more vigilant in the last decade or two with regard to certain phenomena such as Export-Processing Zones (EPZs) and groups facing legislative or practical hurdles such as migrant workers. In the case of EPZs, their existence owes much to governments' restrictions on the application of local and international labour laws. In the case of migrant workers, unions at least in some advanced countries have paid more attention to their needs in recent years.[6]

Generally speaking, the policies and behaviour that frame the contemporary mode of globalization deal many workers some good cards and some bad cards, sometimes more of the latter than the former. Bad cards have always played through to the Committee of Experts as well as to the Committee on Freedom of Association. In this sense, globalization is bound to be a factor behind the rise in the non-achievement of freedom of association rights.

9
Achievements in the Area of Forced Labour

9.1   Introduction

No government officially condones forced or compulsory labour today, though leaders of the Burmese junta practice it and quite a number of developing countries have still not removed all vestiges of compulsory mobilization for development purposes. Others allow the employment of prisoners under conditions that the CEACR finds to be in contradiction of Convention No. 105. The State has actually receded into the background as organizer of forced labour. Today, it is primarily private actors – employers, landlords, intermediaries, recruitment agents and the like – who force and threaten others to work against their will (ILO, 2001b). Trafficking, which has been called the underside of globalization, has emerged as a new factor that frequently, albeit not inevitably, results in forced employment (ILO, 2003d and 2003e).

By December 2004, the numbers and proportions of ratification of the two forced labour Conventions were sufficiently high to cover most countries' *implementation* problems. Of the 159 countries, 149 (94 per cent) had ratified Convention No. 29 and 146 (92 per cent) Convention No. 105.

The time lags between extensive recent ratifications and the detection of *implementation* problems that feed through to CRGs are by no means absent in the area of forced labour despite the previously high level of ratifications. Extensive recent ratifiers number 46 countries with a total of 62 ratifications.

To normalize the forced labour data, the first-stage maxima[1] are reweighted in the case of *adherence* to 7.1 points up to 1999 and 6.3 afterwards, and in the case of CRGs to 18.9 points up to 1999 and 16.6 afterwards. *Implementation*'s maxima stay unchanged at 17.1 and 15 points, respectively.

9.2   Global and regional evolution

The long-term trendlines covering at least ten years that can be established for 154 countries were counted and regionalized in percentage
terms in Table 9.1 for the area of forced labour. At the global level,
just over two thirds of the CRG trends improved, just under a third
worsened. The ratio of 2.2:1 is a little higher than the overall ratio of
1.8:1 in Table 7.1, which implies that developments are more positive
in this area than for all areas taken together. The regions' long-term
trends put Latin America (ratio 3.8:1) ahead of 'favourably inclined'
Asian-Pacific countries (3.5:1), Europe (3:1), Africa (2.3:1), the Caribbean/
Canada/US group (1.6:1) and the 'other' Asian-Pacific countries (1.2:1). If
the Table's two sets of subregions are re-aggregated, the Americas (2.6:1)
trail Europe and Africa ranks before the Asian-Pacific region (1.5:1) in
terms of improving to worsening CRG trends.

Table 9.1   Achievement of forced labour rights, by region, 1985–2004 (%)

	Worse*	Better**	Unchanged
Global			
CRGs	31	68	2
Adherence gaps	15	57	28
Implementation gaps	46	41	13
Africa			
CRGs	30	68	2
Adherence gaps	23	49	28
Implementation gaps	55	30	15
Asia-Pacific 'favourably inclined'			
CRGs	22	78	0
Adherence gaps	0	56	44
Implementation gaps	33	56	11
Asia-Pacific 'other'			
CRGs	45	52	3
Adherence gaps	10	76	14
Implementation gaps	52	24	24
Caribbean, Canada, US			
CRGs	38	62	0
Adherence gaps	15	62	23
Implementation gaps	54	38	8
Latin America			
CRGs	21	79	0
Adherence gaps	11	68	21
Implementation gaps	26	74	0

Table 9.1 Achievement of forced labour rights, by region, 1985–2004 (%) – *continued*

	Worse*	Better**	Unchanged
Europe			
CRGs	24	73	3
Adherence gaps	14	46	41
Implementation gaps	41	49	11

Annotations same as for Table 7.1.

Of the long-term *adherence* trendlines, 57 per cent improved during the last 20 years, largely due to ratification of Conventions. About one in seven worsened due to failure to report to the CEACR or under Declaration auspices. That 28 per cent of the *adherence* trends did not change reflects the decades-old high degree of ratification of Convention Nos. 29 and 105 and the fact that a large proportion of countries reported correctly on them.

Among the *implementation* trendlines, about two in five improved, a slightly higher proportion worsened (ratio 0.9:1). In no other area examined in this book are the global *implementation* trends so closely balanced (the overall ratio in Table 7.1 is 0.5:1), which is cause for optimism. When one looks at regional variations one has to take account of the regions' different starting positions in the mid-1980s, which are approximated by the data in Figure 9.1, where the Americas, Asia-Pacific and Europe are at a similar level at the beginning of the period but Africa can be seen to start off with rather more *observations*. The count of trendline movements underlying Table 9.1 gives Latin America, where about three in four *implementation* trends have gone in the right direction, the best ratio (2.8:1). The 'favourably inclined' Asian-Pacific countries and Europe also have positive ratios (1.7:1 and 1.2:1, respectively). The Caribbean/Canada/US group is in negative territory (ratio 0.7:1), Africa and the 'other' Asian-Pacific group strongly so (both with a ratio of 0.5:1).

The contrast between the predominantly improving *adherence* and the marginally worsening *implementation* trendlines in the area of forced labour would, if graphically portrayed, resemble the scissors movement found in Chapter 7 for all Conventions, principles and rights, but the two parts of the scissors would not be far apart in the case of forced labour.

9.3   Ranking of countries

Table 3 of the Rights Gap Indicators contains the ranks of countries according to their 2000–04 average CRG score and distributed by category of 'high', 'medium' and 'non-ratifiers'. In the area of forced labour, 'high' ratifiers are defined as having adopted both Convention Nos. 29 and 105, and 'medium' ratifiers as having adopted one or the other Convention, by 31 December 2004.

The size of the correlation coefficient between the average *Core Rights Gaps* of all countries in 1995–99 and 2000–04 is marginally higher for forced labour (+0.63, and +0.69 if long-standing ratifiers are correlated) than for overall CRGs (+0.58 and +0.67, respectively, all significant at 1 per cent). This suggests that the variations in countries' achievements of the fight against forced labour have been comparatively limited in the last ten years or so.

General patterns in the area of forced labour rendered visible by the categorizations and stylistic identifications differ partly from those in Tables 1 and 2. In the forced labour Table 3, italicized long-standing ratifiers occupy the top positions among high ratifiers when ranked according to 2000–04 average scores, and capitalized extensive recent ratifiers are dispersed rather than close to the top. Finland distinguishes itself by being free from *adherence* and *implementation* problems throughout the 20 years under review; two countries, Norway and Portugal, have perfect scores during three of the four five-year periods; one country, Malta, has no problems during two of these periods; and three others, Sweden, Costa Rica and Honduras, are free from forced labour problems at the end of the period. The observer is comforted by the idea that a fundamental human right in the labour field can be realized fully today by a significant number of countries.

The positive impression in the area of forced labour is reinforced by the distribution of countries according to the categorization of 'good', 'medium' and 'poor' performers. When applying the standard cut-off points (<50 per cent, 25–50 per cent and >50 per cent of the maximum score) to CRGs in 2000–04, 89 countries (56 per cent) turn out to be good overall achievers, 53 (33 per cent) are medium achievers and 17 (11 per cent) are poor achievers, which is a better distribution than in the area of freedom of association (25, 52 and 24 per cent, respectively).

However, not all is well even in the area of forced labour. Some countries have chalked up exceedingly high CRG scores, such as Pakistan (0.962 points in 1985–89), the Central African Republic (0.932

in 1985–89), Tanzania (0.743 in 1985–89, 0.734 in 1990–94) and Sierra Leone (0.802 in 2000–04). African countries are over-represented among the worst performers in the area of forced labour. Six of the ten worst 2000–04 CRGs in Table 3 belong to long-standing ratifiers in Africa, one to a Caribbean country (Belize) and two to Asian-Pacific countries (Japan and Myanmar). Myanmar was the object of a Commission of Inquiry of the International Labour Organization and, in 2000, of a decision by the Organization's annual conference that asked its member States to consider sanctioning the country for its continued violation of Convention No. 29.

Noticeably worsening forced labour CRGs afflict, for instance, Mexico (51 in 2000–04, down from 3 in 1995–99), France (rank 123, down from 61), the United Arab Emirates (138, down from 26) and Niger (140, down from 13). The database's trendlines indicate that rising *implementation* problems are principally responsible for their unsatisfactory performance.

As regards the illustration countries, seven of the eight have now ratified both forced labour Conventions, Japan only Convention No. 29. Jordan (CRG rank 25 in 2000–04) outperforms the other countries. Although it has been the object of a number of *direct requests* by the CEACR, the country's *implementation* trendline points in the right direction, down. The Czech Republic (rank 67) did not report as often as it ought to have done; it also received *direct requests* on both Conventions; and its average forced labour CRG is still not as good as it ought to be at a level of 0.141 points. Barbados (rank 69) experienced increasing reporting problems and decreasing *direct requests* on both Conventions, which resulted in an unchanging forced labour CRG. It dropped 26 ranks between 1995–99 and 2000–04 because other countries performed better. Ireland (rank 77 in 2000–04) received *direct requests* as well as *observations* from the CEACR on both Conventions, but all its trendlines point reassuringly downward. Togo (rank 93) did not ratify Convention No. 105 until 1999, which partly explains its scores and ranks; a few *direct requests* on Convention No. 29 and a recent *observation* on Convention No. 105 account for the rest. Guatemala (rank 144) has grappled with *implementation* problems in the form of *direct requests* and, most of all, *observations*, with an upward trend. Uganda (rank 158) has not always reported when it should; and in the last five years the CEACR has addressed nine *observations* to its government on the two Conventions combined. And Japan (rank 150) has both *adherence* and *implementation* problems, with five *observations* being formulated by the CEACR during the last five years.

9.4 Focus on implementation

9.4.1 Full measurement

To distinguish 'good' from 'medium' and 'poor' forced labour performers, the standard cut-off points (<25 per cent, 25–50 per cent and
>50 per cent of the maximum score) are applied to countries' *imple-
mentation* data in 2000–04, which selects 106 countries as good achievers (67 per cent, the highest proportion in all four areas), 40 as medium
achievers (25 per cent) and 13 as poor achievers (8 per cent, the lowest
proportion in all four areas). The distribution assigns relatively few
countries to the worst achievers because of Sierra Leone's very high
score, 0.833 points. If the next three countries with identical *implementation* scores of 0.600 points (Pakistan, Chad and Uganda) were taken
as a yardstick, there would be 53 per cent good achievers but only
26 per cent medium achievers and 21 per cent poor achievers. Still, the
distribution in the area of forced labour is quite positive compared
with the other areas.

Table 9.2 enables a dynamic comparison to be made of the 20 worst
implementers' performance by identification of the direction of changes
of short-term trends. All but the United Arab Emirates, Guatemala,
Mauritania and Turkey are long-standing ratifiers, including the
advanced industrial society among the worst *implementers*, the United
Kingdom, which has attracted the CEACR's attention on account of
foreign domestic workers, prison labour and its merchant shipping legislation. Pakistan has the dubious distinction of being the only country
in the system with a score indicating total *implementation* failure,
1 point in 1985–89, though the Central African Republic is not far
behind with 0.967 points during the same period. Across the 20 countries, the average score dipped during 1990–94, but it has increased
ever since. In 1995–99 and 2000–04 there were twice as many larger
than smaller *gaps* among the worst *implementers*. The examination of
this group, therefore, confirms the earlier judgement that not all is well
in the area of forced labour – things are getting worse at the 'bad' end
of the distribution of countries.

One may have a different perception of forced labour if one compares the regional *implementation* trendlines in Table 9.1 with the
bottom-rank performers' *implementation* scores in Table 9.2. This is
explicable by the fact that different parts of reality are selected by
the full range of *implementation gaps* in Table 9.1 and the worst
scores in Table 9.2. If one analyses the data in detail one finds that
the bulk of the countries achieve reasonable scores. By contrast,

Table 9.2 The 20 worst forced labour implementers in 2000–04 and short-terms trends

Country	1985–99	1990–94	1995–99	2000–04	Rank	Country	Changes in gaps		
	1	2	3	4			2/1	3/2	4/3
Kenya	0.600	0.400	0.500	0.400	140	*Kenya*	Smaller	Larger	Smaller
Niger	0.100	0.067	0.033	0.400	141	*Niger*	Smaller	Smaller	Larger
Nigeria	0.467	0.467	0.300	0.400	142	*Nigeria*	Same	Smaller	Larger
Thailand	0.500	0.667	0.333	0.400	143	*Thailand*	Larger	Smaller	Larger
Trinidad & T.	0.433	0.233	0.333	0.400	144	*Trinidad & T.*	Smaller	Larger	Larger
UAE	0.067	0.067	0.033	0.400	145	*UAE*	Same	Smaller	Larger
United Kingdom	0.133	0.200	0.467	0.400	146	*United Kingdom*	Larger	Larger	Smaller
GUATEMALA	0.333	0.233	0.400	0.433	147	GUATEMALA	Smaller	Larger	Larger
MAURITANIA	0.333	0.300	0.300	0.433	148	MAURITANIA	Smaller	Same	Larger
TURKEY	0.133	0.067	0.167	0.433	149	TURKEY	Smaller	Larger	Larger
Cameroon	0.633	0.333	0.667	0.467	150	*Cameroon*	Smaller	Larger	Smaller
Jamaica	0.333	0.267	0.300	0.467	151	*Jamaica*	Smaller	Larger	Larger
Algeria	0.500	0.267	0.567	0.500	152	*Algeria*	Smaller	Larger	Smaller
Belize	0.167	0.100	0.400	0.533	153	*Belize*	Smaller	Larger	Larger
C. African Rep.	0.967	0.700	0.300	0.567	154	*C. African Rep.*	Smaller	Smaller	Larger
Tanzania	0.800	0.800	0.700	0.567	155	*Tanzania*	Same	Smaller	Smaller
Chad	0.267	0.333	0.600	0.600	156	*Chad*	Larger	Larger	Same
Pakistan	1.000	0.600	0.763	0.600	157	*Pakistan*	Smaller	Larger	Smaller
Uganda	0.300	0.267	0.363	0.600	158	*Uganda*	Smaller	Larger	Larger
Sierra Leone	–	–	–	0.833	159	*Sierra Leone*	–	–	–
Average score	0.425	0.335	0.390	0.492	–	Ratio larger:smaller	0.2:1	2:1	2:1

– Not applicable. Annotations same as for Table 7.2.

most of those in the *implementation* doldrums face growing problems. They include countries from all continents; but 11 of the 20 countries in Table 9.2 are from Africa where both traditional and modern forms of forced labour persist and where weak governments are sometimes unwilling and sometimes incapable of doing much about the phenomenon, hoping that it will somehow disappear through future development. The fact the United Kingdom and Turkey figure among the 20 worst *implementers* should tell them otherwise. Forms of forced labour that are associated with trafficking pose intractable problems, even in advanced countries; and subcontractors who engage in practices that are akin to forced labour are

not limited to developing countries but have proliferated in techno-
logically advanced sections of European agriculture, horticulture and
construction, among other sectors.

9.4.2 Proxy measurement

The forced labour *implementation* proxy, which portrays the dominant
tendency by netting out the improving, unchanging and worsening
scores of individual countries, is presented in the same combination as
the freedom of association proxy, that is, the Figure dispenses with
the global trend of *observations* that would be positioned well above
the regional forced labour data and point slightly upward. Instead,
Figure 9.1 includes the global trend of cases of progress, which is the
broken line at the bottom that is sloping slightly downward – in
the wrong direction. These two trendlines form the by now well-
known scissors movement, but the opening of the two scissors is
small in the case of forced labour. Still, the fact that both global trends
point in the wrong direction suggests that even the area of freedom
from forced labour is in a real crisis today.

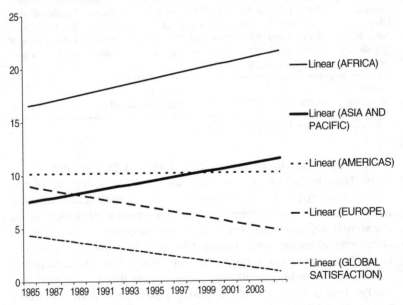

Figure 9.1 Trends in regional observations and global satisfaction in the area of
forced labour, 1985–2004

Regionally, there were contrasting developments if one compares the worst performer, Africa,[2] and the Asian-Pacific region, both of which encountered growing numbers of problems, with the Americas, where the overall trend was flat, and with Europe, where the level of *observations* declined.

If one crosschecks with the regional evolution in expressions of *satisfaction* (data not shown here, but the global trend of cases of progress is included in Figure 9.1), one finds a practically flat trend for the Asian-Pacific region, a marginally downward-sloping line for Africa and slightly downward-sloping lines for the Americas and Europe, that is, movements that go in the wrong direction. Legislative or practical measures evidently do not reduce several old and new forms of forced labour (see Box 9.1). The rather low number of cases of progress, even in the Americas and Europe, suggests that some problems get resolved but that others continue to cloud the picture.

Box 9.1   Forced labour is everywhere

Since the beginning of 2003, slavery in Sudan has hit international media headlines. But old and new forms of forced labour have been rediscovered elsewhere in Africa (in Niger, for example, see Oumanou, 2001). Forced labour practices at village level and for national development purposes have not totally disappeared yet from the continent. In Asia, millions of bonded labourers toil the soil and make bricks in, for example, India (see Mishra, 2001 and 2002) and neighbouring Pakistan. The Gulf countries' practice of taking the passports and other documents from the menial labourers and household workers they import from abroad also frequently results in forced labour situations. Within-country trafficking in Africa, Asia and Latin America supplies labour for plantations, private households, brothels, and so on. Across-border trafficking into Asian, African, North and Central American countries as well as into Europe incurs forced labour in private households, brothels, even construction and modern agriculture.

Changing the approach from visualization to quantification in order to compare the incidence of *observations* with cases of progress, the forced labour data are time-lagged by two years in the same way as the overall data in Chapter 7. For the whole period, 803 *observations* compare with 45.5 cases of progress, a ratio of 17.6:1. During the initial five years the ratio was 12.4:1, during the final five years nearly 35:1. As the number of *observations* is not greatly higher during the final than during the initial five years, the worsening of the ratio is due essentially to the decline in cases of progress, which is signalled graphically by the bottom line in Figure 9.1. The achievement of a world free from forced labour is not making progress in spite of some perfect, and large numbers of reasonable, scores. In effect, the movement has gone in the wrong direction in the last 20 years or so.

The check of how long-standing ratifiers performed in respect of forced labour throws more light on the matter. The 97 countries that fall into this group received a total of 701.5 *observations* and 31 expressions of *satisfaction*, a ratio of 22.6:1. During the initial five years the ratio was 15:1; during the last five years, when no more than 4.5 cases of progress were recorded among long-standing ratifiers, the ratio was 48.4:1. Even though these countries have had several decades to deal legislatively and practically with old and new forms of forced labour, they nevertheless account for a disproportionately large number of *observations*; their long-term ratio exceeds that of all countries; and their short-term ratios tripled between the initial and the final years. As the spotless records at the top of Table 3 make clear, there are quite a number of outstanding performers among long-standing ratifiers. However, there are even more that perform exceedingly badly. When all are put together, the picture is depressing because, on average, countries regress rather than progress in the fight against forced labour.

Are the upward sloping long-term *implementation* trendlines due to a hardening of the criticisms on the part of the Committee of Experts? Has it substituted *direct requests* by *observations*? Given that the global trendline for *direct requests* (data not shown here) points upward in the same way as the global trendline for *observations* does, this is as little the case for forced labour as it was for the overall situation in Chapter 7 and for freedom of association in Chapter 8. The CEACR does not change its yardsticks.

9.5   Conclusions regarding forced labour gaps

The *gap* system performs credibly at the level of the two core Conventions concerning forced labour. There are no other indicators that cover the same area or which could be taken as proxies.

In terms of the extent of and changes in achieving freedom from forced labour, the conclusions in this area are mixed. A few countries perform outstandingly well, a sizeable number perform reasonably well, quite a few others *implement* badly, and more of the bad *implementers* regress than progress. Globally, *observations* increased slightly and expressions of *satisfaction* decreased very slightly. Putting the two together, it must be concluded that the fight against forced labour is far from over.

Regionally, contrasting developments among (and within) the major regions are at the origin of the global evolution. Whereas both Africa and the Asian-Pacific region face situations of predominantly worsening *implementation* problems, improvements in long-term trends outweigh undesirable developments in the Americas and Europe. In the latter two regions, some of the problems experienced seem to find solutions some of the time.

The technological underpinnings of contemporary globalization, as well as the cost-reducing pressures and deregulation associated with it, facilitate trafficking and subcontracting practices in advanced countries that lend themselves to the emergence of pockets of forced labour in agriculture, horticulture, construction, the sex industry, and so on. The two regions most given to dense legislative regulation of the labour market, the Americas and Europe, appear to have kept such pockets of forced labour at bay in recent years. Anecdotal evidence makes it appear that they have been less successful in respect of the spread of trafficking itself.

It is worrying that the change in the role of the State – from pursuing 'equity to efficiency' (Nayyar, 2003, p. 17) – entails the danger of hollowing out labour inspection, which is crucial to the fight against forced labour. On top of this hollowing out comes the uneven distribution of the phenomenon of forced labour and of labour inspection across the economy. While forced labour is absent in large enterprises and medium-size enterprises, negligible in small enterprises but extensive in the informal economy, especially in ethnic niches, labour inspectors regularly visit large and medium-size enterprises, occasionally small enterprises but practically never the informal economy. Their deployment across enterprises is the opposite of what a policy aimed at flushing out forced labour would require. The phenomenon cannot be suppressed by border control; it has to be fought within countries.

10
Achievements in the Area of Child Labour

10.1 Introduction

The two core Conventions in this area aim to effectively abolish undesirable work by children. Convention No. 138 requires countries to fix the end of compulsory schooling as the minimum age for admission to employment and to raise it progressively where it is low, which reflects industrial nations' experience in this field, buttressed by moral as well as human capital considerations.[1] Many developing countries felt that this Convention did not suit their circumstances well. Most shunned ratification on grounds of traditions, lack of enforcement capacity and the – misguided – belief that it is better to have children help gain income in poor households than to have them at school. By the beginning of the *gap* system's review period, January 1985, only 28 countries had ratified Convention No. 138, half of them were advanced or communist countries at the time. Since the early 1990s, perceived threats of trade sanctions on the part of the United States and the European Union on goods made by exploited children, the ILO Director-General's ratification campaign since 1995 and the Declaration on Fundamental Principles and Rights at Work of 1998 have greatly raised the number of ratifications. By the end of the review period in December 2004, 125 countries had *adhered* to Convention No. 138. But it remains the least ratified of all core Conventions, 21 per cent of the countries in the *gap* system have so far not taken that step.

Convention No. 182, which entered into force in 2000, prioritizes the immediate elimination of the worst forms of child labour such as slavery, prostitution, pornography and work that is hazardous for children below 18 years of age. This Convention has enjoyed the fastest rate of ratification of any binding instrument of the International

Labour Organization (see also Box 3.2). By December 2004, 89 per cent had ratified it.

Measurement of *implementation* problems in this area is hampered, on the one hand, by the low level of ratification of Convention No. 138 at the beginning of the *gap* system's review period and, contrariwise, by the enormously fast rate of ratification of Convention No. 182 in the space of a few years and the associated time-lag effects (see Chapter 6.1). Due to the inter-linkages between *adherence* and *implementation*, only the 28 long-standing ratifiers' *implementation* of Convention No. 138 could be examined by the CEACR at the start of the *gap* system,[2] which means that the great majority of countries would initially be without *implementation gaps*. Due to Convention No. 182, there is not a single high ratifier in Table 4 of the Rights Gaps Indicators that is not at the same time a capitalized extensive recent ratifier, and only three of the medium ratifiers are not extensive recent ratifiers – Israel (CRG rank 93), Cuba (rank 124) and Venezuela (rank 133). Due to the definitions, 26 of the italicized long-standing ratifiers are simultaneously extensive recent ratifiers, that is, they are long-standing ratifiers for Convention No. 138 and recent ratifiers of Convention No. 182. Israel and Cuba are the only long-standing ratifiers of Convention No. 138 that have not taken the step to adopt Convention No. 182.

For the new indicator system, the time-lag effects of a total of 220 ratifications of the two child labour Conventions between 1996 and 2004 on *implementation* and CRGs are widespread and sizeable but variable in their impact on five-year averages, depending on the year of ratification. An illustration with reweighted points makes this clear. If a country had abstained until the end of the previous century from ratifying Convention No. 138, its *adherence* dimension would show 14.3 'raw' points each year until 1999, or 3.6 points after reweighting, and its CRG would be 3.6 points as well (disregarding all other Conventions). If the country ratified the two child labour Convention in 2000, its *adherence* and CRG scores would disappear – 0 points – in 2000–01. The government's first reports on the two Conventions would be due in 2002 and hopefully received in time for appraisal by the Committee of Experts. If the CEACR then put forward, as it tends to do in the case of first reports, no more than a *direct request* on each Convention, the country's *implementation* dimension and CRG would be charged with a total of 5 points in 2002. If the second report by the government, due and received two years later, led the CEACR to address an *observation* on each Convention to the country, a total of

10 points would appear in 2004; the average *implementation* and CRG score for the whole of 2000–04 would be 15/5=3 points; and the average CRG would decrease by 0.6 points relative to the previous period's. (If the reports had not been received on time and/or the Committee had not been able to examine them immediately – it was indeed overwhelmed by the number of reports on the child labour Conventions and deferred scrutiny of some country's situation to later sessions – the difference would be much greater.) If the ratifications had occurred in 2001, everything else being equal, the 2000–04 CRG would comprise the 3.6 points from the *adherence* dimension in 2000 and the 5 points from the *implementation* dimension in 2003, which would average 1.7 points – the CRG would be 1.9 points lower than the previous period's average. If the ratifications had been registered in 2003, everything else being equal, the *adherence* dimension would feed the CRG with 3×3.6 points during 2000–02; there would be no *implementation* score during 2004; and the 2000–04 CRG would average 2.2 points, which is a decrease of 1.4 points relative to the previous period's average.

Until the time-lag effects have dissipated, presumably by 2005–09, individual countries' child labour CRGs and, particularly, their *implementation* scores of 2000–04 must be treated with caution. Furthermore, the low number of *observations-cum-satisfaction* in this area, 117.5 out of a total of 3,268.5 in the new indicator system, makes the trendlines of individual countries and regional aggregates subject to change when a few critical comments by the CEACR enter the system. Regional ratios need not be shown in respect of Convention Nos. 138 and 182 at this stage.

To normalize the child labour data, the first-stage maxima[3] are reweighted in the case of *adherence* to 3.6 points up to 1999 and 6.3 afterwards, and in the case of CRGs to 9.5 points up to 1999 and 16.6 afterwards. *Implementation's* values are not affected by reweighting and stay unchanged at 8.6 and 15 points, respectively.

10.2   Global and regional evolution

The long-term trendlines covering at least ten years that can be established for 154 countries were counted and regionalized in percentage terms in Table 10.1 for the area of child labour. More than three quarters of the global CRG trends improved as opposed to about a fifth that worsened, a ratio of 3.6:1, which is twice the overall ratio of Table 7.1.

Table 10.1   Achievement of child labour rights, by region, 1985–2004 (%)

	Worse*	Better**	Unchanged
Global			
CRGs	21	78	1
Adherence gaps	14	77	10
Implementation gaps	71	5	23
Africa			
CRGs	13	87	0
Adherence gaps	11	81	9
Implementation gaps	62	6	32
Asia-Pacific 'favourably inclined'			
CRGs	0	100	0
Adherence gaps	11	89	0
Implementation gaps	56	11	33
Asia-Pacific 'other'			
CRGs	7	93	0
Adherence gaps	7	90	3
Implementation gaps	72	0	28
Caribbean, Canada, US			
CRGs	31	69	0
Adherence gaps	15	77	8
Implementation gaps	69	0	31
Latin America			
CRGs	32	63	5
Adherence gaps	5	74	21
Implementation gaps	79	0	21
Europe			
CRGs	41	59	0
Adherence gaps	27	59	14
Implementation gaps	84	11	5

Annotations same as for Table 7.1.

Of the global *adherence* trendline movements, 77 per cent improved, almost exclusively due to ratification of Conventions, and one in seven worsened because of non-ratification of Convention No. 182 and failure to report to the Committee of Experts or under Declaration auspices.

As regards *implementation*, the relationship between improving and worsening trends is highly negative. This is primarily due to the difficulties of successfully applying the broad Convention No. 138, where countries incurred a number of *observations* but were not gratified much by expressions of *satisfaction* on the part of the CEACR. It is also due to the fact that Convention No. 182 has already entailed a few *observations*, but the positive reactions that governments might have had have not yet entered the *gap* system. Therefore, at the global level merely eight *implementation* trends improve compared with 110 that worsen (a ratio of 0.1:1), though there is a very large number of unchanging lines. Unfortunately, one must expect a string of *direct requests* and *observations* on Convention No. 182 in the future, which would jack up the numbers of worsening trendlines even more but hopefully also be followed subsequently by expressions of *satisfaction*. For the time being, it is clear that the world is not winning the fight against child labour – it is losing it.

10.3   Ranking of countries

Table 4 of the Rights Gap Indicators contains the ranks of countries according to their 2000–04 average CRG score and distributed by category of 'high', 'medium' and 'non-ratifiers'. In the area of child labour, 'high' ratifiers are defined as having adopted both Convention Nos. 138 and 182, and 'medium' ratifiers as having adopted one or the other Convention, by 31 December 2004.

There is no correlation between the average *Core Rights Gaps* of all countries in 1995–99 and 2000–04 (the coefficient is +0.13, for longstanding ratifiers as well), which reflects the enormous number of ratifications of the 'new' child labour Convention that was added to the indicator system at the turn of the century.

General patterns rendered visible by the categorizations and stylistic identifications are particular to the area of child labour. For example, Table 4 contains many CRGs of 0.377 points in 1985–89, 1990–95 and 1995–99. They stem from the non-ratification of Convention No. 138 prior to the existence of Convention No. 182, which inflicts a maximum *adherence gap* of 0.250 points on countries that becomes a *Core Rights Gap* of 0.377 points. Secondly, the States that formed an integral part of the former Soviet Union, Belarus (CRG rank 17 in 2000–04) and Ukraine (rank 96), or were then its satellites, Poland (rank 50) and Bulgaria (rank 75), and which are long-standing ratifiers of Convention No. 138, were not deemed to have an *implementation* problem during 1985–89 and thus have 0 CRG scores. The subsequent regime change, and possibly the poverty that accompanied it initially, made the Committee of Experts point to problems in Belarus during 1990–94

(1 *direct request* and 2 *observations*) and in Ukraine, Poland and Bulgaria during 1995–99 (1 *direct request* each). Of course, there were other countries with 0 CRG scores during the 1980s and 1990s. Examples are Finland (rank 15 in 2000–04), the Netherlands (rank 49) and Uruguay (rank 105).

At the other end of the scale, the largest CRGs are attributed by the new indicator system to Dominica, 0.740 points in 1990–94 (CRG rank 156 in 2000–04) and to Azerbaijan, 0.523 points in 2000–04 (rank 159). Dominica's score is the result of two *direct requests* and four *observations* on Convention No. 138, Azerbaijan's of four *direct requests* and four *observations*.

Distinguishing 'good' from 'medium' and 'poor' performers by application of the standard cut-off points (<25 per cent, 25–50 per cent and >50 per cent of the maximum score) to countries' CRGs in 2000–04 selects 48 countries (30 per cent) as good achievers, 76 countries (48 per cent) as medium achievers and 35 countries (22 per cent) as poor achievers in the area of child labour, which is not an unusual distribution.

As regards the illustration countries, Togo and Ireland figure among the long-standing ratifiers of Convention No. 138 (CRG ranks 41 and 88 in 2000–04). Neither has had a spotless *implementation* record over the years. The Czech Republic (CRG rank 131) has not ratified Convention No. 138; and it must have a real problem in the child labour area because the CEACR addressed a *direct request* and an *observation* to the government on Convention No. 182 in 2004. The other countries' *implementation* scores in 2000–04 are the result of two *direct requests* each in the case of Japan (CRG rank 24) and Barbados (rank 25), three *direct requests* in the case of Jordan (rank 18) and four *direct requests* and three *observations* in the case of Guatemala (rank 148). Uganda has persistent reporting problems, which depress its CRG (rank 70).

10.4 Focus on implementation

10.4.1 Full measurement

The selection of 'good' from 'medium' and 'poor' performers by application of the standard cut-off points (<25 percent, 25–50 per cent and >50 per cent of the maximum score) to countries' *implementation gaps* in 2000–04 assigns 113 countries (71 per cent) to the good achievers, 34 countries (21 per cent) to the medium achievers and 12 countries (8 per cent) to the poor achievers in the area of child labour. There are relatively few worst achievers because of El Salvador's high score of 0.467 points.

A dynamic comparison can be made of the 20 worst *implementers'* performance on the basis Table 10.2, which identifies the direction of changes of short-term trends. The prevailing trend is encapsulated in the continuously rising average scores at the bottom. *Implementation* problems have grown rather than diminished during the system's review period. Three countries had continuously worsening scores, Guatemala, Mauritius and Azerbaijan. None of the worst *implementers* had continuously improving scores.

Table 10.2   The 20 worst child labour implementers in 2000–04 and short-term trends

Country	1985–99	1990–94	1995–99	2000–04	Rank	Country	Changes in gaps		
	1	2	3	4			2/1	3/2	4/3
HONDURAS	0.200	0.133	0.200	0.200	140	*HONDURAS*	Smaller	Larger	Same
MOROCCO	0.000	0.000	0.000	0.200	141	MOROCCO	Same	Same	Larger
IRELAND	0.067	0.067	0.200	0.200	142	*IRELAND*	Same	Larger	Same
LIBYA	0.200	0.067	0.333	0.200	143	*LIBYA*	Smaller	Larger	Smaller
URUGUAY	0.000	0.000	0.333	0.200	144	*URUGUAY*	Same	Larger	Smaller
BOLIVIA	0.000	0.000	0.000	0.233	145	BOLIVIA	Same	Same	Larger
TURKEY	0.000	0.000	0.000	0.233	146	TURKEY	Same	Same	Larger
UKRAINE	0.000	0.000	0.067	0.233	147	*UKRAINE*	Same	Larger	Larger
ANTIGUA & B.	0.200	0.267	0.200	0.267	148	*ANTIGUA & B.*	Larger	Smaller	Larger
KENYA	0.467	0.267	0.400	0.267	149	*KENYA*	Smaller	Larger	Smaller
INDONESIA	0.000	0.000	0.000	0.300	150	INDONESIA	Same	Same	Larger
COSTA RICA	0.067	0.200	0.400	0.300	151	*COSTA RICA*	Larger	Larger	Smaller
GUATEMALA	0.000	0.133	0.267	0.333	152	GUATEMALA	Larger	Larger	Larger
MALAWI	0.000	0.000	0.000	0.333	153	MALAWI	Same	Same	Larger
DOMINICA	0.133	0.733	0.400	0.333	154	*DOMINICA*	Larger	Smaller	Smaller
MAURITIUS	0.000	0.133	0.200	0.333	155	MAURITIUS	Larger	Larger	Larger
UAE	0.000	0.000	0.000	0.367	156	UAE	Same	Same	Larger
AZERBAIJAN	–	0.000	0.200	0.400	157	AZERBAIJAN	–	Larger	Larger
DOMINICAN REP.	0.000	0.000	0.000	0.433	158	DOMINICAN REP.	Same	Same	Larger
EL SALVADOR	0.000	0.000	0.067	0.467	159	EL SALVADOR	Same	Larger	Larger
Average score	0.070	0.100	0.163	0.292	–	Ratio larger/ smaller	1.7:1	5.5:1	2.6:1

– Not applicable. Annotations same as for Table 7.2.

10.4.2 Proxy measurement

The correlation to test whether the child labour *implementation* proxy is a valid shortcut of the full *implementation* dimension provides a coefficient of +0.87 in respect of 2000–04, significant at the 1 per cent level. This is a high degree of correlation, and the proxy can therefore be considered to constitute a valid shortcut to the measurement of *implementation* scores in this area.

The *implementation* proxy that portrays the dominant tendency and which is shown Figure 10.1 includes the global trendline of *observations*, which points steeply in the wrong direction; but it dispenses with the global trendline concerning cases of progress that would be positioned right at the bottom, starting at a value of 0 and ending with a value of 1. The limited number of data entries impacts strongly on the direction and slope of the lines and calls for some prudence in interpreting the results. Still, all *observation* trends unmistakably point in the same – wrong – direction. The achievement of freedom from child labour seems to be regressing rather than progressing, notably in the Americas and Africa.[4]

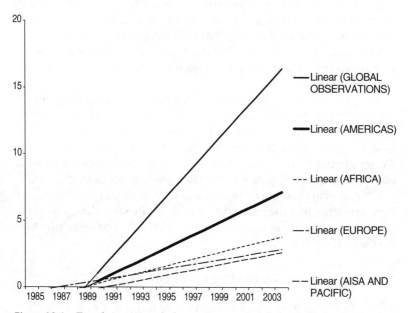

Figure 10.1 Trends in regional observations and global satisfaction in the area of child labour, 1985–2004

The trendlines of cases of progress (data not shown here) do point upward, which is the right direction; but if they were put on the same scale as the *observations* in Figure 10.1, they would constitute an indistinguishably thick line at the bottom because of the few cases involved. The child labour area is reminiscent of the freedom of association area in that critical *observations* by the CEACR are numerous and growing strongly while the figure for cases of progress, although increasing, remains small.

The quantitative comparison of the incidence of *observations* with cases of progress according to the usual time-lagged method is, for once, restricted to a single Convention, that is, the 'old' Convention No. 138 which is at the basis of the battle against child labour – the 'new' Convention No. 182 being in a sense a specification and elaboration of parts of the first international standard in this area. For the whole of the period, one finds 59.5 *observations* and 9.5 cases of progress, a ratio of 6.3:1. During the initial five years the CEACR did not put forward any *observations*; during the final five years the ratio of *observations* to cases of progress was 5.3:1 – small progress towards the ideal of 1:1. It should be noted, however, that the CEACR did not find any reason to express *satisfaction* toward any African country at any time; in the Americas one country was credited with 'half' a case of progress (Costa Rica in 2003); and in the Asia-Pacific region only a single country earned a full expression of *satisfaction* (Israel in 1997).

As regards Convention No. 182 itself, 24 *observations* were addressed to governments since it entered into force. No case of progress has been recorded yet.

If the calculation is repeated for long-standing ratifiers, again only for Convention No. 138, the mere 28 countries that fall into this group have a total of 41 *observations* and 6 expressions of *satisfaction*, a ratio of 6.8:1. During the last five time-lagged years, 16 *observations* and 3 cases of progress occurred, a ratio of 5.3:1, which suggests that one or the other long-standing ratifier has made some progress in this area.

The cross-check of how *direct requests* have evolved (data not shown here) confirms that their trendline points in the same direction as the trendline for *observations*, upward. Thus, there has been no substitution of one by the other.

10.5   Conclusions regarding child labour gaps

Any indicator system will encounter difficulties if a new variable is added in mid-stream. The *gap* system, where Convention No. 182 had to be added to incorporate new developments in human rights, is no exception. The perturbation went more or less unnoticed when overall CRGs, *adherence* and *implementation gaps* were estimated in Chapter 7 because the additional data were dwarfed by the other variables – there is safety in numbers. In the child labour area, however, it manifests itself strongly. *Adherence gaps* and CRGs have been deflated instantly while the time-lag effects on *implementation gaps* are pronounced and will take a few years to work themselves out of the system. Despite these interfering factors, I prefer to keep the child labour Conventions in the system at its gestation stage. Temporary or permanent exclusion would amputate the field of human rights assessment. Empirically, the child labour data usefully demonstrate how the *gap* system performs at low levels of ratification and when a surge of ratification sets in.

In terms of the extent of and changes in the elimination of child labour, the conclusions in this area are much the same as those of the previous areas. While the global CRGs and the *adherence gaps* have declined, the global *implementation gaps* have grown. Although there are slight variations in the achievements of the four regions at this stage, they all seem to face growing *implementation* problems.

Most developing countries have had large numbers of working children on their soil before the onset of trade-driven globalization in the 19th century and before capital-driven globalization engulfed the whole world late in the 20th century. But yesteryear's tilling of the parents' land is quite different from the pressures of today's globalization, which has moved children into hazardous work that is more harmful to growing bodies than to adults' and which is tied into international trading patterns, such as carpet weaving in Egypt or spraying pesticides around banana plantations in Central America. The inverse distribution of labour inspection and forced labour across the economy that was mentioned in the preceding Chapter also holds true for child labour, which means one cannot expect much to happen unless labour inspection is stepped up where it is most needed. This applies particularly to developing countries' brittle inspection systems.

Trafficking of under-age children, within countries and across borders, is facilitated by the technological underpinnings of contemporary globalization; and this has led to the emergence of new pockets of child labour in developed countries. Fortunately, globalization also spreads awareness, and sometimes mobilizes resources, to tackle the problem of children at work that they should not be carrying out. Judging by the *gap* system, however, globalization wins rather than countries' attempts to eliminate child labour.

11
Achievements in the Area of Non-discrimination

11.1 Introduction

The quest for equality among women and men, different races, ethnically, socially, politically or religiously defined groups began in earnest a good century ago in respect of women, extended to different races in many advanced countries during the 1960s and to ethnic groups in the 1970s. Twin brother of democracy, it progressively touched many parts of the world. Is there light at the end of the discrimination tunnel?

By December 2004, the numbers and proportions of ratification of the two non-discrimination Conventions were sufficiently high to cover most countries' *implementation* problems. Of the 159 countries, 148 (93 per cent) had ratified Convention No. 100 and 145 (91 per cent) Convention No. 111.

The time lags between extensive recent ratifications and the detection of *implementation* problems that feed through to CRGs (Chapter 6.1) are notable in the area of non-discrimination despite the previously high level of ratifications. Extensive recent ratifiers number 46 countries with a total of 68 ratifications.

To normalize the non-discrimination data, the first-stage maxima[1] are reweighted in the case of *adherence* to 7.1 points up to 1999 and 6.3 afterwards, and in the case of CRGs to 18.9 points up to 1999 and 16.6 afterwards. *Implementation's* values stay unchanged at 17.1 and 15 points, respectively.

11.2 Global and regional evolution

The long-term trendlines covering at least ten years that can be established for 154 countries were counted and regionalized in percentage terms in Table 11.1 for the area of non-discrimination. In terms of global CRG trends, a little over half improved, 44 per cent worsened, a ratio of 1.2:1, which is a little below the overall ratio of 1.8:1 in Table 7.1 and suggests that this area is afflicted by widespread problems. Regionally, the group of Asian-Pacific countries that I called 'favourably inclined' towards the values of the International Labour Organization does not seem at all favourably inclined towards equality, its ratio of improving to worsening trends is strongly negative at 0.6:1. The Latin American countries' ratio is just as low. Europe also has a

Table 11.1   Achievement of non-discrimination rights, by region, 1985–2004 (%)

	Worse*	Better**	Unchanged
Global			
CRGs	44	52	4
Adherence gaps	16	53	31
Implementation gaps	66	23	11
Africa			
CRGs	43	53	4
Adherence gaps	26	57	17
Implementation gaps	66	21	13
Asia-Pacific 'favourably inclined'			
CRGs	56	33	11
Adherence gaps	11	44	44
Implementation gaps	78	11	11
Asia-Pacific 'other'			
CRGs	24	76	0
Adherence gaps	17	79	3
Implementation gaps	59	14	28
Caribbean, Canada, US			
CRGs	38	54	8
Adherence gaps	8	62	31
Implementation gaps	69	31	0
Latin America			
CRGs	58	37	5
Adherence gaps	11	53	37
Implementation gaps	68	26	5
Europe			
CRGs	54	43	3
Adherence gaps	11	27	62
Implementation gaps	65	32	3

Annotations same as for Table 7.1.

negative ratio (0.8:1), and its poor performance is reflected in the later Figure 11.1. Africa's ratio is just above par; the Caribbean/Canada/US group scores satisfactorily in this area (1.4:1); and the 'other' Asian-Pacific countries have the best ratio of improving to worsening trends (3.1:1). When the Table's two sets of subregions are re-aggregated, the Asian-Pacific region averages out at a ratio of 2.1:1 and the American region at 0.9:1.

Of the global *adherence* trendlines, more than half moved in the right direction and only one in six worsened. The fact that 31 per cent of the *adherence* lines did not change is a reflection of the decades-old high degree of ratification of Convention Nos. 100 and 111 and correct reporting on them.

Implementation, once more, turns out to be the real problem. Only 23 per cent of the global trendlines moved in the right direction, a full two thirds worsened, a negative ratio of 0.4:1. When one looks at regional variations one has to take account of the different starting positions in the mid-1980s, which are approximated by Figure 11.1, where Europe has more *observations* to start with than the other major regions that are at a similar level. In Table 11.1, all regional ratios of improving to worsening lines are negative. The 'favourably inclined' Asian-Pacific group scores worst as far as non-discrimination *implementation* trends are concerned (ratio of 0.1:1) and has the highest proportion of worsening trendlines.[2] The 'other' Asian-Pacific group does not much better (0.2:1), nor does Africa (0.3:1). The two subregions of Latin America and the Caribbean/Canada/US (each 0.4:1) and Europe (0.5:1) are but marginally better *implementers*.

The contrast between the mainly improving *adherence* and the predominantly worsening *implementation* trendlines in the area of non-discrimination would, if graphically portrayed, resemble the scissors movement found in Chapter 7 for all Conventions, principles and rights. The opening between the two parts of the scissors would be quite large.

11.3 Ranking of countries

Table 5 of the Rights Gap Indicators contains the ranks of countries according to their 2000–04 average CRG score and distributed by category of 'high', 'medium' and 'non-ratifiers'. In the area of non-discrimination, 'high' ratifiers are defined as having adopted both Convention Nos. 100 and 111, and 'medium' ratifiers as having adopted one or the other Convention, by 31 December 2004.

The correlation coefficient between the average non-discrimination *Core Rights Gaps* of all countries in 1995–99 and 2000–04 is much lower (+0.25, and +0.30 if long-standing ratifiers are correlated) than for overall CRGs (+0.58 and +0.67, respectively, all significant at 1 per cent), which implies that there have been many changes in the area of non-discrimination in recent years.

The categorizations and stylistic identifications of countries in Table 5 help to detect certain general patterns. Firstly, more of the capitalized extensive recent ratifiers can be found closer to the top than the bottom ranks, which is partly due to the time-lag effects associated with recent ratification. St. Kitts and Nevis, Gambia and Papua New Guinea, at the very top, demonstrate the workings of the time-lag effects and of the resulting ranks. The case of St. Kitts and Nevis may suffice to illustrate this with normalized data. Scored by the new indicator system as from 1997, the country did not ratify the non-discrimination Conventions until 2000. Up to 1999 it incurred 0.250 points on the *adherence* scale that translate into 0.377 points on the CRG scale. In 2000–01 it was not charged with either *adherence* or *implementation* points. The first reports by the government were due in 2002 but not received, which loaded 0.063 reporting points on the *adherence* dimension, equivalent to 0.094 points on the CRG scale. The reports were again requested and not received in 2003. The Committee of Experts was tolerant and waited another year. The report on Convention No. 111 arrived in 2004 and promptly incurred a *direct request*; but the report on Convention No. 100 did not arrive; and the year's CRG score of 0.198 points reflects the 0.031 non-reporting points of the *adherence* dimension and the 0.167 *direct request* points of the *implementation* dimension. Averaged over the five-year period, St. Kitts and Nevis has a CRG of 0.077 points, which is 0.300 points less than its previous average and moves it from rank 137 in 1995–99 to rank 1 in 2000–04, perhaps only temporarily.

Secondly, more of the italicized long-standing ratifiers can be found closer to the bottom rather than the top ranks. For example, among the 20 bottom-ranked high ratifiers, 15 are long-standing ratifiers but only one country (Trinidad and Tobago) is an extensive recent ratifier.

Thirdly, European countries are outscored by a number of non-European countries. Disregarding extensive recent ratifiers, examples are Uzbekistan (2000–04 CRG rank 2), Nicaragua (rank 5) and Lebanon (rank 10) – all countries that have something to prove internationally. Macedonia (rank 6) is the best-placed European country – it also has something to prove internationally – followed by Italy (rank 12) and San Marino (rank 19).

Distinguishing 'good' from 'medium' and 'poor' performers by application of the standard cut-off points (<25 per cent, 25–50 per cent and >50 per cent of the maximum score) to countries' CRGs in 2000–04 puts no more than 22 countries (19 per cent) in the group of good achievers but 75 countries (47 per cent) in the group of medium achievers and, most of all, 62 countries (39 per cent) in the group of poor achievers, a distribution that leans toward the side of poor performers – a signal of deep-seated problems in the area of non-discrimination.

The worst CRGs are attributed by the new indicator system to India (0.641 points in 1990–94, CRG rank 153 in 2000–04), Guinea (0.630 points in 1995–99, CRG rank 156 in 2000–04) and Jamaica (0.621 points in 1990–94, CRG rank 85 in 2000–04). Germany, which in the mid-1980s was the object of a Commission of Inquiry concerned with discrimination on political grounds, had very high CRGs (0.543 points in 1990–94 and still 0.151 points in 2000–04, CRG rank 31) that derived from equal remuneration problems and, principally, discrimination questions associated with the country's unification.

Worsening CRGs afflict countries as different as Sweden (rank 151 in 2000–04, down from 55 in 1995–99) and Bolivia (rank 152, down from 64). The database indicates that, in addition to the countries' spotty reporting record on Convention No. 111, Sweden received *observations* on both Conventions and Bolivia on Convention No. 111, which were formulated during 2000–04, thus pushing up the CRGs of this period.

Among the illustration countries are four long-standing ratifiers of both Conventions: Togo (CRG rank 27 in 2000–04), which has had an almost perfect reporting record in this area but seven *direct requests* addressed to it in 1995–99 and a further three in 2000–04; Barbados (rank 65), which has been the object of an uninterrupted string of *direct requests* on Convention No. 111 and, up to the mid-1990s, of *observations* on both non-discrimination Conventions that ended with a full case of progress in 1998; Jordan (rank 72), which has received a series of *direct requests* on both Conventions throughout the review period and, more recently, three *observations* on Convention No. 111; and Guatemala (rank 157), which has also seen a continuous stream of *direct requests* on both Conventions and recently *observations* as well, one of which entailed a full expression of satisfaction in 1999. Ireland (rank 8) and Japan (rank 143) ratified Convention No. 100 in 1974 and 1967, respectively; Ireland added Convention No. 111 in 1999; but Japan has not yet ratified that core standard. The Czech Republic (rank

158) assumed responsibility for both Conventions upon entry into the International Labour Organization – but has had rising CRGs ever since. The Committee of Experts has never been content with its *implementation* of Convention No. 111 and, more recently, has addressed *observations* to the government on Convention No. 100 as well. Uganda (rank 113) has not ratified either of the two Conventions. Its *adherence* score is just below the maximum of 0.250 points because five of six reports due under the Declaration were received.

The fact that some degree of correlation exists between decreasing *adherence gaps* and increasing *implementation gaps* due to the inter-linkages built into the system can also seen in the area of non-discrimination. For 2000–04, the coefficient is –0.55; but it is of negligible magnitude if only long-standing ratifiers' scores are correlated (–0.12).

11.4   Focus on implementation

11.4.1   Full measurement

Distinguishing 'good' from 'medium' and 'poor' performers by application of the standard cut-off points (<25 per cent, 25–50 per cent and >50 per cent of the maximum score) to countries' *implementation* scores in 2000–04 selects 45 countries (28 per cent) as good achievers, 65 countries (41 per cent) as medium achievers and 49 countries (31 per cent) as poor achievers in the area of non-discrimination. Like the distribution of CRGs, the *implementation* distribution leans toward the side of poor performers.

Table 11.2 enables a dynamic comparison to be made of the 20 worst *implementers'* performance by identifying the direction of change of short-term trend. All but Slovenia and the Czech Republic are long-standing ratifiers, which is a sobering thought if one considers the prospects of extensive recent ratifiers. None of the 20 countries had continuously improving scores, but six had continuously worsening scores: Paraguay, St. Lucia, Morocco, Spain, Guatemala and the Czech Republic. Eleven countries had scores above the level of 0.500 points during one or several periods, compared with only two countries that exceeded the 0.500 points level under freedom of association. The *implementation* picture of the achievement of non-discrimination is very sombre indeed. It is evidently one thing to mandate rights to women, different races, ethnic or other groups and quite another for governments to ensure that they have concrete effects in practice.

Table 11.2 The 20 worst non-discrimination implementers in 2000–04 and short-term trends

Country	1985–99	1990–94	1995–99	2000–04	Rank	Country	Changes in gaps		
	1	2	3	4			2/1	3/2	4/3
Slovenia	–	0.167	0.167	0.433	140	Slovenia	–	Same	Larger
Venezuela	0.133	0.100	0.267	0.433	141	*Venezuela*	Smaller	Larger	Larger
Paraguay	0.200	0.267	0.300	0.433	142	*Paraguay*	Larger	Larger	Larger
Brazil	0.167	0.500	0.400	0.433	143	*Brazil*	Larger	Smaller	Larger
St. Lucia	0.067	0.267	0.367	0.433	144	*St. Lucia*	Larger	Larger	Larger
Finland	0.467	0.267	0.200	0.433	145	*Finland*	Smaller	Smaller	Larger
Greece	0.367	0.233	0.133	0.433	146	*Greece*	Smaller	Smaller	Larger
Iceland	0.167	0.400	0.200	0.433	147	*Iceland*	Larger	Smaller	Larger
Norway	0.300	0.400	0.233	0.467	148	*Norway*	Larger	Smaller	Larger
Dominican Rep.	0.367	0.433	0.200	0.467	149	Dominican Rep.	Larger	Smaller	Larger
Bulgaria	0.167	0.300	0.300	0.500	150	*Bulgaria*	Larger	Same	Larger
Sweden	0.333	0.600	0.233	0.500	151	*Sweden*	Larger	Smaller	Larger
Bolivia	0.133	0.233	0.233	0.500	152	*Bolivia*	Larger	Same	Larger
Morocco	0.233	0.400	0.500	0.533	153	*Morocco*	Larger	Larger	Larger
Guinea	0.500	0.467	0.633	0.533	154	*Guinea*	Smaller	Larger	Smaller
India	0.267	0.667	0.333	0.533	155	*India*	Larger	Smaller	Larger
Spain	0.267	0.367	0.400	0.567	156	*Spain*	Larger	Larger	Larger
Guatemala	0.100	0.233	0.300	0.567	157	*Guatemala*	Larger	Larger	Larger
Sierra Leone	–	–	–	0.583	158	*Sierra Leone*	–	–	–
Czech Rep.	–	0.167	0.367	0.600	159	Czech Rep.	–	Larger	Larger
Average score	0.249	0.340	0.304	0.491	–	Ratio larger/ smaller	3.3:1	1:1	18:1

– Not applicable. Annotations same as for Table 7.2.

11.4.2   Proxy measurement

To test whether the non-discrimination *implementation* proxy is a valid shortcut of the full *implementation* dimension, simple correlations were carried out. The coefficient between the proxy and the corresponding full *implementation* data in 2000–04 comes to +0.86, significant at the 1 per cent level. This is a high degree of correlation, and the proxy can therefore be considered a valid shortcut to the measurement of *implementation* scores.

The *implementation* proxy, which portrays the dominant tendency of individual countries' achievements, is presented in Figure 11.1 in the combination that dispenses with the global number of *observations*, which would appear way above the regional non-discrimination trend-lines and point very strongly in the wrong (upward) direction, and includes instead the global number of cases of progress, which is the line at the bottom that also slopes in the wrong (downward) direction. In the case of non-discrimination, too, the two global trendlines would form a scissors movement. Here, the opening of the scissors would be rather large.

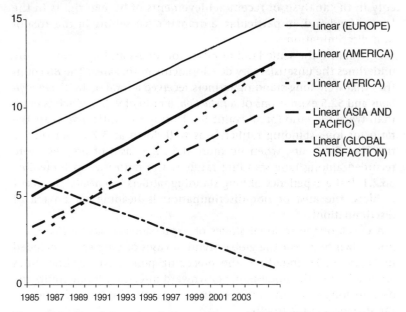

Figure 11.1 Trends in regional observations and global satisfaction in the area of non-discrimination, 1985–2004

As regards the major regions, all four major regions are afflicted by severe *implementation* problems. Europe comes out worst, followed by the Americas, Africa and the Asia-Pacific region. The European and Asian-Pacific data may be biased a little upward through the addition of countries that formed part of them at the end of the review period (10 in Asia-Pacific, 11 in Europe, 2 in Africa and 1 in the Americas). Figure 11.1 suggests that achievements, being the opposite of the *observations-cum satisfaction* lines portrayed in Figure 11.1, plummet more rapidly in Africa than elsewhere.

Changing the approach from visualization to quantification in order to compare the incidence of *observations* with cases of progress, the non-discrimination data are time-lagged in the same way as the overall data in Chapter 7. For the whole period, 580.5 *observations* compare with 61.5 cases of progress, a ratio of 9.4:1. During the initial five years the ratio was a low 3.8:1, during the final five years the ratio of *observations* to cases of progress jumped to 25.7:1. If one compares the two end periods, while the number of *observations* has more than doubled, the number of cases of progress has decreased by two thirds – an instance of the scissors movement found repeatedly in the analysis of recent achievements of human rights in the labour field and, in particular, a dramatic worsening in the area of non-discrimination.

Calculating the same kind of ratios for long-standing ratifiers only underlines the unsatisfactory developments in this area. The 86 countries that were long-standing ratifiers received a total of 483.5 *observations* and 52.5 expressions of *satisfaction*, a ratio of 9.2:1, which is more than twice the ratio for all countries. During the initial five years the ratio for long-standing ratifiers was well down at 3.7:1; but during the final five years, when no more than 2.5 cases of progress were recorded among long-standing ratifiers, the ratio was an incredible 66.2:1. If the experience of long-standing ratifiers is repeated by recent ratifiers, the area of non-discrimination is heading for an era of discrimination!

A check of the regional slopes of expressions of *satisfaction* (data not shown here, but the global trend of cases of progress is included in Figure 11.1) underlines the preceding points. All regional lines are heading in the undesirable downward direction. If one limits the data to long-standing ratifiers, there is practically no difference in the steepness of the trends.

Has the Committee of Experts hardened its attitude and moved deliberately from *direct requests* to *observations*? The indications given for several countries above do not support such a hypothesis, and in the full database the global trendline for *direct requests* points upward (data not shown here) in the same way as the global trendline for *observations* does. The CEACR does not change its yardsticks.

11.5 Correlations?

Very few indicators are designed to measure the achievement of equality of opportunity and treatment in the world of work that can be correlated with CRGs, *adherence* and *implementation gaps*. Remuneration apart, a strong initial handicap of comparability is that all existing indicators are limited to one of the seven contingencies, gender, for which equality should be ensured – the six others are not captured. Even without the additional oddities of time-lag effects on *implementation* and CRG scores, one should be sceptical if there were more than weak-to-modest correlations with other indicators and proxies. To demonstrate the validity of this assumption, I shall re-run the correlations for long-standing ratifiers.

What do the data show? Table 11.3 presents the correlations starting with the CIRI human rights database, which includes a category labelled women's economic rights. This CIRI scale appears homogeneous

Table 11.3 Correlations of countries' non-discrimination gaps with other indicators

	CRGs				CRGs	Adh.	Imp.
	1985–89	1990–94	1995–99	2000–04			
Basic labour or economic rights indicators							
CIRI (avg. 1995–99 or 2000–03)[1]							
Women's economic rights	–	–0.11	–0.19	0.08	0.03	0.04	
Cuyvers and van den Bulcke (1999 or later)[2]							
Formal non-discrimination index	–	–0.25	–0.32	0.06	–0.90	0.45	
Real non-discrimination index	–	0.11	0.00	0.09	0.14	0.02	
Non-discrimination index	–	0.07	–0.15	0.10	–0.24	0.19	
Development proxies							
UNDP (2000)[3]							
Gender-related Development Index	0.04	–0.06	–0.23	0.13	–0.07	0.15	
Gender Empowerment Measure	0.27	0.18	–0.14	0.16	0.02	0.13	

Annotations same as for Table 7.3.
[1] Same as note 2 of Table 7.3.
[2] Same as note 5 of Table 8.4.
[3] UNDP, 2002. 133 and 60 countries, respectively.

compared with the workers' rights scale introduced in Chapter 7.4 and quite close to the International Labour Organization's non-discrimination principles and rights concerning women. What is totally different, however, is CIRI's judgement of 'societal discrimination' based on US State Department *Country Reports on Human Rights Practices* or, where these are silent, Amnesty International *Annual Reports*. CIRI grades countries according to a four-points scale, where three points correspond to a situation where all or nearly all rights are guaranteed by law and the government enforces the law; two points identify countries with some rights for women and where the government tolerates a low level of societal discrimination against them; one point is accorded where women enjoy the same limited rights but where the government tolerates a moderate level of societal discrimination against them; and zero points are given to countries with worse legislation and governmental toleration of a high level of discrimination against women. The interplay of the source material and of the coding decisions, again, gives rise to unexpected scores such as Saudi Arabia scoring 1 in 2000 but 0 during other years, or the average scores of 1.5 points for Myanmar and of 1.75 for both South Africa and Spain during 2000–03. Such data cannot be expected to correlate well with the objectified *gap* data. Indeed, they do not correlate at all. When the correlations are re-run for long-standing ratifiers, the coefficients do not change much.

Cuyvers and van den Bulcke (forthcoming), whose data were introduced in Chapter 8.5, limit the construction of their non-discrimination indexes to gender issues. The 'Formal' index comprises a ratification and a reporting component in respect of the two relevant core Conventions as well as of five other Conventions. It should correlate highly with the adherence *dimension*, which it does. The 'Real' index evaluates, *inter alia*, differences in access to wage employment generally, to certain professions and unequal enrolment at school. It sounds similar to the *implementation* dimension but its construction is uncertain and its scope is broader. Correlations with *gaps* are doubtful. In effect, they are non-existent. The authors' composite Gender non-discrimination index is the sum of the 'Formal' and 'Real' indexes; and as the scope of the two constituent indexes is quite far removed from the scope of the *gap* system, the correlation coefficients with the composite index would be spurious if they were larger than the coefficients with the components themselves. But they are not. When the correlations are re-run for long-standing ratifiers, they are of the same order of magnitude.

UNDP genderized its HDI in the mid-1990s and added a Gender Empowerment Measure to its range of indicators. The Gender-related

Development Index simply adjusts the HDI for grouped inequalities between the two sexes, that is, for the facts that in many countries women live longer, are less enrolled in schools, are more illiterate and have lower non-agricultural wages than men.[3] Again, there is no conceptual link to the achievement of fundamental human rights, though one might anticipate empirically that gender equality is more likely to be high the more educated and knowledgeable a country's female population is. The correlation coefficients are unsurprisingly low, partly because non-gender aspects are not captured by the UNDP. When the correlations are re-run for long-standing ratifiers, they remain at the same level.

UNDP's Gender Empowerment Measure is built on the percentages of parliamentary seats held by women, female legislators/senior officials/managers and female professional/technical workers plus the ratio of female to male earned income. The measure can be criticized conceptually in terms of the rather limited notion of empowerment (see Charmes and Wieringa, 2003). One can also point to empirical facts that show (i) a greatly disproportionate influence of the income indicator on the results (*ibid.*, p. 432), (ii) a non-linear relationship between indicators of gender equity and women's representation in parliament (Anker, 2003), and (iii) a lack of relationship between female legislators/senior officials/managers and countries' development levels (*ibid.*).[4] And the Gender Empowerment Measure can also be criticized for leaving out the fundamental human right to equality without which empowerment would seem difficult and haphazard. It is not astonishing, therefore, that UNDP's Gender Empowerment Measure does not correlate with CRGs, *adherence* or *implementation gaps*. When the correlations are re-run for long-standing ratifiers, they are not significantly different.

The new indicator system not only measures non-discrimination by reference to more than the distinction between men and women and with objective data, but the correlations also confirm once more its unique status and value, which is unmatched by any existing indicator.

11.6   Conclusions regarding non-discrimination gaps

The *gap* system performs credibly at the level of the two core Conventions concerning non-discrimination. There are no other indicators that cover the same area or which could be taken as proxies.

In terms of the extent of and changes in ensuring freedom from non-discrimination, the conclusions in this area are similar to those in the other areas but more negative. While the global *adherence gaps* have declined and the global *implementation gaps* have strongly increased, there are fewer reasonable CRG scores and higher numbers of worst *implementers* in the area of non-discrimination than in other areas, and the problems of the 20 worst implementers listed in Table 11.2 have almost invariably worsened. The global trendline for expressions of *satisfaction*, not surprisingly, points in the wrong direction. The four regions experience quite similar developments.[5]

Freedom from discrimination is clearly in crisis, and the crisis is definitely getting worse – the light at the end of the global discrimination tunnel appears to be receding. Awareness about the moral unacceptability and economic inefficiency of discrimination against women, members of different races, ethnic groups, and so on, has spread widely, thanks in part to modern means of communication. Legislation has been adopted to outlaw old habits and legitimize new orientations. Equality-promotion and monitoring bodies have been set up to move things forward. And yet there is a widespread feeling today among many groups who are the object of discrimination that, after initial strides, the movement forward has lost steam and is in danger of backsliding – most notably in respect of equal pay for work of equal value that is the subject of Convention No. 100 but also in respect of equal access to work and equality of treatment in work covered by Convention No. 111. If non-discrimination is to be achieved in practice it will take more energetic, durable and well-resourced political determination than has been mustered up to now.

12
Typical Country Patterns and Conclusions

12.1 Illustration of typical country patterns across all areas

Looking at the same country area after area may sometimes not enable one to see the forest for the trees. This section, therefore, highlights two of the illustration countries by pulling together their 2000–04 CRGs and *implementation gaps* across the four areas. Barbados and Guatemala are chosen because their data are easy to distinguish, but it could have been any other pair from another region. Although no two countries are alike, Figure 12.1 indicates a pattern that is quite common.

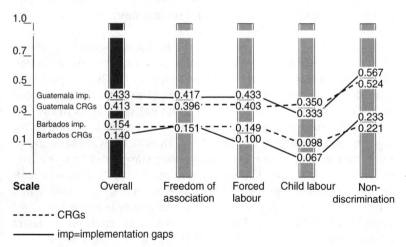

Figure 12.1 Illustration of normalized CRGs and implementation averages: Barbados and Guatemala, 2000–04 (approximate scale)

For most of the countries that have ratified seven or eight core Conventions the normalized *implementation gaps* will generally be larger than the normalized CRGs. Guatemala is a case in point. Two factors combine to that end. First, while non-ratification heavily and continuously charges indicator 1 and CRGs with points, these points disappear with ratification. Occasional and comparatively small non-reporting points may take their place, but they tend to be dwarfed by *implementation* points deriving from *direct requests* or *observations* put forward by the CEACR and from *interim* reports in the case of freedom of association. Second, to normalize the *adherence* dimension, it is first downgraded to one fourth of its 'raw' weight. Thus, when Conventions get ratified one after the other, the whole of the *adherence* dimension contributes less and less to CRG scores and *implementation* starts to dominate the picture. If there were no *adherence* problems at all, the CRG and *implementation gaps* would move in unison.

In countries with reasonably low overall *gaps*, such as Barbados, the scores in the four areas tend to stay in a fairly narrow range. This might reflect prevailing political cultures. But there are many exceptions to this rule, such as Barbados' non-discrimination *implementation gap* of 0.233 points.

Countries with rather sizeable overall *gaps* tend to have a large spread of *gaps* across the four areas because, despite exceptions, they do not necessarily score poorly across all freedoms. One or the other of these may be a relatively small *gap*, Guatemala's child labour *gaps* being an example. Guatemala's non-discrimination *gaps* are very high and pull up the overall figures or average.

The 2000–04 child labour scores, the lowest in Figure 12.1, exemplify the time lag between extensive recent ratification, the detection of *implementation gaps* and their influence on CRGs (Chapter 6.1). Barbados has a small *implementation gap* in this area. Having ratified both Conventions in the year 2000, it did not send either of the first reports that were due in 2002, for which it incurred a small *reporting gap*. The reports arrived one year later, and the CEACR got round to examining them one year later, addressing a *direct request* to the government on each child labour Convention, which sum to a normalized value of 0.067 points. As regards Guatemala, the country had ratified Convention No. 138 in 1991 and proceeded to adopt Convention No. 182 in 2001. The government's first report on the latter Convention was due and received in 2003, but the CEACR commented on it only in 2004 when it had reports on both Conventions before it; and in that year it addressed two *direct requests* as well as two *observations* to the government. This full complement of comments, together with two earlier *direct requests* and an *observation* on Convention No. 138 in the course of 2000–04, account for the large size of Guatemala's CRG and *implementation gap* in the area of child labour.

Freedom of association *gaps* tend to be comparatively high, and the disproportionately large number of *observations-cum-satisfaction* in this area (30 per cent of the total in Barbados's case, 32 per cent in Guatemala's) strongly influences the overall or average score. Forced labour *gaps* and non-discrimination *gaps* are mostly smaller, though Barbados's and Guatemala's non-discrimination *implementation gaps* do not conform to the general pattern. Child labour *gaps* are still somewhat hostage to the low ratification level of Convention No. 138 and the late integration of Convention No. 182 into the system. Future CRGs and *implementation gaps* in this area will probably be higher.

12.2 Conclusions

All human rights indicators must capture two dimensions. One is the commitment to rights in law, the other is the actual effect given to them in practice. The new indicator system constructs the first dimension through a ratification indicator and three related indicators (though one will be operational only after this book has been published). Together they measure what I call, for short, *adherence*. The second dimension is built up through three indicators and assesses the extent to which countries *implement* what they already *adhered* to in principle. In fact, both dimensions scale the opposite, that is, the lack of *adherence* and the failure to *implement*. The two are then combined in a single index, denoted *Core Rights Gaps*, which comprehensively depicts the non-achievement of fundamental human rights in the world of work. Over time, CRGs emancipate themselves from *adherence* and are influenced progressively by *implementation* problems. The new indicator system thus mirrors the shift from the importance of espousing a policy, which is the decisive first step, to giving it practical effect in all respects over an indefinite period of time.

The *gap* system's measurement methods respect the criteria that must be met to ensure a credible conversion of qualitative information into quantitative data – validity, transparency, replicability, non-truncation and, most important of all, objectivity. Utility in the sense of ease and cost-effectiveness of data collection, and relevance in the sense of linking data to policies, should come on top, which is the case for the *gap* system.

Among the innovations introduced by the *gap* system is the fact that the weights of indicators 2–7 are expressed as a proportion of the value of the ratification indicator and that the absolute size of that indicator is in itself of no consequence to the end result. The weights of indicators 2–7, far from being arbitrary, are reasoned and do not have an inordinate impact on measurements. For an individual country, a drastic increase or decrease of one or the other or of all weights might change the perception of where that country's principal problems lie; but one would have to give the *implementation* indicators unreasonably low weights to dilute the evidence presented in this book that, for each pair of core Conventions, it is *implementation* which causes most problems throughout the world. Modifications of the weights of indicators 2–7 might affect the measurement of countries' comparative achievements – ranks – but, again, the changes would have to be drastic to jumble countries' relative positions. The reason for the inherent stability of the *adherence* and *implementation* measurements is the proportional relationship of indicators 2–7 to the value of ratifying a Convention, which has the effect of making countries move pretty much in parallel when the weights are changed slightly. Only when the *Core Rights Gaps* themselves are estimated by the addition of the *adherence* and *implementation* dimensions does the weight of one relative to the other impact significantly on countries' ranks. Here, a question of judgement is involved as to how important *implementation* is relative to *adherence*.

The indicator system elaborated in this book has been introduced with data that reach back for 20 years, a period that should be viewed as its gestation period and which provides historical information. Now that ratifications tend to become exceptional, the fact that they are not necessarily and certainly not instantly followed by up-to-date *implementation* scores and CRGs will work itself out of the system. While one would hope to see future ratifications of core Conventions, by the coming five-year period, 2005–09, one should be able to make comparisons among countries that are not influenced by the effects associated with extensive recent ratifications. The Declaration progress indicator (indicator 4) will kick in during that period, too. When the new indicator system has matured, it will provide up-to-date *implementation* scores and CRGs, and it can then be used to monitor developments for any or all countries and regions at intervals of two years or longer.

But already today, at the system's gestation stage, one can clearly see certain empirical results. They show that, on the one hand, countries have *adhered* increasingly to the values embodied in the core Conventions and the Declaration on Fundamental Principles and Rights at Work of the International Labour Organization. On the other hand, they have encountered growing problems of *implementation*. Today's problems of fundamental human rights in the world of work lie in the effect given to them – or, rather, not given to them. *Implementation* problems tend to get worse as time goes by, notably and most disturbingly on the part of long-standing ratifiers' commitments regarding freedom of association and non-discrimination. In the area of freedom of association, while solutions are found to some problems, large numbers of old problems remain unresolved and new problems emerge to darken the horizon. Problems outpace solutions, widening the gap between them. No other area is afflicted by as many *implementation* problems. This could in small part be due to preferences on the part of workers' organizations to get involved in the reporting process on ratified Conventions, which would have a differential impact on the number of critical *observations* by the CEACR. Their right to comment on governments' reports may lead them to pick up questions of freedom of association more often than questions such as the abolition of child labour. But this is unverifiable at present and certainly does not tell the whole story.

In the area of freedom from forced labour, one finds but a small increase in global *implementation* problems and rays of hope in the American and European regions, where improving trends outweigh worsening trends. In the case of child labour, the measurement of achievements suffers from the insertion of Convention No. 182 into the system at the end of the 20th century, an influence that will wane in the coming years. The relatively low degree of ratification of Convention No. 138 has impaired the detection of *implementation gaps*, though the present indicators show that, where problems are commented upon by the CEACR, they have tended to worsen in all major regions. For freedom from non-discrimination, the conclusions are very negative. This area is characterized by comparatively fewer reasonable CRGs, comparatively higher numbers of worst *implementers*, a strong increase in global *implementation gaps* and almost invariably worsening problems on the part of the worst *implementers* identified in Table 11.2, including on the part of long-standing ratifiers.

In the areas of forced labour, child labour and non-discrimination, broad policies, unspecific legislation and half-hearted measures seem to prevail. They rarely eliminate such deep-seated phenomena effectively. The Committee of Experts is bound to detect that policies are too general, that laws and implementing regulations are deficient in scope and detail, and that the measures do not impact as much or as widely as they should. It has to point this out time and again. The resulting *observations* inflate the trends. The few expressions of *satisfaction* do not counter them much. Furthermore, the CEACR perceives that the weakening labour administration and inspection systems in many developing and transition countries have the effect of undermining governments' capacities to do what their own policies, legislation and measures hold them to do. The Experts would fail in their duty if they did not point out the gap between aspirations and means to deal with them. *Observations* are their most powerful tool to draw public attention to *implementation* problems.

Are there common factors that underlie developments in the various areas? I see elements of the policies and behaviour determining contemporary globalization playing a role. When globalization spread from conservative administrations in the United States and the United Kingdom to other countries as well as to international financial institutions in the mid-1980s, it was defined in opposition to command economies and import-substitution regimes. All sorts of virtues were attributed to an idolized market. Globalization certainly benefited mobile workers with scarce skills and, for example, young women in Export-Processing Zones. But its policy prescriptions posed many problems to ordinary workers in traditional industries, para-statal enterprises or public services. Legislation cut down their entitlements and freedoms at the same time as their jobs were threatened or privatized. Trade unions faced employers determined to impose their reading of the market, especially where privatization had occurred. In the area of freedom of association, globalization is demonstrably at the origin of the rise in *implementation* problems. In the areas of forced labour and child labour, the revolution in communications technology that facilitated globalization's spread across the globe has raised awareness of phenomena that were supposed to have been assigned to the dustbin of history; it has spurred trafficking that incurs forced labour; and it has moved under-age children into export-oriented production. Only the area of non-discrimination appears not to be influenced by the policies and behaviour that promote contemporary globalization in a general way. Here, the worsening *implementation gaps* reflect good intentions gone awry – they have not been followed sufficiently by practical measures.

Human rights in the labour field are in crisis today. There is a yawning gap between the political values that countries embrace publicly and the realities on their soil. The current form of globalization and the policies associated with it have put social and human rights on the back burner. That is dangerous because globalization has so far failed more people than it has benefited, and a backlash is underway. While fundamental human rights in the labour field are not a cure for globalization's ills, and even though their legitimacy does not depend on economic side effects, without them the world is more likely to continue splitting into winners and losers, domestically as well as internationally, which does not augur well for stability. It is urgent, therefore, to reverse current trends by full realization of the values embodied in the human rights this book has dealt with. The *gap* system enables one to follow future developments. It has a purpose and a future.

Appendix   Rights Gaps Indicators

Table 1 Countries' normalized overall Core Rights Gaps since 1985 (averages sorted by 2000–04 order of best to worst performers)[1]

Countries by groups	1985–89 Score	1990–94 Score	1995–99 Score	1995–99 Rank	2000–04 Core Rights Gaps Score	2000–04 Core Rights Gaps Rank	2000–04 Adherence gaps Score	2000–04 Adherence gaps Rank	2000–04 Implementation gaps Score	2000–04 Implementation gaps Rank
124 High ratifiers[2] including 41 extensive recent and 18 long-standing ratifiers										
GAMBIA	0.308	0.308	0.300	126	0.061	1	0.030	78	0.027	8
San Marino	0.182	0.160	0.040	1	0.065	2	0.013	49	0.053	12
Italy	0.171	0.122	0.101	7	0.074	3	0.000	3	0.080	23
ST. KITTS & N.	–	–	0.308	128	0.079	4	0.054	109	0.013	4
SOUTH AFRICA	–	–	0.178	44	0.082	5	0.002	16	0.087	25
Ireland	0.178	0.184	0.157	28	0.092	6	0.005	20	0.093	31
Nicaragua	0.280	0.227	0.148	23	0.098	7	0.000	4	0.107	37
NAMIBIA	0.308	0.308	0.285	111	0.102	8	0.033	83	0.067	19
SEYCHELLES	0.250	0.298	0.255	89	0.106	9	0.006	24	0.107	34
Austria	0.215	0.213	0.169	35	0.111	10	0.005	21	0.113	44
Portugal	0.171	0.142	0.181	47	0.117	11	0.000	6	0.127	52
Hungary	0.179	0.213	0.132	16	0.118	12	0.006	23	0.120	46
Poland	0.225	0.190	0.098	5	0.119	13	0.012	45	0.113	42
Luxembourg	0.093	0.074	0.094	3	0.121	14	0.023	67	0.100	33
Finland	0.141	0.127	0.105	9	0.123	15	0.000	2	0.133	57
Malta	0.172	0.150	0.137	19	0.125	16	0.006	32	0.127	51
KAZAKHSTAN	–	0.308	0.299	124	0.126	17	0.063	125	0.053	11
SWITZERLAND	0.214	0.207	0.148	24	0.129	18	0.000	9	0.140	61
Israel	0.105	0.058	0.084	2	0.130	19	0.036	89	0.093	30
CAMBODIA	–	–	0.253	88	0.133	21	0.058	118	0.067	17
Sweden	0.124	0.206	0.100	6	0.135	22	0.009	36	0.133	55
Togo	0.171	0.185	0.170	36	0.135	23	0.000	10	0.147	72
EQUATORIAL G.	0.241	0.252	0.259	92	0.137	25	0.061	123	0.067	15
Jordan	0.263	0.239	0.189	54	0.138	26	0.027	74	0.113	43
BAHAMAS	0.241	0.243	0.256	91	0.140	27	0.029	77	0.113	39
Benin	0.151	0.184	0.203	59	0.140	28	0.014	51	0.133	59
ZIMBABWE	0.299	0.278	0.214	68	0.141	29	0.020	61	0.127	49
Senegal	0.187	0.206	0.296	122	0.142	30	0.000	8	0.153	78
Romania	0.231	0.278	0.244	77	0.142	31	0.000	7	0.153	76

Table 1 Countries' normalized overall Core Rights Gaps since 1985 (averages sorted by 2000–04 order of best to worst performers)[1] – *continued*

Countries by groups	1985-89	1990-94	1995-99		2000–04					
					Core Rights Gaps		Adherence gaps		Implemen-tation gaps	
	Score	Score	Score	Rank	Score	Rank	Score	Rank	Score	Rank
124 High ratifiers[2] including 41 extensive recent and 18 long-standing ratifiers										
Netherlands	0.213	0.155	0.166	33	0.144	32	0.012	44	0.140	63
PAPUA N. G.	0.327	0.317	0.288	117	0.144	33	0.017	59	0.133	56
SLOVAKIA	–	0.123	0.101	8	0.149	36	0.011	41	0.147	67
Germany	0.239	0.253	0.192	56	0.150	37	0.012	43	0.147	74
ST. VINCENT & G.	0.308	0.308	0.253	87	0.150	38	0.057	116	0.087	24
Guyana	0.179	0.227	0.125	13	0.151	39	0.013	46	0.147	68
Iceland	0.152	0.170	0.124	12	0.152	40	0.003	18	0.160	81
Belgium	0.146	0.134	0.141	21	0.152	41	0.013	50	0.147	73
GRENADA	0.256	0.204	0.176	42	0.152	42	0.074	127	0.067	16
ALBANIA	–	–	–	–	0.153	43	0.016	55	0.144	66
Barbados	0.219	0.214	0.251	85	0.154	45	0.020	62	0.140	64
Lithuania	–	0.220	0.141	22	0.157	46	0.017	58	0.147	69
Mali	0.114	0.168	0.203	60	0.159	47	0.014	53	0.153	75
Lebanon	–	–	0.179	45	0.159	48	0.049	98	0.107	35
Ukraine	0.171	0.135	0.184	51	0.160	49	0.000	11	0.173	91
MOZAMBIQUE	–	–	0.209	64	0.161	50	0.051	104	0.107	36
Croatia	–	0.167	0.207	62	0.162	51	0.006	28	0.167	84
Greece	0.306	0.309	0.136	18	0.162	52	0.006	29	0.167	83
BOTSWANA	0.308	0.308	0.138	20	0.163	53	0.033	80	0.133	54
BURKINA FASO	0.277	0.277	0.226	72	0.168	54	0.006	26	0.173	90
Honduras	0.189	0.211	0.183	49	0.174	56	0.006	30	0.180	99
Argentina	0.213	0.264	0.248	81	0.174	57	0.006	25	0.180	101
Cape Verde	0.269	0.227	0.180	46	0.175	59	0.057	115	0.113	40
Tunisia	0.248	0.227	0.178	43	0.178	61	0.009	37	0.180	97
Norway	0.171	0.134	0.127	14	0.178	62	0.000	5	0.193	108
MALAWI	0.234	0.271	0.213	67	0.180	63	0.006	31	0.187	102
Spain	0.134	0.190	0.176	40	0.180	64	0.006	33	0.187	105
Uruguay	0.192	0.128	0.131	15	0.180	65	0.006	34	0.187	103
Cyprus	0.148	0.179	0.215	69	0.181	67	0.017	57	0.173	92
Russian Fed.	–	0.167	0.134	17	0.183	68	0.019	60	0.173	87
LESOTHO	0.218	0.231	0.192	57	0.183	69	0.029	76	0.160	80
Slovenia	–	0.079	0.118	10	0.185	70	0.020	63	0.173	86
Ivory Coast	0.163	0.234	0.251	86	0.187	71	0.047	96	0.140	65
Yemen	–	0.202	0.250	82	0.188	72	0.013	47	0.187	104
Panama	0.294	0.273	0.267	99	0.188	73	0.003	19	0.200	116

Table 1   Countries' normalized overall Core Rights Gaps since 1985 (averages sorted by 2000–04 order of best to worst performers)[1] – *continued*

Countries by groups	1985-89 Score	1990-94 Score	1995-99 Score	1995-99 Rank	2000-04 Core Rights Gaps Score	Core Rights Gaps Rank	Adherence gaps Score	Adherence gaps Rank	Implementation gaps Score	Implementation gaps Rank
124 High ratifiers[2] including 41 extensive recent and 18 long-standing ratifiers										
CONGO	0.306	0.283	0.286	112	0.191	74	0.050	100	0.140	62
Peru	0.287	0.460	0.317	134	0.191	75	0.025	71	0.173	93
ERITREA	–	0.308	0.300	125	0.192	76	0.036	87	0.160	79
CHILE	0.281	0.260	0.236	75	0.192	77	0.011	38	0.193	107
St. Lucia	0.194	0.221	0.342	142	0.196	78	0.059	121	0.133	60
FIJI	0.285	0.232	0.281	111	0.197	79	0.075	128	0.113	41
UK	0.285	0.313	0.310	130	0.197	80	0.000	12	0.213	123
France	0.126	0.159	0.164	32	0.198	81	0.011	39	0.200	114
Costa Rica	0.129	0.207	0.296	120	0.198	82	0.006	27	0.207	121
Egypt	0.241	0.283	0.225	71	0.199	83	0.012	42	0.200	115
Cuba	0.183	0.295	0.169	34	0.201	85	0.028	75	0.180	98
Belarus	0.134	0.134	0.162	29	0.203	87	0.000	1	0.220	124
Macedonia	–	0.044	0.097	4	0.203	88	0.080	131	0.113	38
Syria	0.247	0.244	0.251	84	0.205	90	0.022	64	0.193	109
Libya	0.302	0.281	0.353	144	0.206	92	0.013	48	0.207	120
Rwanda	0.185	0.233	0.369	149	0.210	93	0.005	22	0.220	126
TANZANIA	0.379	0.389	0.384	151	0.215	94	0.034	88	0.187	106
ZAMBIA	0.244	0.196	0.163	30	0.215	95	0.025	70	0.200	113
COMOROS	0.179	0.197	0.247	80	0.220	98	0.089	136	0.120	47
MAURITIUS	0.279	0.230	0.220	70	0.221	99	0.049	99	0.173	88
Bulgaria	0.135	0.175	0.171	37	0.225	100	0.003	17	0.240	132
Antigua & B.	0.135	0.246	0.182	48	0.227	101	0.059	119	0.167	82
Swaziland	0.205	0.213	0.266	96	0.228	104	0.041	91	0.193	110
Ecuador	0.309	0.320	0.339	141	0.230	106	0.002	14	0.247	136
Gabon	0.250	0.305	0.244	78	0.232	107	0.053	108	0.180	100
Bosnia-Herz.	–	–	0.157	27	0.233	108	0.055	110	0.180	95
Azerbaijan	–	0.097	0.212	66	0.236	111	0.037	90	0.207	118
Ghana	0.322	0.310	0.372	150	0.238	112	0.044	93	0.200	117
BURUNDI	0.346	0.265	0.260	93	0.240	113	0.025	68	0.227	127
SRI LANKA	0.269	0.303	0.299	123	0.241	114	0.026	72	0.227	128
Niger	0.118	0.138	0.176	41	0.243	116	0.017	56	0.240	133
KENYA	0.333	0.280	0.323	135	0.246	118	0.045	95	0.207	119
INDONESIA	0.279	0.309	0.273	102	0.248	119	0.002	15	0.267	142
Morocco	0.250	0.364	0.385	152	0.256	122	0.033	82	0.233	131
MADAGASCAR	0.332	0.323	0.392	153	0.262	125	0.043	92	0.227	129
BELIZE	0.183	0.190	0.266	97	0.263	126	0.023	66	0.253	137

Table 1   Countries' normalized overall Core Rights Gaps since 1985 (averages sorted by 2000–04 order of best to worst performers)[1] – *continued*

Countries by groups	1985–89 Score	1990–94 Score	1995–99 Score	2000–04						
				Core Rights Gaps		Adherence gaps		Implementation gaps	
				Score	Rank	Score	Rank	Score	Rank
124 High ratifiers[2] including 41 extensive recent and 18 long-standing ratifiers									
C. African Rep.	0.443	0.359	0.237	76	0.263	127	0.014	52	0.267	144
NIGERIA	0.296	0.275	0.323	136	0.267	130	0.052	105	0.220	125
Brazil	0.260	0.320	0.353	145	0.268	131	0.033	81	0.247	135
Dominican Rep.	0.377	0.283	0.211	65	0.273	132	0.002	13	0.293	152
Dominica	0.124	0.275	0.175	38	0.277	133	0.025	69	0.267	143
Jamaica	0.375	0.384	0.336	140	0.277	134	0.050	101	0.233	130
Algeria	0.246	0.273	0.296	121	0.278	135	0.016	54	0.280	150
Philippines	0.257	0.292	0.308	129	0.280	136	0.033	84	0.260	141
Kyrgyzstan	–	0.073	0.205	61	0.281	137	0.078	129	0.200	111
ETHIOPIA	0.274	0.288	0.335	140	0.285	139	0.047	97	0.247	134
Denmark	0.215	0.194	0.156	25	0.287	140	0.023	65	0.280	148
Cameroon	0.288	0.296	0.412	156	0.288	141	0.034	86	0.267	146
MAURITANIA	0.336	0.384	0.328	138	0.291	142	0.027	73	0.280	149
Bangladesh	0.362	0.257	0.315	132	0.294	143	0.034	85	0.273	147
Czech Republic	–	0.123	0.189	53	0.294	144	0.044	94	0.260	139
Chad	0.226	0.305	0.358	147	0.296	145	0.051	103	0.253	138
TRINIDAD & T.	0.324	0.323	0.287	115	0.303	147	0.051	102	0.260	140
Paraguay	0.302	0.339	0.366	148	0.319	150	0.059	120	0.267	145
Guinea	0.325	0.240	0.407	155	0.330	151	0.053	107	0.287	151
Venezuela	0.224	0.172	0.288	116	0.332	152	0.030	79	0.320	155
Bolivia	0.209	0.230	0.316	133	0.335	154	0.052	106	0.293	154
TURKEY	0.287	0.250	0.273	103	0.356	156	0.009	35	0.373	158
Pakistan	0.480	0.457	0.418	157	0.385	157	0.058	117	0.340	156
Guatemala	0.255	0.247	0.392	154	0.413	158	0.011	40	0.433	159
21 Medium ratifiers[3] including 6 extensive recent and 8 long-standing ratifiers									
TURKMENISTAN	–	0.308	0.163	31	0.133	20	0.108	141	0.000	1
ESTONIA	–	0.264	0.175	39	0.136	24	0.060	122	0.067	18
Uzbekistan	–	0.132	0.121	11	0.154	44	0.120	148	0.007	3
GuineaBissau	0.247	0.315	0.278	107	0.168	55	0.087	135	0.067	20
New Zealand	0.251	0.273	0.231	73	0.176	60	0.078	130	0.087	28
MALAYSIA	0.302	0.305	0.265	95	0.181	66	0.082	133	0.087	27
Iran	0.367	0.211	0.280	109	0.200	84	0.098	139	0.087	29
Kuwait	0.268	0.258	0.245	79	0.205	89	0.056	114	0.147	70
THAILAND	0.332	0.371	0.277	106	0.218	97	0.113	145	0.087	26
Saudi Arabia	0.195	0.322	0.234	74	0.228	102	0.090	138	0.127	50

Table 1 Countries' normalized overall Core Rights Gaps since 1985 (averages sorted by 2000–04 order of best to worst performers)[1] – *continued*

Countries by groups	1985–89 Score	1990–94 Score	1995–99 Score	1995–99 Rank	2000–04 Core Rights Gaps Score	Core Rights Gaps Rank	Adherence gaps Score	Adherence gaps Rank	Implementation gaps Score	Implementation gaps Rank
21 Medium ratifiers[3] including 6 extensive recent and 8 long-standing ratifiers										
Latvia	–	0.103	0.276	105	0.228	103	0.090	137	0.127	53
EL SALVADOR	0.364	0.381	0.208	63	0.233	109	0.055	112	0.180	96
Mongolia	0.194	0.234	0.188	52	0.234	110	0.100	140	0.120	45
Canada	0.301	0.329	0.326	137	0.243	115	0.082	132	0.153	77
Djibouti	0.211	0.169	0.343	143	0.245	117	0.109	142	0.120	48
UAE	0.280	0.280	0.199	58	0.251	120	0.069	126	0.180	94
Mexico	0.172	0.179	0.189	55	0.252	121	0.055	113	0.200	112
Australia	0.156	0.142	0.184	50	0.264	128	0.055	111	0.213	122
Uganda	0.281	0.253	0.266	98	0.312	148	0.124	150	0.173	85
Japan	0.308	0.258	0.311	131	0.347	155	0.062	124	0.293	153
Sierra Leone	–	–	–	–	0.439	159	0.082	134	0.367	157
14 Low ratifiers[4] including 4 extensive recent and 2 long-standing ratifiers										
KIRIBATI	–	–	–	–	0.144	34	0.117	147	0.000	2
Surinam	0.174	0.153	0.157	26	0.149	35	0.111	144	0.013	5
BAHRAIN	0.296	0.294	0.255	90	0.174	58	0.116	146	0.033	9
China	0.315	0.294	0.271	100	0.202	86	0.149	155	0.020	7
VIETNAM	–	0.308	0.251	83	0.206	91	0.138	153	0.040	10
KOREA, REP.	–	0.319	0.272	101	0.217	96	0.121	149	0.073	21
Singapore	0.320	0.311	0.300	127	0.229	105	0.126	151	0.080	22
US	0.308	0.280	0.278	108	0.257	123	0.164	156	0.060	14
Qatar	0.289	0.294	0.262	94	0.261	124	0.137	152	0.100	32
Oman	–	–	0.290	118	0.266	129	0.171	157	0.060	13
Laos	0.305	0.289	0.275	104	0.285	138	0.217	159	0.020	6
India	0.288	0.480	0.286	113	0.297	146	0.111	143	0.173	89
Sao Tome & P.	0.273	0.241	0.287	114	0.312	149	0.144	154	0.147	71
Myanmar	0.283	0.365	0.357	146	0.334	153	0.171	158	0.133	58

[1] Three groups are distinguished by way of categorizations reflected in subheadings. Italicizing identifies 28 long-standing ratifiers, defined as countries that adhered before 1985 to such core Conventions as were listed as having been ratified by them on 31 December 2004; and capital letters identify 51 extensive recent ratifiers, defined as countries that ratified 3 or more core Conventions between 1 January 1996 and 31 December 2004, which include the UK and the UAE but not the US.

[2] Countries that had ratified 7 or 8 core Conventions by 31 December 2004.

[3] Countries that had ratified 5 or 6 core Conventions by 31 December 2004.

[4] Countries that had ratified 4 or less core Conventions by 31 December 2004.

Table 2 Countries' normalized freedom of association gaps since 1985 (averages sorted by 2000–04 order of best to worst performers)[1]

Countries by groups	1985–89 Score	1990–94 Score	1995–99 Score	Rank	Core Rights Gaps Score	Rank	Adherence gaps Score	Rank	Implementation gaps Score	Rank
128 High ratifiers[2] including 30 extensive recent and 78 long-standing ratifiers										
Ireland	0.021	0.106	0.000	1	0.000	1	0.000	28	0.000	4
SURINAM	0.000	0.000	0.034	6	0.000	2	0.000	52	0.000	13
KIRIBATI	–	–	–	–	0.000	3	0.000	31	0.000	5
San Marino	0.059	0.000	0.000	2	0.010	4	0.013	85	0.000	11
Italy	0.011	0.017	0.017	4	0.016	5	0.000	29	0.017	20
ST. KITTS & NEVIS	–	–	0.211	105	0.030	6	0.038	116	0.000	10
Sweden	0.000	0.118	0.073	17	0.037	7	0.006	71	0.033	29
SOUTH AFRICA	–	–	0.093	19	0.037	8	0.006	69	0.033	28
Israel	0.000	0.000	0.005	3	0.042	9	0.013	82	0.033	26
GAMBIA	0.211	0.211	0.205	82	0.042	10	0.013	81	0.033	23
Hungary	0.101	0.185	0.051	8	0.048	11	0.000	25	0.050	31
France	0.000	0.027	0.056	9	0.048	12	0.000	19	0.050	30
TURKMENISTAN	–	0.211	0.095	23	0.051	13	0.064	128	0.000	15
MALAWI	0.156	0.161	0.106	31	0.063	15	0.000	33	0.067	41
Finland	0.101	0.152	0.135	45	0.063	16	0.000	18	0.067	34
Luxembourg	0.017	0.000	0.039	7	0.073	17	0.013	84	0.067	40
Slovakia	–	0.000	0.056	10	0.075	18	0.014	91	0.067	43
BAHAMAS	0.122	0.116	0.119	42	0.081	19	0.022	101	0.067	32
EQUATORIAL G.	0.211	0.211	0.211	101	0.081	20	0.063	125	0.033	22
St. Lucia	0.144	0.211	0.389	152	0.084	21	0.026	105	0.067	42
Grenada	0.160	0.095	0.109	33	0.088	22	0.031	110	0.067	35
Spain	0.034	0.084	0.067	14	0.095	23	0.000	50	0.100	60
Austria	0.051	0.168	0.101	27	0.095	24	0.000	4	0.100	44
Iceland	0.073	0.089	0.106	30	0.095	25	0.000	26	0.100	51
Greece	0.196	0.280	0.118	39	0.095	26	0.000	21	0.100	50
Togo	0.118	0.185	0.112	35	0.095	27	0.000	55	0.100	61
Belgium	0.067	0.101	0.152	53	0.095	28	0.000	7	0.100	45
Namibia	0.211	0.211	0.168	63	0.095	29	0.000	37	0.100	56
KAZAKHSTAN	–	0.211	0.211	102	0.098	30	0.044	119	0.067	37
Latvia	–	0.009	0.212	106	0.100	31	0.006	66	0.100	52
PAPUA NEW G.	0.278	0.295	0.245	123	0.100	32	0.006	68	0.100	57
Slovenia	–	0.000	0.067	15	0.105	33	0.013	88	0.100	59
ERITREA	–	0.211	0.205	83	0.105	34	0.013	80	0.100	49
Albania	–	–	–	–	0.106	35	0.000	1	0.111	62
Ivory Coast	0.118	0.236	0.207	97	0.111	36	0.020	98	0.100	47
Russian Fed.	–	0.084	0.067	16	0.111	37	0.000	47	0.117	69

Table 2 Countries' normalized freedom of association gaps since 1985 (averages sorted by 2000–04 order of best to worst performers)[1] – *continued*

Countries by groups	1985–89 Score	1990–94 Score	1995–99 Score	2000–04 Rank	Core Rights Gaps Score	Core Rights Gaps Rank	Adherence gaps Score	Adherence gaps Rank	Implementation gaps Score	Implementation gaps Rank
128 High ratifiers[2] including 30 extensive recent and 78 long-standing ratifiers										
Benin	0.039	0.128	0.128	44	0.111	38	0.000	8	0.117	63
Poland	0.286	0.269	0.135	46	0.111	39	0.000	44	0.117	68
Cyprus	0.067	0.084	0.117	37	0.116	40	0.006	65	0.117	66
ST. VINCENT & G.	0.211	0.211	0.166	60	0.120	42	0.031	111	0.100	58
CAPE VERDE	0.200	0.200	0.191	74	0.121	43	0.013	79	0.117	64
CAMBODIA	–	–	0.202	79	0.125	45	0.038	113	0.100	46
Djibouti	0.027	0.100	0.284	132	0.125	46	0.038	118	0.100	48
MOZAMBIQUE	–	–	0.093	20	0.127	47	0.000	36	0.133	77
Dominica	0.077	0.137	0.095	22	0.127	48	0.000	14	0.133	74
Malta	0.152	0.118	0.112	36	0.127	49	0.000	35	0.133	76
Nicaragua	0.393	0.331	0.135	47	0.127	50	0.000	39	0.133	78
SEYCHELLES	0.212	0.278	0.213	107	0.137	52	0.013	86	0.133	79
Comoros	0.067	0.078	0.104	29	0.141	54	0.038	117	0.117	65
Guyana	0.151	0.161	0.101	28	0.143	55	0.000	23	0.150	88
Netherlands	0.240	0.131	0.118	40	0.143	56	0.000	38	0.150	90
Croatia	–	0.253	0.236	117	0.143	57	0.000	12	0.150	84
Mongolia	0.122	0.134	0.061	12	0.146	58	0.045	121	0.117	67
Chad	0.196	0.302	0.219	108	0.147	59	0.025	102	0.133	73
TANZANIA	0.178	0.206	0.276	130	0.148	60	0.006	72	0.150	91
BOTSWANA	0.211	0.211	0.095	24	0.148	61	0.027	106	0.133	71
Azerbaijan	–	0.042	0.185	70	0.152	64	0.013	77	0.150	82
Barbados	0.112	0.089	0.201	75	0.152	65	0.013	78	0.150	83
Gabon	0.207	0.274	0.145	51	0.154	66	0.014	89	0.150	86
Mali	0.034	0.101	0.117	38	0.158	67	0.000	34	0.167	98
Romania	0.140	0.168	0.185	71	0.158	68	0.000	46	0.167	101
Burkina Faso	0.191	0.235	0.206	95	0.158	69	0.000	10	0.167	93
Portugal	0.067	0.152	0.219	109	0.158	70	0.000	45	0.167	100
Antigua & B.	0.095	0.212	0.094	21	0.162	71	0.045	120	0.133	70
Algeria	0.135	0.167	0.161	58	0.163	72	0.006	61	0.167	92
CHILE	0.211	0.211	0.168	67	0.163	73	0.006	64	0.167	95
LIBYA	0.222	0.256	0.251	124	0.169	74	0.013	87	0.167	97
Ghana	0.157	0.257	0.285	134	0.173	83	0.019	93	0.167	96
Lithuania	–	0.140	0.056	11	0.174	84	0.000	32	0.183	103
SWITZERLAND	0.139	0.206	0.152	54	0.174	85	0.000	53	0.183	105
Ukraine	0.101	0.067	0.202	76	0.174	86	0.000	57	0.183	106
ZIMBABWE	0.211	0.211	0.166	61	0.184	92	0.072	129	0.133	106

Table 2   Countries' normalized freedom of association gaps since 1985 (averages sorted by 2000–04 order of best to worst performers)[1] – *continued*

Countries by groups	1985-89 Score	1990-94 Score	1995-99 Score	2000-04 Rank	Core Rights Gaps Score	Core Rights Gaps Rank	Adherence gaps Score	Adherence gaps Rank	Implementation gaps Score	Implementation gaps Rank
128 High ratifiers[2] including 30 extensive recent and 78 long-standing ratifiers										
FIJI	0.251	0.173	0.206	96	0.187	93	0.056	123	0.150	108
Nigeria	0.185	0.140	0.228	116	0.190	96	0.020	99	0.183	104
Uruguay	0.118	0.084	0.022	5	0.190	97	0.000	59	0.200	116
Germany	0.135	0.135	0.168	64	0.190	98	0.000	20	0.200	109
Norway	0.168	0.101	0.168	65	0.190	99	0.000	40	0.200	112
Senegal	0.157	0.135	0.184	69	0.190	100	0.000	49	0.200	113
Dominican Rep.	0.284	0.236	0.202	77	0.190	101	0.000	15	0.200	108
Honduras	0.135	0.275	0.219	110	0.190	102	0.000	24	0.200	110
UK	0.253	0.303	0.253	125	0.190	103	0.000	58	0.200	115
Tunisia	0.118	0.084	0.140	48	0.195	104	0.006	73	0.200	114
CONGO	0.283	0.194	0.224	114	0.204	105	0.038	114	0.183	102
Niger	0.055	0.128	0.161	59	0.205	106	0.019	94	0.200	111
Bulgaria	0.101	0.106	0.123	43	0.206	108	0.000	9	0.217	119
Sri Lanka	0.189	0.173	0.167	62	0.206	109	0.000	51	0.217	121
Syria	0.179	0.235	0.253	126	0.206	110	0.000	54	0.217	122
C. African Rep.	0.273	0.240	0.228	115	0.206	111	0.021	100	0.200	107
Bolivia	0.118	0.202	0.385	151	0.211	112	0.006	62	0.217	118
Lesotho	0.084	0.072	0.089	18	0.216	115	0.013	83	0.217	120
Costa Rica	0.135	0.202	0.333	144	0.222	116	0.000	11	0.233	125
Argentina	0.168	0.219	0.354	148	0.222	117	0.000	2	0.233	123
Sierra Leone	–	–	–	–	0.223	118	0.031	112	0.208	117
Yemen	–	0.213	0.245	122	0.227	119	0.006	74	0.233	131
Czech Republic	–	0.000	0.066	13	0.227	120	0.007	75	0.233	126
Jamaica	0.380	0.323	0.319	142	0.233	124	0.014	90	0.233	125
ZAMBIA	0.227	0.227	0.143	50	0.237	125	0.019	96	0.233	133
Trinidad & T.	0.280	0.324	0.285	133	0.237	126	0.019	95	0.233	130
Rwanda	0.126	0.140	0.336	145	0.238	127	0.000	48	0.250	132
BURUNDI	0.211	0.174	0.147	52	0.243	129	0.006	63	0.250	134
MADAGASCAR	0.217	0.245	0.237	119	0.243	130	0.006	67	0.250	135
Cameroon	0.152	0.285	0.368	149	0.243	131	0.027	107	0.233	124
MAURITANIA	0.261	0.245	0.209	100	0.245	132	0.029	109	0.233	128
Cuba	0.101	0.152	0.118	41	0.253	134	0.000	13	0.267	138
Philippines	0.253	0.269	0.207	98	0.253	135	0.000	43	0.267	142
INDONESIA	0.206	0.313	0.265	129	0.253	136	0.000	27	0.267	140
Panama	0.202	0.302	0.308	139	0.253	137	0.000	41	0.267	141
Sao Tome & P.	0.211	0.095	0.160	57	0.258	138	0.046	122	0.233	129

Table 2   Countries' normalized freedom of association gaps since 1985 (averages sorted by 2000–04 order of best to worst performers)[1] – *continued*

Countries by groups	1985–89 Score	1990–94 Score	1995–99 Score	Rank	2000–04 Core Rights Gaps Score	Rank	Adherence gaps Score	Rank	Implementation gaps Score	Rank
128 High ratifiers[2] including 30 extensive recent and 78 long-standing ratifiers										
Swaziland	0.168	0.219	0.308	140	0.258	140	0.006	70	0.267	143
Belize	0.034	0.083	0.157	56	0.269	141	0.020	97	0.267	137
Egypt	0.152	0.269	0.202	78	0.269	142	0.000	16	0.283	144
Guinea	0.202	0.151	0.289	136	0.273	143	0.025	103	0.267	139
Bosnia-Herz.	–	–	0.109	32	0.284	144	0.058	124	0.250	133
Australia	0.034	0.067	0.219	111	0.301	145	0.000	3	0.317	146
Peru	0.207	0.609	0.455	154	0.301	146	0.000	42	0.317	147
Belarus	0.101	0.067	0.168	66	0.317	147	0.000	6	0.333	149
Bangladesh	0.219	0.219	0.185	72	0.317	148	0.000	5	0.333	148
Macedonia	–	0.000	0.100	25	0.320	149	0.064	127	0.283	145
Denmark	0.174	0.168	0.185	73	0.348	150	0.019	92	0.350	151
Ecuador	0.292	0.320	0.286	135	0.354	151	0.007	76	0.367	152
Kyrgyzstan	–	0.013	0.204	81	0.368	152	0.064	126	0.333	150
Japan	0.269	0.135	0.236	118	0.380	153	0.000	30	0.400	155
Turkey	0.240	0.232	0.308	141	0.380	154	0.000	56	0.400	156
Ethiopia	0.185	0.202	0.403	153	0.386	155	0.027	108	0.383	153
Paraguay	0.354	0.325	0.369	150	0.394	156	0.038	115	0.383	154
Guatemala	0.202	0.280	0.518	156	0.396	157	0.000	22	0.417	157
Pakistan	0.229	0.353	0.303	138	0.416	158	0.025	104	0.417	158
Venezuela	0.291	0.207	0.455	155	0.459	159	0.000	60	0.483	159
17 Medium ratifiers[3] including 1 extensive recent and 14 long-standing ratifiers										
Estonia	–	0.105	0.101	26	0.063	14	0.000	17	0.067	33
Singapore	0.212	0.251	0.237	120	0.118	41	0.109	139	0.033	27
Guinea-Bissau	0.228	0.278	0.156	55	0.123	44	0.116	141	0.033	24
Uzbekistan	–	0.105	0.111	34	0.130	51	0.145	144	0.017	21
NEW ZEALAND	0.227	0.211	0.205	84	0.139	53	0.175	145	0.000	7
Lebanon	–	–	0.209	99	0.150	62	0.109	134	0.067	39
Jordan	0.257	0.206	0.221	112	0.150	63	0.109	132	0.067	36
Mauritius	0.217	0.206	0.170	68	0.182	87	0.109	136	0.100	54
Malaysia	0.206	0.296	0.282	131	0.182	89	0.109	135	0.100	53
Morocco	0.240	0.397	0.344	147	0.182	90	0.109	138	0.100	55
Kuwait	0.240	0.289	0.237	121	0.213	113	0.109	133	0.133	75
Brazil	0.200	0.206	0.338	146	0.213	114	0.109	130	0.133	72
Mexico	0.206	0.257	0.254	127	0.229	121	0.109	137	0.150	89

Table 2 Countries' normalized freedom of association gaps since 1985 (averages sorted by 2000–04 order of best to worst performers)[1] – *continued*

Countries by groups	1985–89 Score	1990–94 Score	1995–99 Score	Rank	2000–04 Core Rights Gaps Score	Rank	Adherence gaps Score	Rank	Implementation gaps Score	Rank
17 Medium ratifiers[3] including 1 extensive recent and 14 long-standing ratifiers										
Uganda	0.189	0.139	0.142	49	0.231	122	0.131	143	0.133	80
Kenya	0.161	0.189	0.204	80	0.232	123	0.113	140	0.150	87
Canada	0.240	0.307	0.322	143	0.245	133	0.109	131	0.167	94
Myanmar	0.206	0.279	0.289	137	0.258	139	0.126	142	0.167	99
14 Non-ratifiers[4]										
Iran	0.211	0.211	0.205	85	0.173	75	0.219	150	0.000	3
Qatar	0.211	0.211	0.205	86	0.173	76	0.219	152	0.000	9
Thailand	0.211	0.211	0.205	88	0.173	77	0.219	153	0.000	14
UAE	0.211	0.211	0.205	87	0.173	78	0.219	154	0.000	16
US	0.211	0.227	0.205	89	0.173	79	0.219	155	0.000	17
Oman	–	–	0.211	103	0.173	80	0.219	151	0.000	8
Bahrain	0.227	0.211	0.205	90	0.173	81	0.219	146	0.000	1
China	0.227	0.261	0.222	113	0.173	82	0.219	147	0.000	2
Saudi Arabia	0.211	0.211	0.205	91	0.178	88	0.225	157	0.000	12
Vietnam	–	0.211	0.205	92	0.183	91	0.231	158	0.000	18
Laos	0.211	0.211	0.211	104	0.188	94	0.238	159	0.000	6
El Salvador	0.261	0.379	0.205	93	0.189	95	0.219	148	0.017	19
India	0.244	0.312	0.205	94	0.205	107	0.219	149	0.033	25
Korea, Rep.	–	0.239	0.256	128	0.242	128	0.225	156	0.067	38

[1] Three groups are distinguished by way of categorizations reflected in subheadings. Italicizing identifies 92 long-standing ratifiers, defined as countries that adhered before 1985 to such freedom of association Conventions as were listed as having been ratified by them on 31 December 2004, and capital letters identify 31 extensive recent ratifiers, defined as countries that ratified one or both of the freedom of association Conventions between 1 January 1996 and 31 December 2004, which do not include the UK, UAE or US.
[2] Countries that had ratified Convention Nos. 87 and 98 by 31 December 2004.
[3] Countries that had ratified either Convention No. 87 or Convention No. 98 by 31 December 2004.
[4] Countries that had ratified neither Convention No. 87 nor Convention No. 98 by 31 December 2004.

Table 3   Countries' normalized forced labour gaps since 1985 (averages sorted by 2000–04 order of best to worst performers)[1]

Countries by groups	1985-89 Score	1990-94 Score	1995-99 Score	2000-04 Rank	Core Rights Gaps Score	Core Rights Gaps Rank	Adherence gaps Score	Adherence gaps Rank	Implementation gaps Score	Implementation gaps Rank
141 High ratifiers[2] including 44 extensive recent and 89 long-standing ratifiers										
Finland	0.000	0.000	0.000	1	0.000	1	0.000	21	0.000	6
Norway	0.060	0.000	0.000	4	0.000	2	0.000	44	0.000	15
Portugal	0.091	0.000	0.000	5	0.000	3	0.000	46	0.000	16
Malta	0.151	0.000	0.019	6	0.000	4	0.000	36	0.000	13
Sweden	0.030	0.030	0.040	12	0.000	5	0.000	55	0.000	19
Costa Rica	0.121	0.189	0.121	30	0.000	6	0.000	12	0.000	4
Honduras	0.391	0.100	0.121	32	0.000	7	0.000	25	0.000	8
KIRIBATI	–	–	–	–	0.024	8	0.016	92	0.000	10
Switzerland	0.060	0.060	0.030	9	0.030	9	0.000	56	0.033	28
Uruguay	0.309	0.258	0.030	10	0.030	10	0.000	63	0.033	29
Israel	0.151	0.030	0.091	22	0.030	11	0.000	28	0.033	24
Cuba	0.453	0.513	0.211	67	0.030	12	0.000	14	0.033	23
Senegal	0.181	0.272	0.511	150	0.030	13	0.000	50	0.033	27
ST. KITTS & NEVIS	–	–	0.377	135	0.038	14	0.025	112	0.000	17
San Marino	0.377	0.377	0.100	24	0.049	15	0.013	88	0.033	26
CAMBODIA	–	–	0.272	90	0.057	16	0.038	123	0.000	2
GAMBIA	0.377	0.377	0.377	128	0.057	17	0.038	126	0.000	7
Iceland	0.181	0.000	0.000	2	0.060	18	0.000	26	0.067	35
Poland	0.242	0.030	0.030	8	0.060	19	0.000	45	0.067	44
Argentina	0.091	0.030	0.060	14	0.060	20	0.000	1	0.067	30
Surinam	0.181	0.091	0.060	15	0.060	21	0.000	54	0.067	46
Venezuela	0.300	0.189	0.070	17	0.060	22	0.000	64	0.067	47
Australia	0.121	0.060	0.091	20	0.060	23	0.000	2	0.067	31
Nicaragua	0.260	0.130	0.091	23	0.060	24	0.000	43	0.067	41
Jordan	0.240	0.168	0.121	33	0.060	25	0.000	30	0.067	36
New Zealand	0.211	0.181	0.140	39	0.060	26	0.000	42	0.067	40
Spain	0.242	0.272	0.242	83	0.060	27	0.000	53	0.067	45
NAMIBIA	0.377	0.377	0.377	132	0.060	28	0.000	40	0.067	39
Panama	0.521	0.242	0.191	63	0.070	29	0.006	65	0.067	42
BOSNIA-HERZ.	–	–	0.236	80	0.077	30	0.051	132	0.000	1
UZBEKISTAN	–	0.189	0.104	25	0.078	31	0.052	133	0.000	21
Guyana	0.089	0.149	0.030	7	0.079	32	0.013	82	0.067	34
Peru	0.523	0.502	0.151	45	0.079	33	0.013	86	0.067	43
Luxembourg	0.060	0.070	0.040	11	0.089	34	0.019	97	0.067	37
Cape Verde	0.298	0.149	0.079	18	0.089	35	0.019	93	0.067	32
ESTONIA	–	0.377	0.136	36	0.091	36	0.000	20	0.100	52

Table 3 Countries' normalized forced labour gaps since 1985 (averages sorted by 2000–04 order of best to worst performers)[1] – *continued*

Countries by groups	1985–89 Score	1990–94 Score	1995–99 Score	2000–04 Rank	Core Rights Gaps Score	Rank	Adherence gaps Score	Rank	Implementation gaps Score	Rank
141 High ratifiers[2] including 44 extensive recent and 89 long-standing ratifiers										
Netherlands	0.242	0.121	0.151	44	0.091	37	0.000	41	0.100	60
Italy	0.317	0.121	0.160	49	0.091	38	0.000	29	0.100	56
Guinea-Bissau	0.200	0.317	0.209	66	0.091	39	0.000	24	0.100	54
Greece	0.553	0.532	0.211	70	0.091	40	0.000	23	0.100	53
Bulgaria	0.249	0.279	0.211	71	0.091	41	0.000	10	0.100	50
Seychelles	0.128	0.217	0.226	76	0.091	42	0.000	51	0.100	62
UKRAINE	0.430	0.249	0.249	86	0.091	43	0.000	61	0.100	64
Ecuador	0.402	0.181	0.302	100	0.091	44	0.000	16	0.100	51
EQUATORIAL G.	0.377	0.377	0.377	126	0.094	45	0.063	135	0.000	5
KAZAKHSTAN	–	0.377	0.377	129	0.094	46	0.063	136	0.000	9
TURKMENISTAN	–	0.377	0.170	54	0.097	47	0.064	137	0.000	20
Tunisia	0.423	0.453	0.351	119	0.100	48	0.006	68	0.100	63
BAHRAIN	0.298	0.319	0.174	55	0.101	49	0.007	72	0.100	48
Iran	0.491	0.121	0.183	60	0.120	50	0.020	104	0.100	55
Mexico	0.049	0.000	0.000	3	0.121	51	0.000	38	0.133	77
Austria	0.181	0.121	0.121	27	0.121	52	0.000	3	0.133	66
Belarus	0.242	0.030	0.121	28	0.121	53	0.000	6	0.133	67
Germany	0.272	0.272	0.121	31	0.121	54	0.000	22	0.133	72
CROATIA	–	0.189	0.136	35	0.121	55	0.000	13	0.133	69
SOUTH AFRICA	–	–	0.151	47	0.121	56	0.000	52	0.133	83
Lithuania	–	0.252	0.170	52	0.121	57	0.000	34	0.133	75
ROMANIA	0.500	0.430	0.174	56	0.121	58	0.000	47	0.133	79
ST. VINCENT & G.	0.377	0.377	0.226	77	0.121	59	0.000	48	0.133	81
ERITREA	–	0.377	0.377	127	0.121	60	0.000	19	0.133	71
MOZAMBIQUE	–	–	0.279	94	0.129	61	0.066	138	0.033	25
SLOVENIA	–	0.189	0.136	37	0.130	62	0.006	67	0.133	82
ZIMBABWE	0.377	0.377	0.226	78	0.130	63	0.006	71	0.133	84
Hungary	0.279	0.181	0.091	21	0.140	64	0.013	83	0.133	74
MALAWI	0.189	0.189	0.151	46	0.140	65	0.013	85	0.133	76
St. Lucia	0.268	0.075	0.155	48	0.140	66	0.033	121	0.100	61
CZECH REPUBLIC	–	0.189	0.147	42	0.141	67	0.013	89	0.133	70
LESOTHO	0.219	0.298	0.249	85	0.142	68	0.034	122	0.100	59
Barbados	0.181	0.189	0.149	43	0.149	69	0.038	128	0.100	49
Grenada	0.247	0.177	0.145	40	0.149	70	0.019	95	0.133	73
Belgium	0.242	0.211	0.121	29	0.151	71	0.000	7	0.167	86
Dominican Rep.	0.540	0.211	0.211	68	0.151	72	0.000	15	0.167	90

Table 3   Countries' normalized forced labour gaps since 1985 (averages sorted by 2000–04 order of best to worst performers)[1] – *continued*

Countries by groups	1985–89 Score	1990–94 Score	1995–99 Score	2000–04 Rank	Core Rights Gaps Score	Rank	Adherence gaps Score	Rank	Implementation gaps Score	Rank
141 High ratifiers[2] including 44 extensive recent and 89 long-standing ratifiers										
El Salvador	0.530	0.389	0.211	69	0.151	73	0.000	18	0.167	92
Egypt	0.332	0.121	0.272	89	0.151	74	0.000	17	0.167	91
RWANDA	0.258	0.379	0.340	116	0.154	75	0.022	109	0.133	80
MACEDONIA	–	0.189	0.208	65	0.162	76	0.107	141	0.000	12
Ireland	0.409	0.321	0.302	101	0.162	77	0.007	75	0.167	94
ETHIOPIA	0.377	0.377	0.340	117	0.169	78	0.072	140	0.067	33
Antigua & B.	0.079	0.168	0.168	51	0.169	79	0.032	118	0.133	65
Libya	0.551	0.440	0.489	147	0.170	80	0.013	84	0.167	96
Gabon	0.362	0.421	0.330	110	0.172	81	0.014	91	0.167	93
Paraguay	0.281	0.432	0.421	141	0.177	82	0.038	127	0.133	78
SLOVAKIA	–	0.189	0.166	50	0.179	83	0.019	99	0.167	98
Zambia	0.391	0.221	0.221	73	0.179	84	0.019	101	0.167	100
CHILE	0.279	0.249	0.221	74	0.181	85	0.020	102	0.167	87
Saudi Arabia	0.091	0.242	0.181	59	0.181	86	0.000	49	0.200	104
Yemen	–	0.040	0.147	41	0.191	87	0.006	70	0.200	106
AZERBAIJAN	–	0.189	0.249	84	0.189	88	0.025	110	0.167	85
Denmark	0.091	0.060	0.070	16	0.199	89	0.032	119	0.167	89
BOTSWANA	0.377	0.377	0.170	53	0.201	90	0.033	120	0.167	88
Lebanon	–	–	0.079	19	0.211	91	0.000	33	0.233	112
BURKINA FASO	0.258	0.289	0.204	64	0.211	92	0.000	11	0.233	109
TOGO	0.249	0.249	0.221	75	0.211	93	0.000	59	0.233	114
Benin	0.200	0.211	0.291	97	0.211	94	0.000	8	0.233	108
INDONESIA	0.349	0.258	0.332	112	0.211	95	0.000	27	0.233	111
Morocco	0.242	0.291	0.381	136	0.211	96	0.000	39	0.233	113
KYRGYZSTAN	–	0.189	0.279	92	0.237	98	0.057	134	0.167	95
Mali	0.091	0.100	0.240	82	0.242	99	0.000	35	0.267	118
INDIA	0.370	0.670	0.400	138	0.252	100	0.007	74	0.267	117
ALBANIA	–	–	–	–	0.264	101	0.042	130	0.222	107
Djibouti	0.328	0.100	0.217	72	0.268	103	0.038	125	0.233	110
Bahamas	0.251	0.268	0.332	111	0.272	104	0.000	4	0.300	120
Fiji	0.209	0.121	0.270	87	0.272	105	0.021	107	0.267	116
RUSSIAN FED.	–	0.264	0.174	57	0.281	106	0.006	66	0.300	125
SRI LANKA	0.249	0.500	0.440	144	0.285	107	0.069	139	0.200	105
Comoros	0.140	0.189	0.349	118	0.289	109	0.031	115	0.267	115
Ghana	0.400	0.260	0.500	149	0.291	110	0.013	81	0.300	124

Table 3 Countries' normalized forced labour gaps since 1985 (averages sorted by 2000–04 order of best to worst performers)[1] – *continued*

Countries by groups	1985–89 Score	1990–94 Score	1995–99 Score	1995–99 Rank	2000–04 Core Rights Gaps Score	Core Rights Gaps Rank	Adherence gaps Score	Adherence gaps Rank	Implementation gaps Score	Implementation gaps Rank
141 High ratifiers[2] including 44 extensive recent and 89 long-standing ratifiers										
Cyprus	0.181	0.130	0.300	99	0.300	111	0.019	94	0.300	123
Ivory Coast	0.140	0.272	0.309	105	0.301	112	0.020	103	0.300	122
Mauritius	0.242	0.181	0.181	58	0.302	113	0.000	37	0.333	133
Kuwait	0.242	0.070	0.191	62	0.302	114	0.000	32	0.333	132
Syria	0.291	0.240	0.281	96	0.302	115	0.000	57	0.333	136
Brazil	0.391	0.362	0.362	120	0.302	116	0.000	9	0.333	128
Bangladesh	0.725	0.181	0.402	139	0.302	117	0.000	5	0.333	127
Swaziland	0.119	0.121	0.130	34	0.309	119	0.045	131	0.267	119
Papua New G.	0.338	0.268	0.230	79	0.332	122	0.020	106	0.333	135
France	0.200	0.432	0.191	61	0.333	123	0.021	108	0.333	130
Burundi	0.543	0.411	0.589	153	0.351	129	0.013	79	0.367	137
CONGO	0.235	0.296	0.371	123	0.358	130	0.038	124	0.333	129
Guinea	0.392	0.130	0.409	140	0.360	131	0.019	96	0.367	138
Thailand	0.481	0.651	0.302	102	0.362	133	0.000	58	0.400	143
UK	0.121	0.181	0.423	142	0.362	134	0.000	62	0.400	146
Kenya	0.543	0.362	0.472	146	0.362	135	0.000	31	0.400	140
UAE	0.258	0.258	0.106	26	0.372	138	0.006	69	0.400	145
Dominica	0.200	0.257	0.140	38	0.381	139	0.013	80	0.400	139
Niger	0.109	0.070	0.049	13	0.382	140	0.013	90	0.400	141
Trinidad & T.	0.411	0.240	0.311	107	0.391	141	0.019	100	0.400	144
TURKEY	0.309	0.258	0.264	88	0.392	142	0.000	60	0.433	149
Nigeria	0.460	0.423	0.319	108	0.403	143	0.027	114	0.400	142
GUATEMALA	0.423	0.249	0.362	121	0.403	144	0.007	73	0.433	147
MAURITANIA	0.509	0.460	0.394	137	0.403	145	0.007	76	0.433	148
Cameroon	0.687	0.321	0.632	154	0.443	147	0.013	87	0.467	150
Jamaica	0.340	0.260	0.281	95	0.452	148	0.020	105	0.467	151
Algeria	0.453	0.279	0.541	151	0.472	151	0.013	78	0.500	152
Tanzania	0.743	0.734	0.672	155	0.524	153	0.007	77	0.567	155
Belize	0.160	0.100	0.372	124	0.542	154	0.039	129	0.533	153
C. African Rep.	0.932	0.691	0.300	98	0.554	155	0.027	113	0.567	154
Pakistan	0.962	0.572	0.691	156	0.572	156	0.019	98	0.600	157
Chad	0.242	0.330	0.553	152	0.581	157	0.025	111	0.600	156
Uganda	0.300	0.270	0.338	113	0.591	158	0.031	117	0.600	158
Sierra Leone	–	–	–	–	0.802	159	0.031	116	0.833	159

Table 3 Countries' normalized forced labour gaps since 1985 (averages sorted by 2000–04 order of best to worst performers)[1] – *continued*

Countries by groups	1985–89 Score	1990–94 Score	1995–99 Score	1995–99 Rank	2000–04 Core Rights Gaps Score	Core Rights Gaps Rank	Adherence gaps Score	Adherence gaps Rank	Implementation gaps Score	Implementation gaps Rank
13 Medium ratifiers[3] including 2 extensive recent and 8 long-standing ratifiers										
Malaysia	0.362	0.211	0.277	91	0.225	97	0.109	143	0.067	38
Latvia	–	0.204	0.319	109	0.265	102	0.116	150	0.100	58
Canada	0.340	0.279	0.340	115	0.286	108	0.109	142	0.133	68
Laos	0.368	0.298	0.238	81	0.304	118	0.142	154	0.100	57
US	0.377	0.226	0.279	93	0.316	120	0.109	147	0.167	99
Philippines	0.309	0.309	0.430	143	0.316	121	0.109	144	0.167	97
QATAR	0.377	0.377	0.302	104	0.346	126	0.109	145	0.200	103
OMAN	–	–	0.302	103	0.351	128	0.113	149	0.200	102
Madagascar	0.530	0.468	0.489	148	0.360	132	0.119	151	0.200	101
Singapore	0.430	0.319	0.309	106	0.437	146	0.109	146	0.300	126
Bolivia	0.377	0.208	0.338	114	0.460	149	0.125	153	0.300	121
Japan	0.249	0.279	0.370	122	0.472	150	0.113	148	0.333	131
Myanmar	0.279	0.500	0.458	145	0.482	152	0.120	152	0.333	134
5 Non-ratifiers[4]										
China	0.377	0.377	0.377	125	0.340	124	0.225	155	0.000	3
Korea, Rep.	–	0.377	0.377	130	0.340	125	0.225	156	0.000	11
Vietnam	–	0.377	0.377	134	0.349	127	0.231	157	0.000	22
Mongolia	0.377	0.377	0.377	131	0.368	136	0.244	158	0.000	14
Sao Tome & P.	0.377	0.377	0.377	133	0.368	137	0.244	159	0.000	18

[1] Three groups are distinguished by way of categorizations reflected in subheadings. Italicizing identifies 97 countries long-standing ratifiers, defined as countries that had adhered before 1985 to such forced labour Conventions as were listed as having been ratified by them on 31 December 2004, and capital letters identify 46 extensive recent ratifiers, defined as countries that ratified one or both of the forced labour Conventions between 1 January 1996 and 31 December 2004, which include the UAE but not the UK or the US.

[2] Countries that had ratified Convention Nos. 29 and 105 by 31 December 2004.

[3] Countries that had ratified either Convention No. 29 or Convention No. 105 by 31 December 2004.

[4] Countries that had ratified neither Convention No. 29 nor Convention No. 105 by 31 December 2004.

Table 4   Countries' normalized child labour gaps since 1985 (averages sorted by 2000–04 order of best to worst performers)[1]

Countries by groups	1985-89 Score	1990-94 Score	1995-99 Score	2000–04 Rank	Core Rights Gaps Score	Rank	Adherence gaps Score	Rank	Implementation gaps Score	Rank
121 High ratifiers[2] including 121 extensive recent and 26 long-standing ratifiers										
SENEGAL	0.377	0.377	0.302	57	0.030	1	0.000	15	0.033	60
SWITZERLAND	0.377	0.377	0.302	58	0.030	2	0.000	16	0.033	63
NAMIBIA	0.377	0.377	0.368	78	0.030	3	0.000	17	0.033	59
SEYCHELLES	0.377	0.377	0.368	79	0.030	4	0.000	18	0.033	61
SOUTH AFRICA	–	–	0.368	80	0.030	5	0.000	19	0.033	62
ZIMBABWE	0.377	0.377	0.368	81	0.030	6	0.000	21	0.033	64
MALAYSIA	0.377	0.377	0.170	27	0.060	7	0.000	12	0.067	86
PORTUGAL	0.377	0.377	0.226	43	0.060	8	0.000	14	0.067	81
UK	0.377	0.377	0.368	77	0.060	9	0.000	20	0.067	73
KUWAIT	0.377	0.377	0.302	61	0.070	10	0.006	28	0.067	84
MALI	0.377	0.377	0.368	88	0.075	11	0.050	84	0.000	22
CHILE	0.377	0.377	0.302	59	0.079	12	0.013	37	0.067	76
GAMBIA	0.377	0.377	0.368	86	0.085	13	0.056	86	0.000	10
CYPRUS	0.377	0.377	0.170	26	0.089	14	0.019	40	0.067	77
FINLAND	0.000	0.060	0.060	3	0.091	15	0.000	2	0.100	103
NORWAY	0.200	0.060	0.060	5	0.091	16	0.000	6	0.100	107
BELARUS	0.000	0.302	0.181	30	0.091	17	0.000	1	0.100	101
JORDAN	0.377	0.377	0.226	42	0.091	18	0.000	13	0.100	99
NICARAGUA	0.121	0.060	0.362	72	0.091	19	0.000	5	0.100	106
C. AFRICAN REP.	0.377	0.377	0.377	123	0.091	20	0.000	22	0.100	95
ECUADOR	0.377	0.377	0.377	124	0.091	21	0.000	23	0.100	96
AUSTRIA	0.377	0.377	0.368	82	0.093	22	0.022	42	0.067	65
MADAGASCAR	0.377	0.377	0.377	126	0.096	23	0.044	74	0.033	47
JAPAN	0.377	0.377	0.368	84	0.098	24	0.025	61	0.067	70
BARBADOS	0.377	0.377	0.377	121	0.098	25	0.025	44	0.067	67
BELIZE	0.377	0.377	0.377	122	0.098	26	0.025	45	0.067	68
PAPUA NEW G.	0.377	0.377	0.377	125	0.098	27	0.025	64	0.067	72
YEMEN	–	0.377	0.377	127	0.098	28	0.025	46	0.067	83
ICELAND	0.377	0.377	0.302	56	0.100	29	0.006	24	0.100	98
PANAMA	0.377	0.377	0.368	90	0.100	30	0.006	29	0.100	112
GERMANY	0.060	0.060	0.060	12	0.101	31	0.047	78	0.033	57
CHINA	0.377	0.377	0.302	64	0.101	32	0.047	81	0.033	56
CONGO	0.377	0.377	0.302	66	0.104	33	0.069	94	0.000	6
BOSNIA-HERZ.	–	–	0.094	19	0.105	34	0.070	96	0.000	2
SAN MARINO	0.377	0.377	0.060	7	0.109	35	0.013	34	0.100	108
HUNGARY	0.377	0.377	0.226	44	0.109	36	0.013	33	0.100	104

Table 4 Countries' normalized child labour gaps since 1985 (averages sorted by 2000–04 order of best to worst performers)[1] – *continued*

Countries by groups	1985–89 Score	1990–94 Score	1995–99 Score	Rank	2000–04 Core Rights Gaps Score	Rank	Adherence gaps Score	Rank	Implementation gaps Score	Rank
121 High ratifiers[2] including 121 extensive recent and 26 long-standing ratifiers										
CAMEROON	0.377	0.377	0.377	132	0.113	37	0.075	100	0.000	3
ALBANIA	–	–	–	–	0.116	38	0.010	31	0.111	113
TANZANIA	0.377	0.377	0.226	45	0.118	39	0.038	72	0.067	82
ITALY	0.200	0.060	0.060	4	0.121	40	0.000	3	0.133	119
TOGO	0.181	0.060	0.181	31	0.121	41	0.000	9	0.133	122
ROMANIA	0.060	0.181	0.362	73	0.121	42	0.000	7	0.133	124
BURUNDI	0.377	0.377	0.377	130	0.125	43	0.063	89	0.033	40
LESOTHO	0.377	0.377	0.377	129	0.126	44	0.044	76	0.067	71
GREECE	0.155	0.140	0.060	6	0.128	45	0.025	50	0.100	97
SPAIN	0.060	0.121	0.060	10	0.128	46	0.025	54	0.100	110
SWEDEN	0.377	0.140	0.060	11	0.128	47	0.025	55	0.100	111
MALTA	0.226	0.121	0.242	51	0.128	48	0.025	53	0.100	105
NETHERLANDS	0.000	0.000	0.060	14	0.131	49	0.047	79	0.067	88
POLAND	0.000	0.000	0.060	15	0.131	50	0.047	80	0.067	87
EGYPT	0.377	0.377	0.302	65	0.131	51	0.047	82	0.067	78
SLOVAKIA	–	0.377	0.151	25	0.132	52	0.007	30	0.133	126
PERU	0.377	0.377	0.368	93	0.132	53	0.088	102	0.000	28
MACEDONIA	–	0.000	0.000	1	0.133	54	0.088	104	0.000	21
MONGOLIA	0.377	0.377	0.377	131	0.134	55	0.069	95	0.033	48
BAHAMAS	0.377	0.377	0.368	85	0.136	56	0.050	83	0.067	66
KOREA, REP.	–	0.377	0.302	62	0.138	57	0.031	67	0.100	100
TUNISIA	0.377	0.377	0.060	13	0.140	58	0.013	35	0.133	123
BELGIUM	0.226	0.121	0.181	32	0.141	59	0.053	85	0.067	74
VIETNAM	–	0.377	0.368	91	0.143	60	0.075	99	0.033	55
BENIN	0.377	0.377	0.377	128	0.145	61	0.056	88	0.067	69
SLOVENIA	–	0.000	0.181	33	0.147	62	0.038	71	0.100	109
DENMARK	0.377	0.377	0.151	24	0.149	63	0.019	39	0.133	117
RWANDA	0.121	0.121	0.242	52	0.151	64	0.000	8	0.167	136
NIGERIA	0.377	0.377	0.368	95	0.151	65	0.100	106	0.000	25
SWAZILAND	0.377	0.377	0.377	134	0.151	66	0.100	105	0.000	33
BOTSWANA	0.377	0.377	0.170	28	0.158	67	0.045	77	0.100	94
CROATIA	–	0.000	0.060	9	0.158	68	0.025	48	0.133	116
SRI LANKA	0.377	0.377	0.368	89	0.158	69	0.025	62	0.133	115
UGANDA	0.377	0.377	0.368	96	0.160	70	0.106	109	0.000	37
LEBANON	–	–	0.368	92	0.162	71	0.088	101	0.033	46
SYRIA	0.377	0.377	0.368	94	0.162	72	0.088	103	0.033	54

Table 4 Countries' normalized child labour gaps since 1985 (averages sorted by 2000–04 order of best to worst performers)[1] – *continued*

Countries by groups	1985–89 Score	1990–94 Score	1995–99 Score	2000–04 Rank	Core Rights Gaps Score	Core Rights Gaps Rank	Adherence gaps Score	Adherence gaps Rank	Implementation gaps Score	Implementation gaps Rank
121 High ratifiers[2] including 121 extensive recent and 26 long-standing ratifiers										
LITHUANIA	–	0.377	0.226	49	0.164	73	0.069	93	0.067	85
LUXEMBOURG	0.060	0.060	0.121	21	0.168	74	0.031	66	0.133	121
BULGARIA	0.000	0.000	0.060	8	0.170	75	0.013	32	0.167	133
NIGER	0.181	0.121	0.317	71	0.170	76	0.013	36	0.167	131
ETHIOPIA	0.377	0.377	0.302	67	0.174	77	0.075	98	0.067	80
THAILAND	0.377	0.377	0.368	100	0.175	78	0.116	115	0.000	34
GUYANA	0.377	0.377	0.226	46	0.177	79	0.038	70	0.133	118
KAZAKHSTAN	–	0.377	0.377	135	0.181	80	0.100	107	0.033	45
MAURITANIA	0.377	0.377	0.368	87	0.187	81	0.044	75	0.133	114
ARGENTINA	0.377	0.377	0.075	18	0.189	82	0.025	57	0.167	129
PHILIPPINES	0.377	0.377	0.226	47	0.189	83	0.025	58	0.167	132
BURKINA FASO	0.377	0.377	0.302	60	0.189	84	0.025	60	0.167	128
FIJI	0.377	0.377	0.377	137	0.189	85	0.125	122	0.000	9
FRANCE	0.377	0.079	0.423	156	0.189	86	0.025	49	0.167	135
IRELAND	0.060	0.060	0.181	35	0.191	88	0.006	25	0.200	142
MOZAMBIQUE	–	–	0.368	98	0.198	89	0.131	124	0.000	23
PARAGUAY	0.377	0.377	0.377	138	0.198	90	0.131	123	0.000	27
KYRGYZSTAN	–	0.000	0.038	2	0.199	91	0.132	129	0.000	18
LIBYA	0.200	0.060	0.377	120	0.209	94	0.019	41	0.200	143
UKRAINE	0.000	0.000	0.060	16	0.211	96	0.000	10	0.233	147
BRAZIL	0.377	0.377	0.368	83	0.214	98	0.022	43	0.200	138
ZAMBIA	0.121	0.060	0.181	36	0.217	100	0.044	73	0.167	137
IVORY COAST	0.377	0.377	0.377	142	0.217	101	0.144	137	0.000	7
GUINEA	0.377	0.377	0.377	143	0.217	102	0.144	138	0.000	12
JAMAICA	0.377	0.377	0.377	144	0.217	103	0.144	139	0.000	16
HONDURAS	0.200	0.121	0.181	34	0.219	104	0.025	51	0.200	140
URUGUAY	0.000	0.000	0.302	55	0.219	105	0.025	56	0.200	144
MOROCCO	0.377	0.377	0.377	133	0.219	106	0.025	63	0.200	141
RUSSIAN FED.	–	0.000	0.242	54	0.225	108	0.069	92	0.133	125
GRENADA	0.377	0.377	0.377	147	0.226	109	0.150	141	0.000	11
ALGERIA	0.181	0.140	0.121	20	0.228	110	0.031	65	0.200	139
TRINIDAD & T.	0.377	0.377	0.368	111	0.231	114	0.153	142	0.000	35
SAUDI ARABIA	0.377	0.377	0.368	105	0.233	116	0.134	131	0.033	52
EQUATORIAL G.	0.121	0.060	0.121	22	0.247	120	0.063	90	0.167	134
TURKEY	0.377	0.377	0.226	48	0.249	121	0.025	59	0.233	146
KENYA	0.441	0.242	0.362	75	0.279	125	0.025	52	0.267	149

Table 4 Countries' normalized child labour gaps since 1985 (averages sorted by 2000–04 order of best to worst performers)[1] – *continued*

Countries by groups	1985–89 Score	1990–94 Score	1995–99 Score	Rank	2000–04 Core Rights Gaps Score	Rank	Adherence gaps Score	Rank	Implementation gaps Score	Rank
121 High ratifiers[2] including 121 extensive recent and 26 long-standing ratifiers										
INDONESIA	0.377	0.377	0.302	63	0.281	126	0.006	27	0.300	150
COMOROS	0.377	0.377	0.377	149	0.283	127	0.188	146	0.000	5
MAURITIUS	0.377	0.121	0.181	38	0.302	134	0.000	4	0.333	155
COSTA RICA	0.060	0.200	0.362	74	0.309	135	0.025	47	0.300	151
BOLIVIA	0.377	0.377	0.170	29	0.320	137	0.072	97	0.233	145
MALAWI	0.377	0.377	0.302	68	0.321	138	0.013	38	0.333	153
ANTIGUA & B.	0.200	0.279	0.219	41	0.345	145	0.069	91	0.267	148
GUATEMALA	0.377	0.140	0.242	53	0.350	148	0.032	68	0.333	152
UAE	0.377	0.377	0.226	50	0.381	155	0.032	69	0.367	156
DOMINICA	0.177	0.740	0.362	76	0.388	156	0.057	87	0.333	154
DOMINICAN REP.	0.377	0.377	0.302	70	0.402	157	0.006	26	0.433	158
EL SALVADOR	0.377	0.377	0.136	23	0.423	158	0.000	11	0.467	159
AZERBAIJAN	–	0.000	0.181	40	0.523	159	0.106	108	0.400	157
25 Medium ratifiers[3] including 22 extensive recent and 2 long-standing ratifiers										
CANADA	0.377	0.377	0.368	97	0.195	87	0.109	110	0.033	41
ST. LUCIA	0.377	0.377	0.377	140	0.208	92	0.138	132	0.000	29
Israel	0.242	0.060	0.060	17	0.209	93	0.119	117	0.033	58
GHANA	0.377	0.377	0.377	136	0.209	95	0.119	116	0.033	44
CHAD	0.377	0.377	0.377	141	0.212	97	0.141	135	0.000	4
ST. KITTS & NEVIS	–	–	0.377	155	0.214	99	0.122	120	0.033	50
PAKISTAN	0.377	0.377	0.377	145	0.222	107	0.147	140	0.000	26
BAHRAIN	0.377	0.377	0.368	101	0.228	111	0.131	125	0.033	39
ESTONIA	–	0.377	0.368	102	0.228	112	0.131	126	0.033	43
SINGAPORE	0.377	0.377	0.368	103	0.228	113	0.131	127	0.033	53
IRAN	0.377	0.377	0.368	112	0.231	115	0.153	143	0.000	15
NEW ZEALAND	0.377	0.377	0.368	107	0.238	117	0.138	134	0.033	49
ERITREA	–	0.377	0.368	108	0.240	118	0.119	119	0.067	79
ST. VINCENT & G.	0.377	0.377	0.377	146	0.242	119	0.141	136	0.033	51
CAMBODIA	–	–	0.302	69	0.249	122	0.125	121	0.067	75
QATAR	0.377	0.377	0.368	99	0.256	123	0.109	112	0.100	93
Cuba	0.060	0.060	0.181	37	0.260	124	0.113	114	0.100	102
US	0.377	0.377	0.368	110	0.286	128	0.109	113	0.133	120
OMAN	–	–	0.377	139	0.289	129	0.131	128	0.100	92
BANGLADESH	0.377	0.377	0.368	104	0.293	130	0.134	130	0.100	89

Table 4 Countries' normalized child labour gaps since 1985 (averages sorted by 2000–04 order of best to worst performers)[1] – *continued*

Countries by groups	1985-89 Score	1990-94 Score	1995-99 Score	2000-04 Rank	Core Rights Gaps Score	Core Rights Gaps Rank	Adherence gaps Score	Adherence gaps Rank	Implementation gaps Score	Implementation gaps Rank
25 Medium ratifiers[3] including 22 extensive recent and 2 long-standing ratifiers										
CZECH REPUBLIC	–	0.377	0.368	106	0.298	131	0.138	133	0.100	90
CAPE VERDE	0.377	0.377	0.368	113	0.299	132	0.178	145	0.033	42
Venezuela	0.019	0.140	0.181	39	0.300	133	0.119	118	0.133	127
MEXICO	0.377	0.377	0.368	109	0.316	136	0.109	111	0.167	130
GABON	0.377	0.377	0.377	148	0.336	143	0.163	144	0.100	91
13 Non-ratifiers[4]										
Australia	0.377	0.377	0.368	114	0.330	139	0.219	147	0.000	1
India	0.377	0.377	0.368	115	0.330	140	0.219	148	0.000	14
Myanmar	0.377	0.377	0.368	116	0.330	141	0.219	149	0.000	24
Surinam	0.377	0.377	0.368	117	0.330	142	0.219	150	0.000	32
Kiribati	–	–	–	–	0.342	144	0.227	151	0.000	17
Guinea-Bissau	0.377	0.377	0.368	118	0.349	146	0.231	152	0.000	13
Latvia	–	0.377	0.368	119	0.349	147	0.231	153	0.000	20
Djibouti	0.377	0.377	0.377	150	0.358	149	0.238	154	0.000	8
Uzbekistan	–	0.377	0.377	153	0.358	150	0.238	155	0.000	38
Sierra Leone	–	–	–	–	0.362	151	0.240	156	0.000	31
Sao Tome & P.	0.377	0.377	0.377	151	0.368	152	0.244	157	0.000	30
Turkmenistan	–	0.377	0.377	152	0.368	153	0.244	158	0.000	36
Laos	0.377	0.377	0.377	154	0.368	154	0.244	159	0.000	19

[1] Three groups are distinguished by way of categorizations reflected in subheadings. Italicizing identifies 28 long-standing ratifiers, defined as countries that had adhered before 1985 to such forced labour Conventions as were listed as having been ratified by them on 31 December 2004 and capital letters identify 143 extensive recent ratifiers, defined as countries that ratified one or both of the child labour Conventions between 1 January 1996 and 31 December 2004, which include the UK, UAE and US.

[2] Countries that had ratified Convention Nos. 138 and 182 by 31 December 2004.

[3] Countries that had ratified either Convention No. 138 or Convention No. 182 by 31 December 2004.

[4] Countries that had ratified neither Convention No. 138 nor Convention No. 182 by 31 December 2004.

Table 5   Countries' normalized non-discrimination gaps since 1985 (averages sorted by 2000–04 order of best to worst performers)[1]

Countries by groups	1985–89 Score	1990–94 Score	1995–99 Score	Rank	Core Rights Gaps Score	Rank	Adherence gaps Score	Rank	Implementation gaps Score	Rank
141 High ratifiers[2] including 40 extensive recent and 82 long-standing ratifiers										
ST. KITTS & NEVIS	–	–	0.377	137	0.077	1	0.031	114	0.033	17
Uzbekistan	–	0.000	0.028	2	0.078	2	0.052	128	0.000	15
GAMBIA	0.377	0.377	0.368	117	0.079	3	0.013	89	0.067	21
PAPUA NEW G.	0.377	0.377	0.377	135	0.089	4	0.019	97	0.067	23
Nicaragua	0.179	0.221	0.121	8	0.091	5	0.000	40	0.100	35
Macedonia	–	0.000	0.028	1	0.097	6	0.064	133	0.000	5
TURKMENISTAN	–	0.377	0.170	23	0.097	7	0.064	134	0.000	12
IRELAND	0.289	0.249	0.281	85	0.100	8	0.006	70	0.100	34
CAMBODIA	–	–	0.302	95	0.108	9	0.031	115	0.067	25
Lebanon	–	–	0.130	11	0.121	10	0.000	32	0.133	45
Benin	0.191	0.160	0.160	18	0.121	11	0.000	7	0.133	42
Italy	0.300	0.342	0.211	43	0.121	12	0.000	30	0.133	39
Burkina Faso	0.402	0.291	0.245	63	0.121	13	0.000	10	0.133	38
BAHAMAS	0.377	0.377	0.368	114	0.126	14	0.044	122	0.067	20
KOREA, REP.	–	0.377	0.189	32	0.130	15	0.006	71	0.133	44
CONGO	0.415	0.396	0.321	99	0.132	16	0.088	135	0.000	1
MAURITIUS	0.377	0.377	0.368	119	0.132	17	0.088	136	0.000	6
KENYA	0.377	0.377	0.368	118	0.136	18	0.050	127	0.067	22
San Marino	0.108	0.121	0.040	3	0.140	19	0.013	79	0.133	40
BELIZE	0.377	0.377	0.302	94	0.140	20	0.013	86	0.133	41
SEYCHELLES	0.377	0.377	0.302	96	0.140	21	0.013	80	0.133	36
TANZANIA	0.377	0.377	0.368	124	0.142	22	0.094	138	0.000	11
ST. VINCENT & G.	0.377	0.377	0.377	136	0.145	23	0.056	129	0.067	24
Ukraine	0.121	0.211	0.151	15	0.151	24	0.000	57	0.167	56
Syria	0.260	0.200	0.160	19	0.151	25	0.000	55	0.167	63
Peru	0.151	0.191	0.211	40	0.151	26	0.000	43	0.167	61
Togo	0.181	0.181	0.217	47	0.151	27	0.000	56	0.167	49
Lithuania	–	0.252	0.221	48	0.151	28	0.000	33	0.167	47
Austria	0.462	0.302	0.242	59	0.151	29	0.000	3	0.167	57
Romania	0.211	0.372	0.362	110	0.151	30	0.000	47	0.167	62
Germany	0.483	0.543	0.372	129	0.151	31	0.000	21	0.167	60
FIJI	0.377	0.377	0.377	132	0.151	32	0.100	141	0.000	2
Guinea-Bissau	0.260	0.347	0.519	153	0.151	33	0.000	23	0.167	52
UAE	0.377	0.377	0.264	70	0.154	34	0.022	101	0.133	37
KAZAKHSTAN	–	0.377	0.340	105	0.157	35	0.044	121	0.100	31
Azerbaijan	–	0.151	0.242	60	0.160	36	0.006	64	0.167	58

Table 5 Countries' normalized non-discrimination gaps since 1985 (averages sorted by 2000–04 order of best to worst performers)[1] – *continued*

Countries by groups	1985-89 Score	1990-94 Score	1995-99 Score	Rank	2000–04 Core Rights Gaps Score	Rank	Adherence gaps Score	Rank	Implementation gaps Score	Rank
141 High ratifiers[2] including 40 extensive recent and 82 long-standing ratifiers									
Mali	0.151	0.251	0.240	57	0.162	37	0.007	77	0.167	54
ALBANIA	–	–	–	–	0.167	38	0.010	78	0.167	46
BOTSWANA	0.377	0.377	0.170	22	0.171	39	0.033	119	0.133	43
VIETNAM	–	0.377	0.151	16	0.171	40	0.013	93	0.167	50
Swaziland	0.270	0.211	0.270	74	0.171	41	0.013	92	0.167	55
EQUATORIAL G.	0.219	0.298	0.287	88	0.177	42	0.057	130	0.100	30
Poland	0.211	0.302	0.121	9	0.181	43	0.000	45	0.200	73
Russian Fed.	–	0.302	0.160	17	0.181	44	0.000	48	0.200	75
Belarus	0.151	0.272	0.181	25	0.181	45	0.000	5	0.200	70
Egypt	0.242	0.423	0.181	28	0.181	46	0.000	17	0.200	65
ZIMBABWE	0.340	0.249	0.211	46	0.181	47	0.000	61	0.200	69
SOUTH AFRICA	–	–	0.264	69	0.181	48	0.000	52	0.200	64
UK	0.460	0.430	0.272	81	0.181	49	0.000	58	0.200	76
Argentina	0.332	0.523	0.332	101	0.181	50	0.000	1	0.200	71
Ivory Coast	0.160	0.121	0.209	39	0.191	51	0.006	68	0.200	72
LUXEMBOURG	0.279	0.219	0.224	50	0.198	53	0.031	116	0.167	48
Yemen	–	0.258	0.298	89	0.200	54	0.013	84	0.200	67
GRENADA	0.377	0.340	0.226	52	0.208	56	0.098	139	0.067	26
Zambia	0.191	0.181	0.130	14	0.209	57	0.019	96	0.200	68
Cuba	0.121	0.453	0.211	41	0.211	58	0.000	14	0.233	82
Guyana	0.221	0.349	0.211	42	0.211	59	0.000	24	0.233	84
EL SALVADOR	0.377	0.377	0.249	65	0.211	60	0.000	18	0.233	83
Portugal	0.332	0.151	0.272	79	0.211	61	0.000	46	0.233	88
Netherlands	0.242	0.311	0.311	98	0.211	62	0.000	38	0.233	86
LESOTHO	0.377	0.377	0.226	53	0.220	63	0.026	106	0.200	66
Mozambique	–	–	0.272	80	0.221	64	0.006	63	0.233	79
Barbados	0.372	0.381	0.381	138	0.221	65	0.006	65	0.233	81
Burundi	0.377	0.226	0.075	4	0.240	71	0.019	95	0.233	77
Jordan	0.240	0.300	0.181	27	0.242	72	0.000	31	0.267	102
Switzerland	0.423	0.272	0.181	31	0.242	73	0.000	54	0.267	97
INDONESIA	0.289	0.319	0.211	45	0.242	74	0.000	28	0.267	101
Malta	0.204	0.362	0.240	58	0.242	75	0.000	35	0.267	87
Hungary	0.121	0.211	0.272	77	0.242	76	0.000	26	0.267	92
Canada	0.332	0.392	0.302	91	0.242	77	0.000	11	0.267	99
Croatia	–	0.075	0.302	92	0.242	78	0.000	13	0.267	100
COMOROS	0.319	0.328	0.338	104	0.242	79	0.100	140	0.100	32

Table 5   Countries' normalized non-discrimination gaps since 1985 (averages sorted by 2000–04 order of best to worst performers)[1] – *continued*

Countries by groups	1985-89 Score	1990-94 Score	1995-99 Score	Rank	Core Rights Gaps Score	Rank	Adherence gaps Score	Rank	Implementation gaps Score	Rank
141 High ratifiers[2] including 40 extensive recent and 82 long-standing ratifiers											
Costa Rica	0.160	0.240	0.372	130	0.242	80	0.000	12	0.267	94
BANGLADESH	0.249	0.340	0.434	146	0.242	81	0.000	4	0.267	90
Cape Verde	0.309	0.279	0.170	21	0.242	82	0.021	100	0.233	78
Kyrgyzstan	–	0.099	0.206	38	0.248	83	0.064	132	0.167	53
Niger	0.209	0.230	0.270	72	0.250	84	0.026	107	0.233	80
Jamaica	0.400	0.621	0.400	141	0.252	85	0.027	111	0.233	85
C. African Rep.	0.230	0.338	0.200	36	0.263	87	0.014	94	0.267	93
Tunisia	0.242	0.181	0.130	13	0.260	88	0.013	91	0.267	98
Belgium	0.151	0.121	0.121	7	0.272	89	0.000	6	0.300	105
Honduras	0.079	0.251	0.181	30	0.272	90	0.000	25	0.300	107
Panama	0.191	0.200	0.221	49	0.272	91	0.000	42	0.300	108
Senegal	0.151	0.181	0.279	83	0.272	92	0.000	51	0.300	104
Uruguay	0.302	0.140	0.342	107	0.272	93	0.000	59	0.300	110
Ecuador	0.211	0.432	0.453	147	0.272	94	0.000	16	0.300	106
Rwanda	0.251	0.311	0.511	152	0.272	95	0.000	49	0.300	103
Cyprus	0.145	0.300	0.330	100	0.279	96	0.025	105	0.267	91
Slovakia	–	0.151	0.091	5	0.281	97	0.006	74	0.300	109
ANTIGUA & B.	0.228	0.368	0.338	103	0.292	98	0.094	137	0.167	51
New Zealand	0.272	0.423	0.302	93	0.302	99	0.000	39	0.333	122
Malawi	0.349	0.498	0.421	144	0.302	100	0.000	34	0.333	121
Iran	0.521	0.221	0.468	149	0.302	101	0.000	29	0.333	120
PAKISTAN	0.500	0.570	0.370	127	0.303	102	0.041	120	0.267	89
Sao Tome & P.	0.230	0.298	0.377	131	0.310	103	0.046	125	0.267	96
Latvia	–	0.031	0.308	97	0.311	104	0.006	72	0.333	111
Libya	0.249	0.279	0.389	139	0.311	105	0.006	62	0.333	112
Israel	0.181	0.191	0.230	54	0.321	106	0.013	90	0.333	115
ETHIOPIA	0.279	0.309	0.230	56	0.332	110	0.020	99	0.333	118
Australia	0.332	0.242	0.121	6	0.332	111	0.000	2	0.367	126
Gabon	0.151	0.209	0.270	73	0.342	116	0.027	109	0.333	119
Ghana	0.511	0.421	0.398	140	0.342	117	0.027	110	0.333	114
Dominica	0.108	0.308	0.260	67	0.350	119	0.032	118	0.333	113
SRI LANKA	0.377	0.302	0.364	112	0.351	120	0.013	81	0.367	124
Algeria	0.272	0.521	0.372	128	0.351	121	0.013	85	0.367	125
Mexico	0.130	0.121	0.174	24	0.362	122	0.000	36	0.400	137
France	0.151	0.160	0.200	37	0.362	123	0.000	20	0.400	128

Table 5   Countries' normalized non-discrimination gaps since 1985 (averages sorted by 2000–04 order of best to worst performers)[1] – *continued*

Countries by groups	1985-89	1990-94	1995-99		2000-04					
					Core Rights Gaps		Adherence gaps		Implementation gaps	
	Score	Score	Score	Rank	Score	Rank	Score	Rank	Score	Rank
141 High ratifiers[2] including 40 extensive recent and 82 long-standing ratifiers										
Saudi Arabia	0.181	0.574	0.272	78	0.362	124	0.000	50	0.400	130
Mongolia	0.049	0.190	0.130	12	0.369	126	0.045	123	0.333	116
Chile	0.362	0.302	0.342	106	0.372	127	0.006	67	0.400	135
Madagascar	0.319	0.289	0.579	155	0.372	128	0.006	73	0.400	129
MAURITANIA	0.277	0.560	0.456	148	0.375	129	0.028	112	0.367	123
Turkey	0.302	0.211	0.242	61	0.381	130	0.013	83	0.400	131
ERITREA	–	0.377	0.368	116	0.381	131	0.013	87	0.400	127
Chad	0.191	0.249	0.402	142	0.381	132	0.013	88	0.400	133
Greece	0.332	0.221	0.130	10	0.392	133	0.000	22	0.433	146
Finland	0.423	0.242	0.181	29	0.392	134	0.000	19	0.433	145
Venezuela	0.130	0.109	0.260	68	0.392	135	0.000	60	0.433	141
Brazil	0.179	0.453	0.362	109	0.392	136	0.000	8	0.433	143
Philippines	0.151	0.272	0.411	143	0.392	137	0.000	44	0.433	138
NIGERIA	0.289	0.319	0.475	151	0.398	138	0.063	131	0.333	117
Denmark	0.332	0.281	0.191	33	0.400	139	0.025	103	0.400	136
Iceland	0.151	0.381	0.191	34	0.402	140	0.006	69	0.433	147
Cameroon	0.091	0.249	0.289	87	0.403	141	0.027	108	0.400	134
TRINIDAD & T.	0.289	0.377	0.225	51	0.411	142	0.013	82	0.433	139
Dominican Rep.	0.379	0.392	0.181	26	0.423	144	0.000	15	0.467	149
Norway	0.272	0.362	0.211	44	0.423	145	0.000	41	0.467	148
Slovenia	–	0.151	0.160	20	0.430	146	0.025	102	0.433	140
Bosnia-Herz.	–	–	0.195	35	0.431	147	0.046	126	0.400	132
Paraguay	0.191	0.251	0.300	90	0.440	148	0.031	113	0.433	142
Bulgaria	0.151	0.281	0.272	75	0.453	149	0.000	9	0.500	150
St. Lucia	0.117	0.308	0.426	145	0.461	150	0.046	124	0.433	144
Sweden	0.311	0.572	0.230	55	0.462	151	0.006	75	0.500	151
Bolivia	0.121	0.230	0.249	64	0.462	152	0.006	66	0.500	152
India	0.242	0.641	0.281	84	0.483	153	0.000	27	0.533	155
Morocco	0.211	0.372	0.472	150	0.483	154	0.000	37	0.533	153
Spain	0.242	0.332	0.362	111	0.513	155	0.000	53	0.567	156
Guinea	0.453	0.441	0.630	156	0.521	156	0.025	104	0.533	154
Guatemala	0.091	0.240	0.272	76	0.524	157	0.007	76	0.567	157
Czech Republic	–	0.151	0.360	108	0.573	158	0.020	98	0.600	159
Sierra Leone	–	–	–	–	0.575	159	0.031	117	0.583	158

Table 5 Countries' normalized non-discrimination gaps since 1985 (averages sorted by 2000–04 order of best to worst performers)[1] – *continued*

Countries by groups	1985–89 Score	1990–94 Score	1995–99 Score	Rank	Core Rights Gaps Score	Rank	Adherence gaps Score	Rank	Implementation gaps Score	Rank
11 Medium ratifiers[3] including 7 extensive recent and 4 long-standing ratifiers										
BAHRAIN	0.377	0.377	0.368	115	0.195	52	0.109	142	0.033	18
THAILAND	0.377	0.377	0.335	102	0.205	55	0.116	149	0.033	19
CHINA	0.377	0.228	0.244	62	0.225	66	0.109	143	0.067	27
ESTONIA	–	0.377	0.252	66	0.225	67	0.109	144	0.067	28
Kuwait	0.289	0.328	0.284	86	0.225	68	0.109	145	0.067	29
NAMIBIA	0.377	0.377	0.368	121	0.228	69	0.131	151	0.033	16
SINGAPORE	0.377	0.377	0.368	122	0.231	70	0.153	152	0.000	9
MALAYSIA	0.377	0.377	0.269	71	0.256	86	0.109	146	0.100	33
Djibouti	0.338	0.258	0.558	154	0.340	114	0.125	150	0.167	59
Qatar	0.298	0.319	0.275	82	0.346	118	0.109	147	0.200	74
Japan	0.400	0.400	0.365	113	0.411	143	0.113	148	0.267	95
7 Non-ratifiers[4]										
Myanmar	0.377	0.377	0.368	120	0.330	107	0.219	153	0.000	7
US	0.377	0.377	0.368	126	0.330	108	0.219	155	0.000	14
Oman	–	–	0.377	134	0.330	109	0.219	154	0.000	8
Surinam	0.377	0.377	0.368	123	0.340	112	0.225	156	0.000	10
Uganda	0.377	0.377	0.368	125	0.340	113	0.225	157	0.000	13
Kiribati	–	–	–	–	0.342	115	0.227	158	0.000	3
Laos	0.377	0.377	0.377	133	0.368	125	0.244	159	0.000	4

[1] Three groups are distinguished by way of categorizations reflected in subheadings. Italicizing identifies 86 long-standing ratifiers, defined as countries that had adhered before 1985 to such non-discrimination Conventions as were listed as having been ratified by them on 31 December 2004, and capital letters identify 47 extensive recent ratifiers, defined as countries that ratified one or both of the non-discrimination Conventions between 1 January 1996 and 31 December 2004, which include the UK and the UAE but not the US.

[2] Countries that had ratified Convention Nos. 100 and 111 by 31 December 2004.

[3] Countries that had ratified either Convention No. 100 or Convention No. 111 by 31 December 2004.

[4] Countries that had ratified neither Convention No. 100 nor Convention No. 111 by 31 December 2004.

Notes

Chapter 1   Basic Labour Rights are Human Rights

1   More specifically, to safeguarding 'the basic rights and interests of workers and to this end, freely promote respect for relevant International Labour Organization conventions, including those on the prohibition of forced and child labour, the freedom of association, the right to organize and bargain collectively, and the principle of non-discrimination' (Commitment 3(i) of the Copenhagen Declaration on Social Development and Programme of Action, UN document A/CONF 166/9 of 19 April 1995).

2   The text of Conventions of the International Labour Organization can be accessed through the ILO public website at http://www.ilo.org/ilolex. The text of the Declaration can be found at http://www.ilo.org/declaration.

3   The full wording of the Declaration's first principle and right, 'Freedom of association and the effective recognition of the right to collective bargaining', is cumbersome and generally abbreviated to freedom of association here. For a recent comprehensive treatment, see ILO, 2000c and 2004b.

4   For an introduction to their scope and contents, see Javillier and Obero, 2001, ch. 1–2; ILO, 2003c, ch. 2–3; for a detailed exposition, ILO 1996.

5   For a recent comprehensive treatment, see ILO, 2001b.

6   For an introduction to their scope and contents, see Javillier and Obero, 2001, ch. 3; and ILO, 2003c, ch. 4.

7   For a recent comprehensive treatment, see ILO, 2002b.

8   For an introduction to their scope and contents, see Javillier and Obero, 2001, ch. 5; and ILO, 2003c, ch. 6.

9   For a recent comprehensive treatment, see ILO, 2003b.

10   For an introduction to their scope and contents, see Javillier and Obero, 2001, ch. 4; and ILO, 2003c, ch. 5.

11   The US Trade Act of 2002 misleadingly leaves out non-discrimination but adds 'acceptable conditions of work with respect to minimum wages, hours of work, and occupational safety and health' among 'internationally recognized worker rights'. See text at http://www.tpa.gov/TPA-text.htm.

12   See Aidt and Tzannatos, 2002. For a recent history of the relationships between the International Financial Institutions, the World Trade Organization and the International Labour Organization with regard to core labour standards, see Hagen, 2003, ch. 4.

13   As Spieler (2003, p. 79) put it: 'Pure reliance on an unregulated market permits the persistence of human rights abuses in workplaces that are the equivalent of direct political oppression by governments'.

14   For the theoretical predictions and existing empirical evidence regarding the link between (broader) employment protection laws and economic costs and benefits in advanced countries, see the OECD's authoritative study in ch. 2 of its 1999 *Employment outlook* (OECD, 1999).

Chapter 2   Can the Achievement of Rights be Measured Quantitatively?

1 This has not discouraged, for example, Apocada (1998) to include as one component of her achievement index of Women's Economic and Social Human Rights the right to work as measured by rates of economic activity.

2 The ILO launched a series of surveys in a number of advanced industrial countries to test whether workers of non-national origin were discriminated when applying for jobs, which they were (see Zegers de Beijl, 2000). Such one-off studies cannot be replicated sufficiently often to supply data for a regular indicator system.

3 Which is published regularly by UNDP in its Human Development Reports (see, for example, UNDP, 2003, table 23) on the basis of ILO data that the ILO itself does not issue in this form because of the limitations it sees in the data itself. UNDP also calculates the share of female legislators, senior officials and managers as a measure of gender empowerment. This has been criticized on both conceptual and empirical grounds (see Anker, 2003) and, in any case, is not a valid measure of achievement of gender equality in the labour field. Incidentally, UNDP's gender-related development index has the same constituent elements as its Human Development Index (GDP per capita, life expectancy and education) but disaggregates them by sex, and it cannot possibly be considered a proxy of gender equality in the world of work.

4 Convention No. 182, article 8, contains an innovative provision in international human rights law, which reads: 'Members shall take appropriate steps to assist one another in giving effect to the provisions of this Convention through enhanced international cooperation and/or assistance including support for social and economic development, poverty eradication programmes and universal education.' For a new ILO study on the initial costs and later benefits of eliminating child labour, see ILO, 2004c.

5 On indicator developments and their application to the field of human rights, it is worthwhile going back to the first major book on the subject, Jabine and Claude, 1992, also to Barsh's acerbic but truthful comments (Barsh, 1993), and to UNDP's *Human Development Report 2000* on the subject of human rights and development (UNDP, 2000). Four recent overviews provide general background information: Green, 2001; Compa, 2002; National Research Council, 2004; and Landman, 2004. Regarding relevant indicator work carried out in the ILO, see Kucera, 2002, and the Special Issue: Measuring Decent Work of the *International Labour Review*, Vol. 142, No. 2 (2003). Micro-level surveys that also yield Decent Work indexes were the subject of a previous Special Issue on Socio-Economic Security of the *International Labour Review*, Vol. 141, No. 4 (2002), where the article by Standing (2002) is the most pertinent.

6 I am willing to burn on a CD the Excel programme and data collected, which at well over 300 MB are too large to transfer electronically, and send it to interested researchers by mail.

Chapter 3   The Architecture and Scope of the Gap System

1 One could do this by giving the principles and rights of freedom of association greater weight relative to forced labour, child labour and non-

discrimination. Or one could do it by bringing the CFA into the system. I have chosen the latter option, essentially because it is more pertinent, distinct and enables greater variety to be applied in scoring than other approaches. In order not to accord the CFA too much weight, a limit will be imposed on this component of potential *implementation gaps*.

2 The logic of proportional reductions of the value of ratification might lead one to call into question the whole of a Convention's value where grave and sustained violations occur. This reasoning could be applied to Myanmar since, in 2000, the International Labour Organization asked its members to consider sanctioning the country for its continued violation of Convention No. 29 – a 'first' in the history of the Organization. An indicator system, however, should not be based on exceptional incidences involving only a single country or few countries: It would be truncated by conception.

3 There may be several reasons for this. One is probably the measurement chosen to represent capacity, that is, countries' percentage share of the ILO's regular budget. Another may be the actual cut-off points selected to distinguish countries with adequate capacity from those with little and least capacity. Failure could also be due to the fact that countries ratify important international Conventions for different reasons (see Hathaway, 2002). Some countries ratify because they perceive it to be in their political interest to commit themselves internationally to the provisions of a Convention; others ratify because they want to express a statement internationally of what they feel is the right thing to do. In the latter case, ratification levels may be quite high even for countries that actually lack the capacity to *implement* many of the Conventions. African countries appear over-represented among the latter and, in my view, sometimes engage in premature ratifications.

4 Polity IV (n.d.) considers a State to be failed when its government cannot exercise effective authority over at least 50 per cent of its established territory. I would put the threshold closer to somewhere between a quarter and a third, which accounts for the exclusion of, for example, Colombia, Nepal and Sudan from the *gap* system.

5 Polity IV (n.d.) data generally remain tentative for a period of up to five years following a regime change, see http://www.cidcm.umd.edu/inscr/polity/index.htm, Executive Summary, p. 3.

6 Iraq is excluded throughout the *gap* system's review period because its recent occupation by the United States and its allies is expected to last rather longer than the duration of a reporting cycle on ratified Conventions. If a country was non-functioning or not independent during one or two years, it should preferably be kept in the indicator system.

Chapter 4   Measuring Adherence

1 For an exposition of the several political-science theories on the ratification of UN Covenants and human rights Conventions, see Hathaway, 2002.

2 One could, for example, take the number of ratifications as per cent of the maximum number of possible ratifications, as Weisband (2000) did to measure commitment.

3 An alternative would be for the indicator system to apply the Organization's rule that countries remain internationally bound to apply the denounced

Convention for ten years and to report on it as well. This rule would be difficult for outsiders to follow in its implications and is therefore dropped in favour of a transparent immediate cut-off without any further implications. In the real world, countries do not denounce a Convention because of compliance problems they may have ten years down the road.

4 Countries are not asked to report where the Committee of Experts perceives them to be confronted by problems beyond their control, 'such as natural calamities or even general economic difficulties' (ILO CEACR, 1987, p. 13), in which case the Committee may defer requesting a report that is otherwise due.

5 Ratifications and denunciations of Conventions are regularly listed in an ILO Governing Body document called *Report of the Director-General*, section Progress in international labour legislation, which is available on the ILO's public website at http://www.ilo.org/public/english/standards/relm/gb/gbdoc.htm. A shortcut to ratification data is the country list at http://www.ilo.org/public/db/standards/normes/appl/appl-ratif8conv.cfm?Lan=EN.

6 The data are a little dispersed and can be found in the following places. ILO, 2000a: on freedom of association and collective bargaining in paragraph 79; forced labour in paragraph 90; child labour in paragraph 97; and discrimination in paragraph 109. ILO, 2001a: on freedom of association and collective bargaining in tables 6 and 7; forced labour in tables 8 and 9; child labour in tables 10 and 11 (the heading of table 11 should read 'Countries that owed reports in this category and *did not* submit them for the annual review of 2001'); and discrimination in tables 12 and 13 (the heading of table 13 should read 'Countries that owed reports in this category and *did not* submit them for the annual review of 2001'). ILO, 2002a: all four principles and rights are covered in Annex tables 1–4 and box 1(B). ILO, 2003a, 2004a and 2005: all four principles and rights are covered in boxes 1 and 2.

7 A hypothetical illustration is provided in Böhning, 2003a, table 5.

8 Which they were unwilling to accept at the time. Thus, unlike for reporting, there are no progress data in the *gap* system covering the initial Declaration years.

Chapter 5   Measuring Implementation

1 Two recent publications are helpful in getting to grips with the plethora of ILO procedures: Gravel *et al.*, 2002, and Gravel and Charbonneau-Jobin, 2003; see also the summary by Swepston, 2003, pp. 66ff. Two classical studies contain a wealth of information on their origins, evolution and performance: Haas's searching evaluation of functionalism (1964, especially ch. 9, 11 and 12) and Landy's descriptive insider analysis (1966, especially ch. 1–2). Haas actually constructed a 'human rights observation score' composed of his evaluation of countries' interest shown in the preparation of new Conventions and faithful implementation upon ratification, and he ranked countries during the initial years of the Cold War, 1947–62 (Haas, 1964, p. 371). However, the mixing of one-time involvement at the stage of preparing standards with the open-ended timeline of applying them in practice does not seem a promising approach to constructing an indicator system.

2 Belarus, Chile, Dominican Republic, Germany, Greece, Haiti, Ivory Coast, Liberia, Nicaragua, Poland and Romania.

3 Towards the end of the Introduction of its report to the International Labour Conference, this Committee usually refers to 'special cases' or it lists in a 'special paragraph' one or several governments that are judged to have a particularly bad record, which could theoretically be instrumentalized for indicator purposes. The Committee can ratchet up the pressure it seeks to exert on governments by spelling out instances of 'continued failure to implement' a particular Convention, which also constitutes an indicator of sorts. However, for a distinct set of indicators these data would not satisfy the non-truncation criterion.

4 Eighteen of the countries included in the *gap* system have attracted the ire of this Committee in respect of core Conventions between 1985 and 2004: Belarus, Central African Republic, Cameroon, Dominican Republic, Ecuador, Ethiopia, Guatemala, India, Iran, Morocco, Myanmar, Nigeria, Panama, Pakistan, Romania, Thailand, Turkey and Venezuela. Several countries were singled out a number of times. Two non-functioning States, Colombia and Sudan, have been prominent targets of the Committee on the Application of Standards.

5 The numbers after the slash relate to 2003 because several Experts retired or withdrew and were not immediately replaced so that in December 2004 only 16 Experts participated in the meeting. The composition of the Committee and its members' qualifications are listed at the beginning of its report (ILO CEACR, various). Most Experts were Professors of Law at one time or another of their career. Several occupied the highest positions in their countries' legal systems. Others were members of national or international arbitration commissions. A few had also been ministers or ambassadors for a while.

6 The Committee of Experts also notes certain developments with 'interest' as opposed to *satisfaction*. 'Interest' is a much lower form of approval than *satisfaction*. At one stage of the development of the *gap* system I considered instrumentalizing this notion alongside that of *satisfaction*. The idea was dropped because (i) there can be two, three or even more mentions of 'interest' in a single comment, which would oblige one to accord a very small weight to any single note of 'interest' in order to keep its cumulative total below the weight of *satisfaction*; and (ii) there is no fixed relationship between expressions of 'interest' and expressions of *satisfaction*, that is, two or more mentions of 'interest' cannot be said to correspond invariably to one mention of *satisfaction*.

7 To measure global and regional degrees of compliance with accepted standards, Weisband (2000, p. 654 ff) related *observations* to the number of ratified Conventions. His *observations* appear to include expressions of *satisfaction*, not only negative *observations*.

8 Complaints were declared receivable in the case of, for example, exiled unions under the Franco regime, *Solidarnosc* in Poland, the forbidden SBSI in Suharto's Indonesia and the KCTU in the Republic of Korea.

9 Oral hearings were held on only six occasions. Recently, the CFA chair has spoken to government delegates at the International Labour Conference, and a tripartite sub-group of the Committee went to the Republic of Korea to meet government representatives in the capital.

10 Such pronouncements could at best top up non-truncated source material.

11 Incidentally, the average duration of the examination of a case by the Committee, from the date of submitting the complaint to the adoption of the Committee's report, is a respectably short period of ten months (Gravel *et al.*, 2002, p. 14).

12 Weisband (2000) also counted *satisfaction* against *observations*, but for his benchmarking purposes he related the number of cases of progress to the number of *observations* received, a measure he called responsiveness. He appeared surprised by the low degree of responsiveness, globally 11–12 per cent during 1964–88–95. His selection of Conventions included the core Conventions except the child labour standards but extended to other human rights Conventions.

13 An apparent typing mistake in the CEACR's report for 2005 credits Mauritania with expressions of *satisfaction* for both Convention No. 87 and Convention No. 98 (p. 12) although no individual *observation* is formulated on the latter Convention (pp. 74–5) and no reference is made in the summary Appendix VII to that Convention (p. 542). The case of progress relating to Convention No. 98 is therefore disregarded.

14 In earlier working papers I had opted for a different attribution of the data for the years 1985–95 (Böhning, 2003a and 2003b), but this book's option is more correct.

15 The CFA figures are not procedurally annual data because complaints are lodged with the ILO *ad hoc* rather than according to time slots predetermined by receivability procedures or other factors. They are annual data in a factual sense because the CFA has to deal with numerous cases during the three sessions that it holds each year – nearly 2,500 cases in the CFA's over 50 years of existence.

16 If a session of the CFA was concerned with only one or two countries and the questions examined were relatively serious and called for much study, the table of contents and the heading of the report in the ILO's *Official Bulletin* may not specify what kind of report has been issued. It is usually an *interim* report. The correct category of report can be established by looking at the CFA's conclusions and recommendations.

17 Satisfaction may be expressed elsewhere than in definitive, to be kept informed or *interim* reports. The CFA may also feel moved to express its satisfaction when a government agrees to a request for a Direct Contact mission. And it may use words such as 'welcome' that are difficult to grade.

18 I had previously opted for a method that filled the years between *interim* reports with the weight of such a report on the grounds that the questions examined continued to be unresolved (Böhning, 2003a and 2003b). This had the effect of marginally inflating the CFA component for some countries.

19 The interval was annual up to 1959 when it became biannual. For less important Conventions the interval was lengthened to four years in 1976, but a biannual rhythm was maintained for the most important Conventions that included existing fundamental Conventions except Convention No. 138. The cycle was extended in 1993 to five years for normal Conventions but maintained at two years for priority Conventions. In 2001 it was decided, *inter alia*, to group countries alphabetically with one group reporting on core Conventions in even years and the other group in uneven years, starting in 2003.

20 The following 90 countries did not have an *interim* report addressed to them during 1985–2004 or during the period when they formed part of the *gap* system: Albania, Antigua and Barbuda, Austria, Azerbaijan, Belgium, Belize, Benin, Bosnia-Herzegovina, Botswana, Burkina Faso, Burundi, Cape Verde, Chad, Comoros, Croatia, Czech Republic, Denmark, Dominica, Egypt, Equatorial Guinea, Eritrea, Finland, France, Gabon, Gambia, Germany, Ghana, Greece, Grenada, Guinea-Bissau, Hungary, Iceland, Iran, Ireland, Israel, Italy, Jamaica, Kazakhstan, Kiribati, Kuwait, Kyrgyzstan, Laos, Lebanon, Lithuania, Luxembourg, Libya, Macedonia, Mali, Mauritius, Mongolia, Mozambique, Myanmar, Namibia, Netherlands, Niger, Norway, Oman, Papua New Guinea, Portugal, Qatar, Rwanda, St. Kitts and Nevis, St. Lucia, St. Vincent and the Grenadines, San Marino, Sao Tome and Principe, Saudi Arabia, Senegal, Seychelles, Sierra Leone, Singapore, Slovakia, Slovenia, South Africa, Sri Lanka, Suriname, Sweden, Switzerland, Syria, Tanzania, Thailand, Togo, Trinidad and Tobago, Turkmenistan, Uganda, United Arab Emirates, Uzbekistan, Vietnam, Yemen and Zimbabwe.

21 A possible shortcoming of the CFA component may be associated with the overriding importance of heeding the criterion of objectivity in that *implementation* problems could be slightly underestimated where the CFA published a report containing definitive conclusions on serious violations without having previously issued an *interim* report.

Chapter 6   Time Lags and Finalization of the System's Features

1 For example, after the surge in ratifications of Convention No. 182 the CEACR managed to review no more than about two thirds of the reports received. Several factors were responsible for the delays: Receipt of incomplete information or of late reports, the need to translate legislative texts and certain documents, as well as simply the volume of work.

2 Chapter 10 on child labour contains another exemplification with reweighted points and Chapter 11 on non-discrimination with normalized points.

3 The most striking example is Convention No. 182 that, adopted in 1999, was *adhered* to by 141 of the 159 countries in the *gap* system by December 2004, a phenomenal rate for the International Labour Organization. It illustrates the concept of 'norm cascading' advanced by Finnemore and Sikkink (1998).

4 Australia, Cuba, Djibouti, Guinea-Bissau, Israel, Laos, Latvia, Myanmar, Sao Tome and Principe, and Venezuela.

5 The best source of information on countries' policies and ratification prospects is contained in governments' replies to ILO questionnaires sent to them each year under the auspices of the Declaration, see ILO, 2000b and the reports with the same title at each subsequent March session of the ILO Governing Body.

6 The range of seven points used by Freedom House (see for example 1999) is an example of a non-comparable scale.

7 Which is the sum of the *adherence* maximum (due to non-ratification of Conventions, 100 points) and of the CFA maximum (15 points). In this 'worst-case scenario', non-reporting and the CEACR component are inactive,

and no bonuses are generated under the Declaration component. The reweighted figures for each area will be specified in the relevant Chapters.

8　A CRG of 81.25 points presupposes that all Conventions are ratified, all reports on ratified Conventions are due in the same year and the Committee of Experts has no reason to express any *satisfaction* during that year. In these circumstances, 6.25 points could derive from (reweighted) non-reporting; a further 60 points could be due to seven or eight *direct requests* plus seven or eight *observations*, depending on the year; and the CFA component could generate a maximum of 15 points. The Declaration component would be inactive in this scenario because all Conventions are ratified. It may be noted in passing that the Committee of Experts can and does formulate *direct requests* and *observations* even if the government has not sent a report. For example, it may remind the government of its reporting obligations by way of a *direct request* and, because workers' and employers' organizations have a constitutional right to inform the ILO of their on views on how the government applies a ratified Convention, the CEACR may formulate an *observation* if the views put forward by a non-governmental organization justify it.

9　The oldest ratifications of core Conventions go back to 1931 and Convention No. 29. They honour Ireland, Liberia, Sweden and the UK, in that order. However, none of these countries is a long-standing ratifier as here defined in respect of the seven pre-1985 Conventions. (Liberia has actually been a nonfunctioning country for many years.)

Chapter 7　Human Rights Achievements – Measuring the Four Freedoms as a Whole

1　Lebanon's score relating to 1994 is excluded from the Tables but not from the calculation of trendlines.

2　Such calculations can be deferred until 2005–09 scores are estimated.

3　Denmark's 1985–99, 1990–95 and 1995–99 *implementation* averages (0.183, 0.160 and 0.145, respectively) were not far apart and on a downward trend. Since the year 2000, however, the country was the object of an unusual number of CEACR *direct requests* and *observations* (14 each), which pushed up its average for 2000–04 to 0.280 points.

4　Australia's *implementation* scores first improved from an average of 0.122 in 1985–99 to 0.107 in 1990–95 and then worsened to 0.152 in 1995–99 and 0.213 points in 2000–04, which suggests that problems have taken root or that its policies have turned a little away from previous respect of fundamental labour rights. Australia also has an *adherence* problem in that it has to date ratified none of the two child labour Conventions.

5　In the case of the United States, one of the forced labour and one of the child labour Conventions (Nos. 105 and 182); in the case of China, one of the equality and both of the child labour Conventions (Nos. 100, 138 and 182).

6　Elsewhere, I have standardized the data in terms of the number of countries per region and how many Conventions they ratified by dividing *observations* and cases of progress by the number of ratifications (Böhning, 2005). Even then, three of the four region's trendlines move in the wrong direction. Only the European region's *observation-cum-satisfaction* are decreasing.

7 Given the expected non-correlations, significance levels need to be specified only where it is important to do so.

8 Argentina, Brazil, Chile, China, Colombia, Czech Republic, Egypt, Hungary, India, Indonesia, Israel, Jordan, Republic of Korea, Malaysia, Mexico, Morocco, Pakistan, Peru, Philippines, Poland, Russian Federation, South Africa, Sri Lanka, Taiwan, Thailand, Turkey and Venezuela. Colombia is a non-functioning State and Taiwan is not a member State of the International Labour Organization; neither forms part of the *gap* system.

9 The contrast between the high correlation of *adherence* scores with Verité's ratification data, on the one hand, and the non-correlation of *adherence* scores with Verité's laws and legal system indicator, on the other, provides indirect evidence of the falling apart of commitment and realization. Landman's distinction between 'laws in principle' and 'laws in practice' comes to mind, see Landman, 2004.

10 The CIRI human rights database, irrespective of the serious misgivings I have about its principal source material and its scoring principles, gives rise to a similar conclusion if one compares its 1995–99 averages with its 2000–03 averages. Of CIRI's 136 averages that are comparable, 49 per cent are worse in 2000–03 than in 1995–99, 23 per cent are unchanged and 28 per cent better.

11 Polity scores that downgraded countries by three or more points since 1990 include Belarus, Ecuador, Egypt, Gambia, Kazakhstan, Pakistan and Venezuela. Congo, Comoros and Niger, among others, underwent considerable ups and downs on the democracy-authoritarianism scale.

Chapter 8   Achievements in the Area of Freedom of Association

1 *Adherence* = 28.6 points up to 1999 and 25 as from 2000, *implementation* = 32.1 points up to 1999 and 30 afterwards, CRGs = 43.6 points up to 1999 and 40 afterwards. The CRG maxima are the sum of the *adherence* maximum (due to non-ratification of Conventions, 28.6 points and 25 points, respectively) and of the CFA maximum (15 points). In this 'worst-case scenario', non-reporting and the CEACR component are inactive, and bonuses that might derive from the Declaration component are left out of consideration.

2 Although not directly comparable in terms of aims, methods, regional composition and review periods, Weisband's finding regarding freedom of association are very different for Asia: 'least commitment, highest records of noncompliance and lowest degrees of responsiveness' (2000, p. 659). The fact that his data end in 1995 may play a role; mixing what I have called 'favourably inclined' Asian-Pacific countries and 'other' Asian-Pacific countries also blurs the picture somewhat. Another of his findings is also worth quoting: 'It does appear that factors such as political system and levels of development do not predict for responsiveness. More suggestive are the political and social cultures, which shape values and attitudes regarding workers, trade unions, and the regulation of labor markets, and the employment relationship' (*ibid.*, p. 661).

3 The time-lag effects of very recent ratifications may keep the ratios for all countries lower than they otherwise might be.
4 Of course, the application of constitutional and legislative provisions depends on the subject matter involved. The abolition of the death penalty requires very little to become reality compared with the abolition of forced labour, child labour or discrimination. Several of the subject matters scored by Botero *et al.* are closer to the death penalty end of the range, others to the forced labour, child labour and discrimination end.
5 Trendlines would be lifted by an increase in comments of workers' organization on governments' report if the CEACR did not put forward *observations* of its own. However, unions' comments are clearly not behind most *observations* and, therefore, not the prime reason for the upward sloping freedom of association trendlines. When the CFA requests the CEACR to study the legislative aspects of a case, there could be a knock-on effect of complaints on *observations*. Unfortunately, precise data are not available at present to test these hypotheses.
6 Hard data are not available at present to substantiate the 'increased vigilance' argument – neither with respect to *observations* by the CEACR nor with respect to cases under examination by the CFA.

Chapter 9   Achievements in the Area of Forced Labour

1 *Adherence* = 28.6 points up to 1999 and 25 as from 2000, *implementation* = 17.1 points up to 1999 and 15 afterwards, CRGs = 28.6 points up to 1999 and 25 afterwards. The CRG maxima are equivalent to the *adherence* maximum due to non-ratification of Conventions because, in this 'worst-case scenario', non-reporting and the CEACR component are inactive, and bonuses that might derive from the Declaration component are left out of consideration.
2 Weisband (2000, p. 657) also found Africa performing worst in the area of forced labour.

Chapter 10   Achievements in the Area of Child Labour

1 A Prussian king, an interested and perceptive observer of social realities, once decreed the end of child labour because children who had worked turned out to be small and feeble soldiers.
2 Seven are from Africa (Algeria, Kenya, Libya, Niger, Rwanda, Togo and Zambia), seven from the Americas (Antigua and Barbuda, Costa Rica, Cuba, Dominica, Honduras, Nicaragua, Uruguay), one from the Asian-Pacific region (Israel) and 13 from Europe (Belarus, Bulgaria, Finland, Germany, Ireland, Italy, Luxembourg, Netherlands, Norway, Poland, Romania, Spain and Ukraine).
3 The child labour 'raw' maxima are 14.3 points for *adherence* up to 1999 and 25 as from 2000, 8.6 points for *implementation* up to 1999 and 15 afterwards, 14.3 points for CRGs up to 1999 and 25 afterwards. The CRG maxima are equivalent to the *adherence* maxima due to non-ratification of Conventions because, in this 'worst-case scenario', non-reporting and the CEACR com-

ponent are inactive, and bonuses that might derive from the Declaration component are left out of consideration.

4 The incidence of child labour was estimated by the ILO to be highest in sub-Saharan Africa, followed by Asia and the Pacific (excluding Arab States), Latin America and the Caribbean, much lower in transition economies and lowest in developed countries (ILO, 2002b, table 4). However, countries' willingness, capacity and success in eliminating child labour are not necessarily equivalent to the size of the problem they confront.

Chapter 11   Achievements in the Area of Non-discrimination

1 *Adherence* = 28.6 points up to 1999 and 25 as from 2000, *implementation* = 17.1 points up to 1999 and 15 afterwards, CRGs = 28.6 points up to 1999 and 25 afterwards. The CRG maxima are equivalent to the *adherence* maximum due to non-ratification of Conventions because, in this 'worst-case scenario', non-reporting and the CEACR component are inactive, and bonuses that might derive from the Declaration component are left out of consideration.

2 One should be aware, however, that the small number of countries in this region, nine, exerts a strong impact on the distribution and ratios if one or two trends change.

3 As for the HDI itself, the values of the Gender-related Development Index derive mainly from the income data rather than life expectancy, adult literacy and school enrolment (see Charmes and Wieringa, 2003, p. 430).

4 Anker (2003, p. 54) concludes that 'economic development and its accompanying increases in income per capita, education and life expectancy are not sufficient to change traditional values and gender stereotypes'.

5 The CIRI human rights database, irrespective of the serious misgivings one may have about its principal source material and its scoring principles, gives rise to a similar conclusion if one compares its 1995–99 averages with its 2000–03 averages. Of the 136 comparable figures, 49 per cent are worse in 2000–03 than in 1995–99, 23 per cent are unchanged and 28 per cent are better.

Bibliographic References[1]

Adcock, R. and Collier, C., 2001 'Measurement validity: A shared standard for qualitative and quantitative research', in *American Political Science Review*, Vol. 95, No. 3 (September), pp. 529–46.

Aidt, T. and Tzannatos, Z., 2002 *Unions and collective bargaining: Economic effects in a global environment* (Washington, D.C.: World Bank).

Anker, R., 2003. Measuring women's access to occupations with authority, influence and decision-making power: Women as legislators, senior officials and managers, unpublished draft (September).

Anker, R., *et al.*, 2003 'Measuring decent work with statistical indicators', in *International Labour Review*, Vol. 142, No. 2, pp. 147–77.

Apocada, C., 1998 'Measuring women's economic and social rights achievement', in *Human Rights Quarterly*, Vol. 20, No. 1 (February), pp. 139–72.

Arif, G. M., 2004 *Bonded labour in agriculture: A rapid assessment in Punjab and North West Frontier Province, Pakistan*, Declaration Working Paper No. 25 (Geneva: ILO, March).*

Bales, K., 1999 *Disposable people: New slavery in the global economy* (Berkeley, etc., University of California Press).

Barsh, R. L., 1993 'Measuring human rights: Problems of methodology and purpose', in *Human Rights Quarterly*, Vol. 15, No. 1, pp. 87–121.

Bhaduri, A., 2002 'Nationalism and economic policy in the era of globalization', in D. Nayyar (ed.), *Governing globalization: Issues and institutions* (Oxford University Press), pp. 19–48.

Block, R. N., Berg, P. and Roberts, K., 2003 'Comparing and quantifying labour standards in the United States and the European Union,' in *International Journal of Comparative Labour Law and Industrial Relations*, Vol. 19, No. 4 (Winter), pp. 441–67.

Böhning, W. R., 2003a *Gaps in basic workers' rights: Measuring international adherence to and implementation of the Organization's values with public ILO data*, Declaration Working Paper 13 (Geneva: ILO, May).*

—— 2003b *Normalised and disaggregated Gaps in basic workers' rights*, Declaration Working Paper 17 (Geneva: ILO, November).*

—— 2005 'Standardised proxies to measure the implementation of core labour standards', in Senghass-Knobloch, E., ed. *Weltweit geltende Arbeitsstandards trotz Globalisierung: Analysen, Diagnosen und Einblicke* (Münster: Lit Verlag).

Bonnet, F., Figueiredo, J. B. and Standing, G., 2003 'A family of decent work indexes', in *International Labour Review*, Vol. 142, No. 2, pp. 213–38.

Botero, J., *et al.*, 2003 *The regulation of labor*, NBER Working Paper 9756 (Cambridge: National Bureau of Economic Research, June), also at http://www.nber.org/papers/w9756.

Chapman, A. and Russell, S., (eds) 2002 *Core obligations: Building a framework for economic, social and cultural rights* (Antwerp, Oxford and New York: Intersentia).

Charmes, J. and Wieringa, S., 2003 'Measuring women's empowerment: An assessment of the Gender-related Development Index and the Gender

Empowerment Measure', in *Journal of Human Development*, Vol. 4, No. 3 (November), pp. 419–35.

CIRI, n.d. *Cingranelli and Richards Human Rights Dataset*, at http://ciri.binghamton.edu/ (last accessed January 2005).

Compa, L., 2002 'Assessing assessments: A survey of efforts to measure countries' compliance with freedom of association standards', a paper for the National Academies' project on international labour standards (September), at www.national-academies.org/ international labour.

—— 2003 'Workers' freedom of association in the United States: The gap between ideals and reality', in Gross, J. A. (ed.), 2003 *Workers' rights as human rights* (Ithaca and London: Cornell University Press), pp. 23–52.

Cuyvers, L. and van den Bulcke, D., forthcoming *'The quantification of respect for selected core labor standards: Towards a social development index?'* (University of Antwerp, September 2004).

Engermann, S. L., 2003 'The history and political economy of international labour standards', in Basu, K., *et al.*, *International labor standards: History, theory, and policy options* (Malden, etc.: Blackwell Publishing for EGDI), pp. 9–83.

Ercelawn, A. and Jauman, M., 2001 *Bonded labour in Pakistan*, Declaration Working Paper No. 1 (Geneva: ILO, June).*

Finnemore, M. and Sikkink, K., 1998 'International norm dynamics and political change', in *Human Rights Quarterly*, Vol. 52, No. 4 (Autumn), pp. 887–917.

Freedom House, 1999 *Freedom in the world: The annual survey of political rights and civil liberties, 1998–1999* (New York), also at http://www.freedomhouse.org.

Ghose, A. G., 2003 *Jobs and incomes in a globalizing world* (Geneva: ILO).

Gravel, E., Duplessis, I. and Gernigon, B., 2002 *The Committee on Freedom of Association: Its impact over 50 years*, 2nd edition (Geneva: ILO).

Gravel, E. and Charbonneau-Jobin, C., 2003 *The Committee of Experts on the Application of Conventions and Recommendations: Its dynamic and impact* (Geneva: ILO).

Green, M., 2001 'What we talk about when we talk about indicators', in *Human Rights Quarterly*, Vol. 23, No. 4 (November), pp. 1062–97.

GRI, 2002 *Global Reporting Initiative: Final report of the measurement working group* (January 22), at http://www.globalreporting.org/workgroup/mea-wg/Mea_Final25-01-02.pdf.

Haas, E. B., 1964 *Beyond the nation state: Functionalism and international organization* (Stanford, CA: Stanford University Press).

Hagen, K. A., 2003 *Policy dialogue between the International Labour Organization and the International Financial Institutions: The search for convergence*, Occasional Papers No. 9/2003 (Geneva: Friedrich Ebert Stiftung).

Hathaway, O., 2002 'Do human rights treaties make a difference?', in *The Yale Law Journal*, Vol. 111, No. 8 (June), pp. 1935–2042.

Hussein, A. H., *et al.*, 2004 *Bonded labour in agriculture: A rapid assessment in Sindh and Balochistan, Pakistan*, Declaration Working Paper No. 26 (Geneva: ILO, March).*

ILO, n.d. *Handbook of procedures relating to international labour Conventions and Recommendations* (Geneva), at http://www.ilo.org/public/english/standards/norm/sources/handbook/index.htm

—— various *Official Bulletin*, Series B, Vol. LXVIII, 1985–LXXXVI, 2003 (Geneva).

—— 1995 *ILO law on freedom of association: Standards and procedures* (Geneva).

—— 1996 *Freedom of association: Digest of decisions and principles of the Freedom of Association Committee of the Governing Body of the ILO*, Fourth (revised) edition (Geneva).

—— 2000a *Review of annual reports under the follow-up to the Declaration on Fundamental Principles and Rights at Work*, Part I, Introduction by the ILO Declaration Expert-Advisers to the compilation of annual reports (Geneva: ILO document GB.277/3/1, March).***

—— 2000b *Review of annual reports under the follow-up to the Declaration on Fundamental Principles and Rights at Work*, Part II, Compilation of annual reports by the International Labour Office (Geneva: ILO document GB.277/3/2, March).***

—— 2000c *Your voice at work*, Report I (B), 88th Session of the International Labour Conference (Geneva).**

—— 2001a *Review of annual reports under the follow-up to the Declaration on Fundamental Principles and Rights at Work*, Part I, Introduction by the ILO Declaration Expert-Advisers to the compilation of annual reports (Geneva: ILO document GB.280/3/1, March).***

—— 2001b *Stopping forced labour*, Report I (B), 89th Session of the International Labour Conference (Geneva).**

—— 2002a *Review of annual reports under the follow-up to the Declaration on Fundamental Principles and Rights at Work*, Part I, Introduction by the ILO Declaration Expert-Advisers to the compilation of annual reports (Geneva: ILO document GB.283/3/1, March).***

—— 2002b *A future without child labour*, Report I (B), 90th Session of the International Labour Conference (Geneva).**

—— 2002c *Every child counts: New global estimates on child labour,* International Programme on the Elimination of Child Labour (Geneva, April).

—— 2003a *Review of annual reports under the follow-up to the Declaration on Fundamental Principles and Rights at Work*, Introduction by the ILO Declaration Expert-Advisers to the compilation of annual reports (Geneva: ILO document GB.286/4, March).***

—— 2003b *Time for equality at work*, Report I (B), 91st Session of the International Labour Conference (Geneva).**

—— 2003c *Fundamental rights at work and international labour standards* (Geneva).

—— 2003d *Trafficking in human beings: New approaches to combating the problem,* Special Action Programme to Combat Forced Labour (Geneva).

—— 2003e *Forced labour outcomes of irregular migration and human trafficking in Europe*, Special Action Programme to Combat Forced Labour (Geneva).

—— 2003f *Programme and budget for the biennium 2004–05* (Geneva: ILO document GB.286/PFA/9).***

—— 2004a *Review of annual reports under the follow-up to the Declaration on Fundamental Principles and Rights at Work*, Introduction by the ILO Declaration Expert-Advisers to the compilation of annual reports (Geneva: ILO document GB.289/4, March).***

—— 2004b *Organizing for social justice*, Report I (B), 92nd Session of the International Labour Conference (Geneva).**

—— 2004c *Investing in every child: An econometric study of the costs and benefits of eliminating child labour* (Geneva).

—— 2004d *Economic security for a better world* (Geneva).

—— 2005 *Review of annual reports under the follow-up to the Declaration on Fundamental Principles and Rights at Work*, Introduction by the ILO Declaration Expert-Advisers to the compilation of annual reports (Geneva: ILO document GB.292/4, March).***

—— CEACR, various *Report of the Committee of Experts on the Application of Conventions and Recommendations, General report and observations concerning particular countries*, Report III (Part 4A), International Labour Conference (Geneva: ILO, 1985–2004). Individual observations and cases of progress, though not the direct requests, are available on Internet for recent years, see for example http://www.ilo.org/ilolex/gbe/ceacr2005.htm.

Jabine, T. B. and Claude, R. P., 1992 *Human rights and statistics: Getting the record straight* (Philadelphia: University of Pennsylvania Press).

Javillier, J.-C. and Obero, A. (eds), 2001 *International labour standards: A global approach*, 75th anniversary of the Committee of Experts on the Application of Conventions and Recommendations [Preliminary version] (Geneva: ILO).

Kucera, D., 2002 'Core Labour Standards and foreign direct investment', in *International Labour Review*, Vol. 141, No. 1–2 (2002/1–2), pp.31–69.

—— forthcoming *Measuring trade union rights: A country-level indicator constructed from coding violations recorded in textual sources*, prepared for the ILO Seminar on Qualitative Indicators of Labour Standards and Workers Rights, 14–15 September 2004.

Landman, T., 2004 'Measuring human rights: Principle, practice and policy' in *Human Rights Quarterly*, Vol. 26, No. 4 (November), pp. 906–31.

Landman, T. and Häusermann, J., 2003 *Map-making and analysis of the main international initiatives on developing indicators on democracy and good governance* (University of Essex-Human Rights Centre for EUROSTAT, July).

Landy, E. A., 1966 *The effectiveness of international supervision: Thirty years of I.L.O. experience* (London and New York: Stevens and Oceana).

Mishra, L., 2001 *A perspective plan to eliminate forced labour in India*, Declaration Working Paper 2 (Geneva: ILO, July).*

—— 2002 *Annotated bibliography of forced/bonded labour in India*, Declaration Working Paper 11 (Geneva: ILO, December).*

Munck, G. L. and Verkuilen, J., 2002 'Conceptualizing and measuring democracy', in *Comparative Political Studies*, Vol. 35, No. 1 (February), pp. 5–34.

National Research Council, 2004 *Monitoring international labour standards: Techniques and sources of information* (Washington, D.C.: National Academies Press).

Nayyar, D., 2003 'Work, livelihoods and rights', Presidential address to the 44th Conference of the Indian Society of Labour Economics, in *Indian Journal of Labour Economics*, Vol. 46, No. 1, pp. 3–13.

O'Brien, R., 2004 'Continuing incivility: Labor rights in a global economy', in *Journal of Human Rights*, Vol. 3, No. 2 (June), pp. 203–14.

OECD, 1996 *Trade, employment and labour standards: A study of core workers' rights and international trade* (Paris).

—— 1999 'Employment protection and labour market performance', in *OECD Employment Outlook*, Chapter 2 (Paris: June), pp. 47–132.

—— 2000 *International trade and core labour standards* (Paris).

—— 2003 *Combating child labour: A review of policies* (Paris).

Oumanou, M., 2001 *Défis et opportunités au Niger: Identification des obstacles à la mise en oeuvre des principes et droits fondamentaux au travail et propositions et* *solutions au Niger,* Document de travail du Programme Déclaration No. 4 (Genève: BIT, août).*

Polity IV, n.d. *Political regime characteristics and transitions, 1800–2002,* at http://www.cidcm.umd.edu/inscr/polity/index.htm (last accessed December 2004).

Rama, M. and R. Artecona, 2002 *A database of labor market indicators,* pdf version.

Sengenberger, W., 2002 *Globalization and social progress: The role and impact of international labour standards,* A report prepared for the Friedrich-Ebert-Stiftung (Bonn: December).

Spieler, E. A., 2003 'Risks and rights: The case for occupational safety and health as a core worker right', in Gross, J. A. (ed.), 2003 *Workers' rights as human rights* (Ithaca and London: Cornell University Press), pp. 78–117.

Standing, G., 2002 'From People's Security Surveys to a Decent Work Index', in *International Labour Review,* Vol. 141, No. 4, pp. 441–54.

Swepston, L., 2003 'Closing the gap between international law and U.S. labor law', in Gross, J. A. (ed.), 2003 *Workers' rights as human rights* (Ithaca and London: Cornell University Press), pp. 53–77.

Tajgman, D. and Curtis, K., 2000 *Freedom of association: A user's guide* (Geneva: ILO).

Thomas, C., 2003 'Information sources and measures of international labour standards on employment discrimination', in *Comparative Labor Law and Policy Journal,* Vol. 24, No. 2, pp. 365–400.

UNDP, 2000 *Human Development Report 2000: Human rights and human development* (New York and Oxford: Oxford University Press).

—— 2002 *Human Development Report 2002: Deepening democracy in a fragmented world* (New York and Oxford: Oxford University Press).

—— 2003 *Human Development Report – Millennium Development Goals: A compact among nations to end human poverty* (New York and Oxford: Oxford University Press).

Verité, 2000 *Report to California Public Employees Retirement System (CalPERS), Emerging Markets Research project,* at http://www.calpers.ca.gov/invest/emergingmkt/verite.pdf.

—— 2004 *Country-level assessments of labor conditions in emerging markets: An approach for institutional investors,* prepared for the ILO Seminar on Qualitative Indicators of Labour Standards and Workers Rights, by D. Viederman and E. Klett, September 14–15.

Von Potobsky, G., 1998 'Freedom of association: The impact of Convention No. 87 and ILO action', in *International Labour Review,* Vol. 137, No. 2, pp. 195–221.

Weisband, E., 2000 'Discursive multilateralism: Global benchmarks, shame, and learning in the ILO labor standards monitoring regime', in *International Studies Quarterly,* Vol. 44, No. 4, pp. 643–66.

Zegers de Beijl, R. (ed.), 2000 *Documenting discrimination against migrant workers in the labour market: A comparative study of four European countries* (Geneva: ILO).

---

1   ILO Working Papers with one asterisk can be accessed at http://www.ilo.org/dyn/declaris/DECLARATIONWEB.WORKINGPAPERS?var_language=EN.

ILO publications with two asterisks can be accessed at http://www.ilo.org/dyn/declaris/DECLARATIONWEB.GLOBALREPORTSLIST?var_language=EN. ILO GB documents can be accessed through the general Governing Body site at http://www.ilo.org/public/english/standards/relm/gb/gbdoc.htm?

Index

NOTES: Page numbers in italics refer to tables and figures